FUTURE ENERGY

FUTURE ENERGY

HOW THE NEW OIL INDUSTRY WILL CHANGE PEOPLE, POLITICS, AND PORTFOLIOS

BILL PAUL

John Wiley & Sons, Inc.

Published by John Wiley & Sons, Inc., Hoboken, New Jersey.
Published simultaneously in Canada.

Wiley Bicentennial Logo: Richard J. Pacifico

For general information on our other products and services or for technical support, please contact our Customer Care Department within the United States at (800) 762-2974, outside the United States at (317) 572-3993 or fax (317) 572-4002.

Wiley also publishes its books in a variety of electronic formats. Some content that appears in print may not be available in electronic books. For more information about Wiley products, visit our web site at www.wiley.com.

Library of Congress Cataloging-in-Publication Data:

Paul, William Henry, 1948–
    Future energy : how the new oil industry will change people, politics and portfolios / Bill Paul.
        p.   cm.
    Includes bibliographical references and index.
    ISBN: 978-0-470-09642-0 (cloth)
    1. Petroleum industry and trade—United States.   2. Petroleum reserves—United States.   3. Energy policy—United States.   4. Energy development—United States.   I. Title.
    HD9565.P32   2007
    333.8'2320973—dc22   2006034739

Printed in the United States of America.

10 9 8 7 6 5 4 3 2 1

Contents

Preface   vii

Acknowledgments   ix

Author's Note   xi

CHAPTER 1
The New Oil Industry   1

CHAPTER 2
Terrorists, Nationalists, and Shock Absorbers   31

CHAPTER 3
Substitute Liquid Fuels, Part One: Biofuel   55

CHAPTER 4
Substitute Liquid Fuels, Part Two: Unconventional
Fossil Fuels   81

CHAPTER 5
The Power of Efficiency   101

CHAPTER 6
Every Drop of Oil We Can Get Is Important   127

CHAPTER 7
The New Oil Economy?   145

CHAPTER 8

The Complete List of 100 Companies to Watch 163
*Why the Chevrolet Corvette Should Be the Symbol
of the New Oil Industry*

APPENDIX A

2012 U.S. Biofuel Market Forecast 179

APPENDIX B

Primer on Why Gasoline's True Cost in 2006 Was More
than $11 a Gallon 181

APPENDIX C

Valuable Energy News Web Sites 191

Glossary 195

Notes 205

Index 217

Preface

Hundreds of millions more people in the world are expected to be driving cars and trucks in 25 years' time, but the world is already struggling with high prices, national insecurity, and environmental anxiety as it tries to meet current demand for oil. Not since demand for whale oil decimated the supply of whales has demand so threatened to exceed available supply. Oil companies are running just to try to stay in place. But the new discoveries are smaller than the old ones and the amount of new crude is insufficient to replace reserves at the rate we are using them up. The world is living on past discoveries as it watches its most important oil fields get dangerously long in the tooth.

Besides these physical ailments, the world has big psychological problems. Oil-consuming nations whistle as they walk past the graveyard, hoping there won't be a sudden cutoff in the flow of oil from the region of the globe most likely to erupt in violence, the Middle East, or a rapid falloff in production by key oil fields because of years of inadequate maintenance. People hear shocking statistics on the toll that oil and other fossil fuels are taking on the environment and, consequently, on their health, but then go fill up their tanks with gasoline because they don't have a choice.

Soon, however, the world will be presented with a golden opportunity to solve its energy-related problems. An energy technology revolution is starting to brew in America and throughout the world. This revolution will create a "new" oil industry that holds the promise of energy independence for the United States and other nations, at the expense of nationalists and terrorists who use oil as a sword of Damocles against the West. This revolution also holds the promise of moderate prices and a cleaner environment. It may even hold the promise of a new method of wealth creation, a way for the average joe to make money.

To fully realize the tremendous potential of this revolution, skillful political leadership that emphasizes compromise over confrontation and the national interest over special interests will be required. Shaping and directing this energy technology revolution will be one of the challenges, if not the biggest challenge, faced by leaders in Washington, Beijing, New Delhi, Tokyo, London, and other energy capitals. Although an oil-man, President George Bush has shown in his speeches that he gets what the energy technology revolution is all about. What's needed now is a Manhattan Project–style program for developing these new technologies in order to wean the world off its deadly dependence on imported oil as quickly as possible.

This energy technology revolution will present a major opportunity for investors all over the world. But first they will need to know what disruptive new technologies are being developed, what companies are developing them, and what other companies will be called upon to implement them by providing the infrastructure of the new oil industry. This book presents a list of 100 companies to watch. Though detailed, this list should be viewed by investors as a starting point for further investigation.

Acknowledgments

I would like to thank my friend Stephen Blauweiss for creating the charts for this book. I would also like to thank everyone who contributed so freely of their time, information, and/or enthusiasm.

Author's Note

The material in this book is presented for information purposes only. Under no circumstances does the information in this book represent a recommendation to buy, sell, or hold individual stocks, groups of stocks, or any other investments. The author does not own stock in any of the companies on the "companies to watch" list.

CHAPTER 1

The New Oil Industry

A newspaper article in the spring of 2006 said that economists believe that if gasoline were to reach $5 a gallon in the United States, "an entire industry would develop aimed at cutting costs and finding new sources of energy that could alter the economy in unforeseen ways."[1]

While Americans may or may not see $5 gasoline, in point of fact this new industry is already taking shape. It is being fueled—though only in part—by crude and gasoline prices that have risen rapidly over the past few years, climbing above $70 a barrel and, in the United States, $3 a gallon, respectively, at the start of the 2006 summer driving season.

In addition to high prices, this new industry—really a "new" oil industry because conventional oil production will continue to play a vital role for the foreseeable future—is gaining momentum because of two of the most widespread fears in the world today. The first is the fear of governments everywhere over their lack of energy security, as reflected in President Bush's now-famous statement that the United States is addicted to imported oil. Call it energy insecurity. The second is the fear of people everywhere over the health of the planet, as reflected in 2006's tidal wave of media interest in global warming. Call it environmental anxiety. It was further reflected in a statement made by a European energy planner that combating climate change should be central to the world's global energy strategy. He made the statement to none other than members of the Organization of Petroleum Exporting Countries (OPEC)—the global oil cartel.[2]

Neither of these global fears is about to disappear, and even if,

1

near-term, the price of oil pulls back due, say, to a recession, long-term
(over the next 25 years) the world is expected to need vastly more energy
than it consumes today, putting a continuous strain on existing sources
of supply.

Indeed, the U.S. Energy Information Administration (EIA), the independent statistical and analytical agency within the U.S. Department of
Energy, has forecast that global petroleum consumption is expected to
grow strongly, reaching about 118 million barrels a day in 2030,[3] compared with roughly 84 to 85 million barrels a day currently. The Paris-
based International Energy Agency (IEA), which acts as an energy policy
adviser to more than two dozen countries, has said global oil demand
could reach 99 million barrels a day by 2015 and 116 million barrels by
2030.[4] Even some oil company executives seriously question whether
such increases are achievable.

Chronically high prices plus pervasive geopolitical risk plus environmental fears equals a recipe for change, for a radical restructuring of the
oil industry.

To be sure, it is both tempting and comforting to think that when oil
prices fall precipitously—as they did in the fall of 2006—America's and
the world's oil problems are over. No doubt there will be several more
sharp price declines over the next quarter century due to factors such as
seasonal patterns, depressed overall economic conditions, and overspec-
ulation. However, in addition to rising worldwide demand for oil, the
upward pressure on oil prices should be maintained over the long haul
by the financial and psychological fallout from a number of confluent
conditions:

- The rising cost of discovering, extracting, and refining crude oil.
- Increasing reliance on other hydrocarbon sources that are more expensive to exploit, particularly coal and tar sands.
- The growing concentration of America's critical energy infrastructure in the hurricane-exposed Gulf of Mexico.
- The generally accepted assessment that the war on terrorism is only
  in the first round.
- Rising demand specifically in oil-producing countries that effectively reduces the amount of oil available for export.
- Growing concern that conventional oil production may have or
  could soon peak.

"There are substantial risks going forward," Kevin Petak, director of energy modeling and forecasting at Energy and Environmental Analysis, Inc., a consulting firm in Arlington, Virginia, told me during an interview conducted *after* oil prices started going down in the fall of 2006.

To what extent the new oil industry succeeds in making nations energy secure and the planet healthier is going to depend on political decisions made in Washington, Beijing, and other world capitals. It will depend especially on how effectively governments coordinate the new oil industry's different sectors, which will need to compete without losing the inherent synergism. *With proper guidance, the new oil industry appears to have the potential to solve many, if not most, of the world's energy-related problems.*

But no matter how good a job governments do, the new oil industry should succeed in helping to bring down the price of gasoline by simultaneously increasing supply and decreasing demand. The former will be achieved through the introduction of liquid transportation fuels that can substitute for gasoline refined from crude oil, while the latter will stem from greater use of fuel-efficient hybrid engines and other improvements in the efficiency of vehicles.

Unfortunately, it is going to take time for all this substitution and efficiency to permeate the market—maybe 10 years or longer, though a lot will depend on governments' policies. Until that day, even with the world pumping as much crude as it can, the medical condition known as "pain at the pump" is unlikely to disappear.

■ ■ ■

Oil means transportation and transportation means mobility. Thus, in one way or another, the new oil industry is going to affect all people and all goods and services, in the process creating a wide range of new investment ideas.

To be sure, it is going to be possible to make an argument for why each of these new investment ideas may fail to achieve liftoff, even the ones that 20 years from now will look like they should have been no-brainers back in 2007. As previously indicated, much will depend on government policy, which will be the target of powerful economic and political interests set on advancing their own agendas even if they conflict with the national interest. In addition, a promising new approach may not get off the ground because it seems too expensive, the cause of too much environmental damage, too exposed to geopolitical risk, or unlikely to gain consumer acceptance.

But while specific winners of the new oil industry have yet to be determined, the overall trend is clear. As much as the information, health care, entertainment, and many other industries have been revolutionized by technology, the energy industry has not been. Now, thanks to the combined impact of high oil prices, energy insecurity, and environmental anxiety, an energy technology revolution is underway in the United States and around the world. It is all about smart energy management and it involves the blending of energy with other industries that have already been revolutionized by technology, such as biotech and communications.

Energy analysts sense that big changes are coming. "There's going to be a tremendous push for energy technology," analyst Petak told me.

Wall Street's heavy hitters sense it, too. As we ate breakfast in a private dining room on the 30th floor (the executive floor) of Goldman Sachs (International) worldwide headquarters in Manhattan, Robert Hormats, the investment banking firm's vice chairman, told me, "Just like the 1990s was the decade for money and innovation in the information industry, we're now heading into a decade of big technological innovation in the energy industry."

Indeed, "Energy is now on the radar screens of venture capital firms who realize that part of the answer to today's energy challenges is focused technological breakthroughs," I was subsequently told by Thomas A. Petrie, chairman, president, and CEO of Petrie Parkman & Co., the well-known energy advisory firm. (In October 2006 Merrill Lynch announced an agreement to acquire Petrie Parkman.)

"This innovation," I was further told by Charles T. Maxwell, an oil industry veteran of 50 years and senior energy analyst at Weeden & Co., the independent research firm for institutional investors, "will take many forms. Over time, we're going to be surprised by both the big and small things that turn up."

In point of fact, there are not one but two energy technology revolutions brewing today. This book deals primarily with the revolution in *mobile* energy production and consumption (think cars and trucks). The other is in *stationary* energy production and consumption (think homes, offices, and factories). The latter revolution is primarily about how electricity can be generated, distributed, and consumed at a reasonable price, without risk to national security, and without destroying the planet—which, of course, is also what the mobile revolution is about, only with "liquid" energy. As time goes on, these two revolutions will increasingly be seen as two sides of the same revolution.

This book explores the different paths that technology and politics could cause the new oil industry to follow and identifies companies and industries that deserve to be watched by investors as events unfold over the next several years. Some bear watching in their own right; others are mentioned because they are illustrative of broader trends.

Hopefully, some readers will disagree with my ranking of the categories in which these companies and industries have been placed. I say "hopefully" because the overall purpose of this book is to get readers to think for themselves, both as investors and as members of a global community that is going to need to discuss in a civil fashion how the energy industry should develop so that the world hits the trifecta: reasonable prices, energy security, and environmental improvement.

This book is intended to provide information, insights, and understanding that enable people to actively participate in this discussion. Being active participants in the ongoing discussions about what direction the global energy industry should take will be the best way for investors to figure out which investment ideas are most likely to pan out over the next five years and longer.

In energy, *every winning investment idea is first a winning political idea.*

Figure 1.1 is the reader's blueprint. It highlights the fact that, while the present-day oil industry has one sector—conventional oil—in the new oil industry, conventional oil will be one of three sectors.

One of the two new sectors we will call *substitute liquid fuels.* This is a term I first came across when reading a 2005 report titled, "Peaking of World Oil Production: Impacts, Mitigation, and Risk Management," on which Robert L. Hirsch served as project leader.[5] As Figure 1.1 indicates, substitute liquid fuels—we'll call them SLFs for short—are going be made both from biomass sources and from hydrocarbon sources other than crude oil.

The second new sector we will call *efficiency.* This refers not only to ways of getting more miles out of a gallon of gasoline. It also refers to the

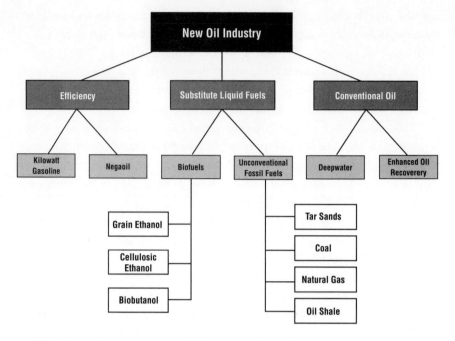

FIGURE 1.1   Components of the New Oil Industry

use of electricity as a *non*liquid alternative fuel, specifically for vehicles which are now under development that will be capable of being plugged in to an ordinary electrical outlet.

To highlight electricity's anticipated new role as a transportation fuel, I thought about giving it a catchy new name. But it is what it is: electricity. To differentiate it from how we generally think of electricity consumption, I finally decided to call it *kilowatt gasoline*. Hopefully Madison Avenue will think of something better by the time these new plug-in vehicles reach dealers' showrooms.

The other box under "Efficiency" has a funny-looking word in it—*negaoil*. To encapsulate the many ways in which efficiency will be improved, I have adapted a concept found in the electric utility industry called *negawatts*, which is a measurement of electricity *not* used as a result of efficiency improvements. The term *negawatts* was coined by energy efficiency guru Amory Lovins, whom I was lucky enough to interview on more than one occasion when I was a staff reporter at the *Wall Street*

Journal covering energy and the environment. Henceforth, negaoil will be used to describe the ways in which oil is *not* used thanks to improved efficiency.

It is worth emphasizing that, while these three sectors will complement one another, they also will need to compete with one another. Except for a brief period in the early 1900s, there has never really been competition for the fuel that goes into people's cars and trucks. The trick for government officials everywhere will be to encourage competition without losing the synergism that will come from having all three sectors working toward the same end.

■　■　■

Before SLFs and efficiency improvements have time to make a real difference, pump prices in the United States could hit $4 a gallon or higher. Even if they don't, it is important to look at the psychological and economic reasons why Americans haven't significantly cut back on their driving in recent years despite steadily rising gasoline prices.

A May 2006 *New York Times* article titled "Why Prices at the Pump May Have Little Bite" made the important point that, "while the price of gasoline may be highly visible and symbolic, filling up the tank simply doesn't eat up that much of most families' budgets."[6] The article noted that only pennies of the American consumer's dollar wind up in the gas tank, and that the rapid rise in gasoline prices over the last few years still has cost consumers only about the price of a movie.

Yes, people complained over the past year or two about pain at the pump. But as gasoline prices were going up, people generally continued to drive more miles than they had the year before, seemingly acquiescing to—very roughly—a half buck annual increase as the price they must pay to keep driving to the mall, the beach, and their kids' soccer practices.

To be sure, for the perhaps one in five Americans at the bottom of the economic totem pole, the pain was all too real. Those at the lower end may have roughly only about $1,500 per year or less available for discretionary spending. Add hundreds of dollars to a low wage earner's gasoline bill and it hurts—not only the wage earner and his or her family but also the retailers, fast food chains, and other businesses that might otherwise get that money.

But as the *Times* article noted, "consumers with a greater ability to absorb the pain of higher gasoline prices buy a disproportionately large amount of the stuff." To be sure, $3 gasoline managed to slow the annual rate of increase in U.S. gas consumption in the first half of 2006. Still, at the start of the 2006 summer driving season an oil industry analyst told a *USA Today* reporter, "People tend to take July and August vacations regardless of the price of fuel."[7] A few weeks later another analyst told another reporter that people seemed to be adjusting to the higher gasoline prices.

If Americans keep adjusting and taking their summer vacations, gasoline prices could hit $4 a gallon by or before 2010. Conceivably, even this forecast could be on the low side.

While the *New York Times* helped me to understand the financial reasons why high gas prices haven't yet changed many Americans' driving behavior, it took Philip Reed to help me unravel the cultural reason.

Reed is the consumer advice editor for the authoritative automotive web site Edmunds.com. From his vantage point in California, the state with some of the highest gasoline prices in the nation, Reed told me, appropriately enough, during the 2006 summer driving season, "We used to have the cowboy on horseback; now we have the cowboy in a pickup truck. There's a little cowboy in all of us. We love to look out as we're driving and see nothing but the road extending in front of us. Americans cherish their freedom of mobility. That freedom is closely intertwined with our definition of democracy."

Further unraveling was provided by Milton Copulos, an economist who, as president of the National Defense Council Foundation, has frequently testified before Congress on energy security issues. In the fall of 2006 Copulos told me, "For Americans, the automobile is not merely a conveyance. It is a statement of personal identity. People have always had the opportunity to go 'over the horizon' if they did not like where they were. That's never going to change."

In a newspaper opinion piece he wrote, the co-author of a 2006 Reason Foundation study on how to deal with America's worsening traffic congestion said there is no evidence that, despite the hassle of sitting in traffic, large numbers of people are prepared to park their cars and turn to public transportation. On the contrary, as David T. Hartgen, a professor of transportation studies at the University of North Carolina at Charlotte, wrote in his report: "As long as we value private mobility and freedom of choice, personal travel will continue to grow, though probably less rapidly in the future." The title of this report was "Building Roads to Reduce Traffic Congestion in America's Cities: How Much and at What Cost?" Notwithstanding the environmental implications, this may not be a bad idea given freedom-loving Americans' desire to look over the horizon.[8]

If we apply the notion of the automobile as the ultimate freedom machine, and then factor in all the time and money that motorists apparently are willing to waste sitting in traffic, even if gasoline were selling for $5 a gallon, pedal-to-the-metal Americans might still be inclined to rationalize that pump prices were a "good deal" compared with other countries. And you know what? They would be right. As the *New York Times* noted in May 2006,[9] if you had been moved to buy a gallon of gasoline in Brussels, Belgium, it would have set you back $6.16 a gallon. In London the price was $6.28 a gallon. In Oslo it was $6.90. In Rome it was *only* $5.53.

Historically, pump prices in Europe have tended to be higher because of higher gas taxes. In Britain, for example, taxes reportedly accounted for upwards of 70 percent of the total price of gas in 2006, compared with less than 25 percent in the United States.

With a long record of being unwilling to stand in the way of their constituents' freedom of mobility, American politicians of both parties have remained on the sidelines despite the win-win situation that higher gasoline taxes might have created by curbing excess demand and raising revenue for a nation that has been at war since September 11, 2001. Twenty-twenty hindsight is always perfect, but if gasoline taxes had been raised when patriotic fervor gripped the nation following the attack on the World Trade Center, in 2006 U.S. pump prices probably would have been even higher than they were; however, the situation probably would not have been nearly so annoying because Americans would have known they were sacrificing to support the troops in Afghanistan and Iraq. Instead, it was all the more maddening knowing that the money was going to oil companies in the form of windfall profits and to governments of countries that hate America's guts—even as America's budget deficit worsened and its dependence on imported oil grew.

Still, while raising gas taxes would have been an appropriate short-term action back in 2001, today it is hard to see it not being a loser because of how Americans feel about their cars and trucks, as well as what the impact of higher gas taxes would be on those with the least amount of discretionary income. Over the long term, the new oil industry is going to have to work with, not against, cultural norms. It's also going to have to pay for itself, which, as I describe later on, it is capable of doing.

■ ■ ■

An important distinction must be made between people's car-*driving* and car-*buying* habits.

Even as Americans have continued to put on the miles in the face of rising gasoline prices, they have started to rethink what sort of car they should be driving. As Reed, the consumer advice editor, put it, "Gas prices haven't changed our behavior, except for car-buying."

According to Reed, in 2006 "ultra-small" cars like the Honda Fit and the Toyota Yaris were the hottest sellers. Reed, who once went undercover as a car salesman, believes Americans have always harbored more interest in smaller, fuel-efficient vehicles than either the auto or oil companies have let on, each industry more interested in protecting its bottom line. Now that gasoline prices have gotten so high, Americans won't be put off any longer, Reed believes. Indeed, in 2006 sales of fuel-efficient hybrid vehicles, while still a very small percentage of total vehicle sales, roared to record highs.

This brings us to the first category on our list of companies to watch. As with nearly all of the categories on this list, this one has more than one company because, for different but related reasons, more than one company appears to be positioned to do well in the same general area. The title of this category is "Automotive Efficiency." It ranks fourth in relative importance. The first two companies to make the list in this category should come as no surprise. They are Toyota and Honda, both of which will be discussed over the course of the book. For now, suffice it to say, "They're the leaders," as consumer automotive expert Reed put it. "Not everything Toyota touches turns to gold," Reed said, but its "winning percentage" is 90 percent, while Honda's is 85 percent.

"America," Reed added, "has very little to point to in fuel efficiency."

■ ■ ■

Many Americans are convinced that the reason why their gasoline costs so much is that oil companies are gouging them. Many Americans' blood boils every time they stick that nozzle into their cars and trucks and wonder why, every blasted time the price of oil goes up, gasoline prices do too, even though oil companies already are making a ton of money. Even when pump prices are going down, polls show that many Americans are convinced that oil companies are manipulating things in order to influence the outcome of an upcoming election. Still, it's when prices are going up that consumer anger goes off the charts. People think: Oil companies don't *have* to raise pump prices, do they?

As painful as it is to admit, just as at any other investor-owned company, oil companies have a fiduciary duty—that is to say, a *legal* responsibility—to their shareholders to run their companies as profitably as possible. Moreover, this idea that oil companies are conspiring to artificially raise prices ignores the very important fact that most of the world's remaining crude oil is controlled not by the familiar names on the signs of the corner gas stations but, rather, by governments of countries like Saudi Arabia and Iran. This conspiracy theory further ignores the fact that gasoline marketers would not be charging as much as they do if there were not people somewhere in the world who were ready, willing, and able to pay those high prices.

Oil, it must always be remembered, is a *global* market.

Were this global market to suffer a major supply disruption that caused an oil price shock, the world might see $4 or even $5 gasoline in a matter of weeks or even days. Indeed, as everyone rushed to top off their tanks in defiance of pleas from their elected leaders, gasoline temporarily might not be available at any price in parts of the United States.

In a sense, in 2006 the world was already in the grip of an oil supply shock, a "slow-motion" shock, as Daniel Yergin, famed energy consultant and Pulitzer Prize-winning oil historian, put it. This slow-motion shock was the result of the lingering effects of hurricanes in the Gulf of Mexico, civil strife in Nigeria, the Iraq war, and other factors and had caused, Yergin said, an aggregate disruption of more than 2 million barrels per day.[10]

The odds strongly favor a *sudden* 2-million-barrels-a-day disruption on top of the slow-motion disruption the world was experiencing in 2006. This was the basic message delivered in 2006 to a committee of the U.S. Senate by energy security experts. Why this is so, and how investors can better cushion their portfolios to absorb the impact of a sudden price shock, are the subjects of Chapter 2. The point to remember here is that

a sudden price shock would serve to exacerbate existing market fundamentals, namely, the strain on global crude oil supplies in the face of
steadily rising demand.

■ ■ ■

Oil is not the only important fossil fuel whose price could skyrocket.
The price of natural gas could too, according to Kevin Petak, the energy
consultant.

Looking out to 2010, Petak, whose specialty is natural gas, told me
that natural gas prices will be vulnerable to what he called "super spikes."
To be sure, thanks to a very mild winter in 2005–2006, in the summer of
2006 the United States had a plentiful supply of natural gas on hand. But
according to Petak, with all of the increased demand from natural
gas–fired power plants, and with domestic production that recently has
been "treading water," to use Petak's words, the shock of an extremely
cold winter could send U.S. natural gas prices as high as $15 to $20 per
thousand cubic feet, which on an energy equivalency basis is equal to $90
to $120 per barrel of oil.

Petak's forecast is important because the prices of oil and natural gas
tend to influence one another. Moreover, thanks to what is called gas-to-
liquids technology (GTL), natural gas could become an important alternative to crude oil in the production of diesel and gasoline, though
obviously not until there is enough natural gas available and the threat of
a super spike has been lifted.

Natural gas is not the only alternative fossil fuel that can be used to
make what in industry jargon is often called "synthetic" oil. As Figure 1.1
indicates, coal, tar sands, and oil shale can be used, too—assuming the
price is right and there is enough supply. Whereas an adequate supply of
natural gas appears to be lacking (at least until sometime after 2010),
there is no supply problem when it comes to the three solid alternative
fossil fuels. However, due to high extraction and refining costs, tar sands,
coal, and oil shale share natural gas's problem of being an expensive alternative to crude-derived gasoline.

While greater reliance on solid hydrocarbons could serve to keep gasoline prices higher than they might otherwise end up in the new oil industry, due largely to their benefits in terms of enhancing national security,
tar sands and coal appear to have bright futures and oil shale may, too.

■ ■ ■

One way to simplify what is happening today in the global oil market is to compare it with what happened in one particularly memorable episode of the TV series *Star Trek*. It was the episode in which Capt. Kirk was transported against his will to the surface of a desolate planet by a superior being. There Kirk was forced to fight for his life against a burly alien. Kirk was on the verge of losing when he came upon the ingredients for making a weapon with which he could defeat the alien. Back up on the *Enterprise*, the crew nervously watched as the action unfolded. (If Kirk died, his crew would, too.) When Dr. McCoy asked if the captain was now going to defeat the alien, Spock cautioned that their captain's time was running out.

Well, of course Kirk wound up having enough time. It was a TV show. In real life, the world ran out of time to prevent what has turned out to be a steep multiyear rise in oil prices. Like Kirk's weapon materials, the answers were in plain view the whole time. But while the world, like Kirk, had enough time to act, the world waited too long.

There is plenty of blame to go around:

- Automakers who, with the notable exception of the Japanese, knuckled under to Wall Street's myopia over quarterly profits and failed to make sufficient long-term investments in efficiency and alternative-fuel vehicles.
- Oil companies that thwarted alternative fuel development and catered to Wall Street by buying the existing reserves of other oil companies instead of pouring that cash into the search for new sources of oil.
- Intransigent environmentalists who were unwilling to admit there was as big a need for new domestic energy sources as there was for conservation and protecting the environment.
- Politicians of both parties who drafted environmental regulations without adequate consideration of the adverse economic consequences of their actions.

Pitted against a na\tion of often self-interested and short-sighted parties, five successive American presidents were unable to wean the United States off its deadly dependence on foreign oil. Richard Nixon had his

"Project Independence," designed to free the nation from dependence on imported energy by 1980. Gerald Ford's idea was energy independence by 1985. Jimmy Carter's plan aimed to achieve energy independence by 1990. George H. W. Bush's national energy strategy was intended to reduce America's dependence on foreign oil, as was Bill Clinton's. Like his predecessors, the current President Bush has a plan and it, too, has a long-term goal, namely, to end America's addiction to imported oil by replacing more than 75 percent of the oil America imports from the Middle East by 2025.[11]

If President Bush's plan had had a short-term goal, and if that plan had been launched immediately after 9/11, in 2006 the United States might have been on the road toward energy independence. As it is, notwithstanding a lot of wishful thinking by politicians in Washington about quick fixes, even if the United States were to launch a crash program today, its foreign oil addiction will worsen over the next few years. It has gotten too late to find enough new sources of crude oil (assuming they exist—a hotly debated topic in oil circles), build enough new refinery capacity, or make a large-scale switch to some substitute fuel like ethanol. Virtually everything that is going to be available to us in 2010 is already in operation, under construction, or far along in the planning stage.

The answers to the world's oil problems remain at its feet: fuels that can substitute for gasoline made from crude oil, and new technologies that enable less gasoline to be consumed. Substitutes and efficiency are the weapons with which the world will slay the alien.

However, before substitutes and efficiency have time to work their magic, there would appear to be no other way to meet the growing global demand for oil than by making oil too expensive for some. Call it price-induced rationing. Who is going to walk the plank? There are the usual suspects, namely, poor countries dependent on oil imports. But cutbacks in their combined consumption almost definitely will not be enough. With gasoline prices already sky-high in Europe and fixed by governments at absurdly low levels in oil-producing countries, the arrow points directly at the world's biggest oil consumer, the United States, and at the world's fastest-growing economies, China and India. Not surprisingly, none has yet shown any interest in walking the plank.

To be sure, if demand continues to push oil prices higher, the result could be a recession. Oil analyst Charley Maxwell would not be surprised if an oil-induced recession hit the United States in 2007 around midyear.

However, as bad as a recession would be for the overall economy, the resulting energy price relief might be limited. Marshall Adkins, energy research chief at the investment banking firm Raymond James & Associates, told me, "If we have a major recession, there will only be a minor blip down in the price of oil." The chief economist at CIBC World Markets, Jeffrey Rubin, has written that a recession "would serve as only a temporary diversion from rising energy prices. Throw in a year of flat global demand like we saw during the 2001 recession, and we would at most buy one to two years of price relief before global demand would quickly return to trend growth and an inevitable collision with supply constraints."[12]

■ ■ ■

But what about the old adage that what goes up must come down?

"Oil prices have always come back down," Vincent Matthews, Colorado's state geologist and an oil industry veteran of more than 35 years, told me. "But this time is different. The world has never seen this type of situation. The world has fundamentally changed. I would never say that prices won't come back down, but it's going to take something we haven't thought about to bring them down this time—something like bird flu."

Glenn Wattley, on the other hand, is convinced that the price of oil, like the price of any other commodity, will come down. Wattley, a Boston-based independent energy analyst and a 30-year observer of energy commodity price trends, expects the price of oil to drop by as much as 50 percent.

Don't get too excited. Wattley told me he wouldn't be surprised if investor emotion, fed by a sensationalistic press, first drove the price of oil as high as $120 a barrel. He believes that oil might then trade in that neighborhood for perhaps two to three weeks before coming back down, though only to around $100 a barrel, where it might stay for six to nine months before coming down again and settling at perhaps around $60 a barrel.

Both Matthews and Wattley are right. The world is fundamentally different, but it still obeys economic laws.

Let me explain. Of all the anecdotes that illustrate why the world has a

"liquid" energy emergency on its hands, maybe the one that best captured the state of affairs in 2006 was reported in the July 2, 2006, *New
York Times Magazine* in an article about China's new love affair with the
automobile. The writer described a dinner he went to with a Chinese automotive journalist and some of the journalist's friends. The Chinese
men had what the article called a "palpable sense of pride" about being
able to drive their own cars. "To them," the article said, "it was China finally entering the world stage and participating fully in human
progress." The article quoted one man as saying, "Once China opened
up and Chinese people could see the other side of the world and know
how people lived there, you could no longer limit the *right* to buy cars."
To which another replied, "This *right* is something that has been ours all
along." Another then commented simply: "Driving is our *right*." (The
extra emphasis is the speakers'.)[13]

In the first eight months of 2006, China's automobile production and
sales rose a very healthy 25 percent or so over the prior year period, fueled in part by monster growth of about 40 percent in passenger sedans.
Goldman Sachs' vice chairman Hormats, a China business expert, told
me the Chinese government believes that the Chinese people's demand
for automobiles eventually will level off because of the inconvenience of
trying to drive around China's already traffic-clogged cities.

Maybe. Then again, if car-loving Americans are willing to sit in traffic,
why would car-loving Chinese be any different? Indeed, in a nation
where other, more tangible freedoms are elusive, the lure of the ultimate
freedom machine might turn out to be even greater than it is in the
United States. One thing is certain: With billions of Chinese—not to
mention a whole lot of Indians and other nationalities—starting to believe that driving is as much their "right" as anyone else's, the world is indeed fundamentally different—and likely to stay forever so.

Not only do millions upon millions more people want to drive, they
are increasingly able to afford to drive. Jeffrey Sachs, the world-
renowned economist and crusader against poverty, said in a speech in
2005 that a billion people live "in a degree of affluence that was unimaginable even a quarter century ago." Another four billion, two-thirds of
the planet, "are what is called middle income . . . not American middle
class, mind you, but above extreme poverty, some newly arrived out of
extreme poverty, like China."[14]

Nevertheless, sooner or later the price of oil will reach a point where the pain at the pump is simply too great a pain in the ass—even in China. In the United States that point could be $4, $5, perhaps not until $6 a gallon. For gasoline to hit $6 a gallon, oil would have to go higher than $120 a barrel, which would not surprise energy analyst Petak, who thinks the world could be in for a "super spike."

Still, there are already signs that the pain at the pump is starting to become too great to bear. Thus now the world must choose: Drive less (fat chance!) or find new ways for an ever-growing number of freedom-loving motorists to keep looking over the horizon.

■ ■ ■

What better place to turn for a simple definition of what oil is than the U.S. Energy Information Administration's online kids' page?

> Oil was formed from the remains of animals and plants that lived millions of years ago in a marine (water) environment before the dinosaurs. Over the years, the remains were covered by layers of mud. Heat and pressure from these layers helped the remains turn into what we today call crude oil. The word "petroleum" means "rock oil" or "oil from the earth."[15]

Although oil prices are expressed in terms of dollars "per barrel," oil isn't kept in barrels, at least not anymore. When oil was first discovered in Pennsylvania back in 1859, it was put into all sorts of barrels, including whiskey and wine barrels. Oilmen, however, quickly realized that they needed a more precise system of measurement, and so they turned to the 42-gallon barrel established by Britain's King Edward IV in the fifteenth century. While oil is still priced in terms of barrels, today it generally gets transported via ship, pipeline, and/or truck.

Oil is often called *black gold* but it actually is brownish in color, turning black when exposed to the atmosphere. While the crude best suited for being refined into gasoline is called *sweet* crude, it does not actually taste sweet the way sugar does. Rather, oil is labeled sweet or *sour* depending on its sulfur content.

Gasoline is but one of a number of products turned out by an oil refinery. Generally speaking, crude is refined into gasoline, distillate fuel oil (home heating oil and diesel fuel), jet fuel, residual fuel oil (used by industry, boats, and electric utilities), and other products such as asphalt and road oil.

Oil is often referred to as the lifeblood of modern civilization because it plays a role in the manufacture of most everything from tanks to toilet paper. Of all oil's economic uses, however, by far the biggest is in transportation. In the United States the transportation sector accounts for roughly two-thirds of all oil consumed, more than twice as much as the next biggest sector, the industrial sector. Transportation's share has steadily grown from about 50 percent a little over three decades ago, as the combined percentage of oil consumed by the residential, commercial, and electric power sectors has fallen and as industrial sector use has held steady at around 25 percent.

Hidden in these statistics is one of the unsung economic success stories of the twentieth century—a success story the world really has no choice but to repeat in the twenty-first century.

As Hirsch indicated in his report, government statistics show that between 1973 and 2003 the gross domestic product (GDP) of the United States grew roughly 140 percent without a big increase in industrial oil use. During the same period total vehicle miles traveled by cars and light trucks more than doubled and oil consumption for transportation purposes rose sharply.

Why did oil consumption rise significantly in the transportation sector but not in the industrial sector? While the transportation sector got more fuel efficient, it continued to rely almost exclusively on oil. By contrast, the industrial sector got more efficient *and* diversified into fuels other than oil. Specifically, during this period there was a changeover from oil-fueled machinery to inherently more efficient electrically powered machinery, the electricity in turn produced from still other energy sources such as coal, natural gas, and nuclear power.

Repeating this success story in the transportation sector will take time. Copulos noted in Congressional testimony that the average age of the vehicle fleet in the United States is roughly eight and a half years, which is roughly only half of a vehicle's average lifespan. So even if, starting today, every vehicle sold in America ran on a fuel other than gasoline, we would not see a big drop in demand for gasoline for a number of years. (Are *you* going to foot the bill for a new car while your current one is still in reasonably good shape?)

Meanwhile, the number of cars and light trucks on global highways continues to grow. By 2020 or sooner, according to an April 2006 *Wall Street Journal* article, there will be one billion cars and light trucks on the world's roads, over 25 percent more than there were in 2006.[16] What this means is that, even after the introduction of large numbers of vehicles that do run on something other than just gasoline, for a time gasoline demand will probably be greater than it is today.

■ ■ ■

Who is to blame for all these additional vehicles that will continue making it harder to keep up with the demand for oil? Nobody, unless you want to blame the rapidly emerging middle classes in India and China for wanting to share in the prototypical American dream, a dream just starting to come into focus in these and other budding economic powers thanks to the global economy's ever-expanding interdependency.

Demand is going to go in only one direction—up. It has been estimated that by 2050 there will be some two billion vehicles on the road—twice as many as are predicted to be on the road in 2020. Yet those of us alive today think that the 750 million or so vehicles now on the road are a huge problem.

While everyone tends to focus on the United States, China, and India, they are only part of the world's "rising demand" problem. Another important part of it is what is happening in the oil-*producing* countries.

We're used to thinking of OPEC as a source of oil. But in addition to exporting their oil around the world, OPEC's members also must satisfy the oil demands of their own people. Due to these and other oil-producing countries' expanding populations and subsidized gasoline prices—neither of which is easily altered—oil demand has started to surge where you might least expect it if you live in a giant oil-consuming nation like China or the United States.

As CIBC economist Jeff Rubin put it in his June 2006 "Monthly Indicators" report:

> All of a sudden, major oil-producing countries are becoming major oil-consuming countries. Russia, Mexico, Venezuela, Saudi Arabia, Iran and Indonesia collectively consumed 9.5 million barrels per day in 2004, nearly 50 percent more than China—the world's second-largest oil-consuming nation. Not surprisingly, many of

those countries posted the greatest growth in domestic oil demand. For example in 2004, Venezuela's oil demand grew by almost 10 percent or nearly three times the world average of that year.[17]

It doesn't take an economist to understand the implication of this trend, which is that the more oil an oil-producing country consumes at home, the less it has available for export unless it ramps up production, which in almost every case simply is not possible.

Why isn't it possible? The explanation often given by the governments of oil-producing countries is that they already pump as much as they can, which is likely true, but not for the reason they would like us to believe. As was explained to me by Charley Maxwell, back in the late 1970s and early 1980s a subtle but decisive change occurred in the way countries' state-owned oil companies operate. What changed was that investment decisions became politicized, made by governments instead of their national oil companies. After a quarter century of this, production is suffering, Maxwell believes. It is a situation that is unlikely to change, he told me, because even though the governments of the oil-producing countries own a majority of the world's oil reserves, they still think that these sorts of investments should be the job of privately owned oil companies.

It should come as no surprise that Saudi Arabian oil officials are loath to let anyone get an inside look.

Then, too, there may be this hidden problem. Say you are the ruler of Saudi Arabia. You are old enough to remember the days before petrodollars made your country fabulously wealthy. You are smart enough to know that when the oil runs out—which it has to, eventually—you could find yourself back where you started. No matter how much a thirsty world may be willing to pay you today for your oil, you must think about tomorrow. At what point do you start protecting the future generations of your country by limiting current production so that your oil reserves last longer?

■　■　■

This is not the first time the world has turned to technology in the wake of high oil prices, energy insecurity, and environmental anxiety. Back in the 1970s, in response to the supply shocks set off by OPEC, the United States toyed with a variety of technologically driven new ideas in the areas of substitutes and efficiency. But after OPEC opened the spigot again, the new thinking was allowed to languish, over the strong objections of the environmental community.

Now the work has begun anew, and this time it should be sustainable because the world's present predicament is different from its last. Specifically, the current strain on global oil supplies is not due to a sudden disruption in supply—not yet, anyway—but rather to a steady buildup of demand that is now reaching the critical stage. Oil is still flowing, just not enough. Service stations have gasoline; it just keeps costing more to fill up, especially during the American summer when U.S. gasoline consumption is very high.

Think of it this way: Supply disruptions are like a heart attack to the economic body, while excessive demand growth is like the long-term buildup of plaque in the body's arteries. Both are killers, but with plaque it may take many years, during which time a person continues to go about his or her daily business while, hopefully, making lifestyle changes that head off the crash cart experience.

The world economy has recently started feeling the effects of many years of plaque buildup that were allowed to go untreated. Like a patient whose blood pressure keeps rising higher into the danger zone, the average U.S. pump price rose from roughly $1.50 a gallon in June 2003 to around $1.93 a gallon in June 2004, to around $2.10 in June 2005, to about $2.85 in June 2006.[18] Like any person whose arteries have become clogged with plaque, the global economy needs to change its ways. Diet and exercise, as the doctor would say—with dietary changes equating to greater use of substitute fuels, and exercise equating to greater efficiency.

Many current oil industry executives were around in the late 1970s and early 1980s, which helps to explain why they see the present oil situation, not withstanding its different characteristics, ending the same way as the last, namely, with a simple price "correction." An August 2006 Reuters poll of oil analysts found that respondents were expecting the price of crude to decline to $64 a barrel in 2007 and to $56 a barrel in 2008. But as Reuters noted in its story on the poll results, one of the analysts polled "cautioned against relying too heavily on past lessons, as the structure of the oil market has changed radically since the 1980s price spike. 'We're in uncharted territory, far from familiar land,' he said."[19]

To be sure, the world is said to have roughly 50 to 60 major new oil-producing projects that are expected to make significant contributions to supply by 2010. Unfortunately, a lot of this new crude will serve only to offset declines in production from mature fields.

This is an important point, one which experts like Maxwell say is not fully appreciated even within the oil industry. Simply put, no oil field lasts forever. Each has what is called a depletion rate. Given that much of the world's oil now comes from fields that are getting long in the tooth, accurately estimating how fast the world's mature oil fields are depleting has never been more important. Maxwell said he factors a 5 percent rate of depletion into his calculations, although he thinks that 6 percent might be closer to the way things really are. He told me that some supply forecasts use much lower depletion rates which, in his opinion, result in a false sense of security.

Marshall Adkins of Raymond James agrees. A petroleum engineer by training, with a quarter century of oil-related experience under his belt, Adkins said 5 to 6 percent is probably "much closer" to the way things really are, and that the actual rate could be as high as 7 or 8 percent.

Another person who seems to agree has been described as somebody who probably knows more about oil than anyone else in Saudi Arabia. His name is Sadad al-Husseini, formerly the Saudis' top executive for exploration and production. According to an August 2005 article in the *New York Times*, al-Husseini believes the world is heading for an oil shortage due to the combined effects of depletion and rising demand. Al-Husseini emphasized that, as the writer of the article paraphrased it, "oil producers deplete their reserves every time they pump out a barrel of oil. This means that merely to maintain their reserve base, they have to replace the oil they extract from declining fields. It's the geological equivalent of running to stay in place."[20]

It should be noted that the depletion rates of oil and natural gas are similar, according to natural gas analyst Petak. "Hydrocarbons are hydrocarbons," he said.

Before long, oil field depletion rates of even 5 to 6 percent may be seen as an underestimation. It all depends on when global crude oil production "peaks."

The "peak oil" debate has been a hot topic in oil circles for many years. This is *not* a debate about when the world will run out of crude. Rather, it is a debate about when the rate at which crude oil is produced can only go down because physical production has topped out.

Imagine you are riding in a roller coaster. As you hit the top and start down the other side, you quickly pick up speed. In a similar fashion, peak oil advocates see production declining rapidly after the peak is reached.

Peaking is an important psychological factor in the global oil market. Pessimists believe the peak has already arrived or will by around 2010. Optimists don't think it will arrive before 2020 and maybe not until 2040 or even later.

But think about this: If even some optimistic experts think conventional oil production could peak while a large number of the world's one billion cars and light trucks are still running on gasoline, there probably is reason for everyone to be concerned about how fast the world's remaining crude can be brought to the surface. Not surprisingly, oil company executives tend to dismiss peak oil talk; however, the chief executive of the French oil company Total has said that unless consumption is cut, production could peak around 2020.[21]

■ ■ ■

In one important way, production appears to have peaked already. As was previously mentioned, the world has two kinds of oil, sweet and sour— or, as they are also called, light and heavy. Light sweet oil's lower sulfur content makes it more desirable because it is cheaper to refine and produces more gasoline per barrel of crude. When the media discusses oil reserves and production, it tends to lump sweet and sour statistics together, which is understandable given that official estimates don't ever seem to break them out. But some geologists believe the world's sweet crude production has started to decline as overall production declines where sweet crude is plentiful, such as in the North Sea.

Meanwhile, in Saudi Arabia, which produces a lot of sour crude, "They say 'we can't help it if we've got the oil the world doesn't want,'" independent petroleum geologist Jeffrey Brown, a peak oil advocate, told me in an interview.

Essentially the world is relying more and more on heavy sour crude. The price of light sweet crude, which is the one that gets all the attention, is rising not just in response to greater demand but also in response to the greater premium that refiners must pay for light sweet crude.

Many oil refineries were built to run on light sweet crude. Some are now being retrofitted to run on heavy sour crude, thereby adding an additional layer of cost that gets passed through to consumers.

But while the issue of a possible peak in sweet oil production is important, it is when the perception that *total* crude oil production has peaked becomes conventional wisdom among the world's oil price setters that the price of crude could soar even if there is a surplus in the market at that time.

Who are these price setters? They include oil companies, financial firms, commodities speculators, and others involved in the minute-by-minute determination of the all-important spot market price of crude. This is a process that can be as much art as science. Prices are often based as much on what people *think* the future will be like as they are on current economic conditions. (Remember, the market is setting prices on cargoes of oil intended for *future* delivery.) Because the market price of oil can come as much from a trader's gut as from his head, prices can rise even during periods when there is a surplus of oil on the market if, for example, price setters are worried about the potential impact of a threatened cutoff of supply by Iran or Venezuela, two big producers whose unpredictable leaders like to froth at the mouth.

Among those who would be only happy to drive prices higher should peak oil become conventional wisdom is the controversial new breed of energy hedge funds on Wall Street. Indeed, as oil prices have risen over the last few years, hedge funds have come under attack for allegedly making a bad situation worse in order to line their own pockets. Still, when these funds have sufficient reasons to drive down the price of oil, that's what they are going to do. These guys thrive on market volatility. The direction is secondary.

It seems unlikely that the doom-and-gloom psychology of peak oil will take hold of the oil market as long as influential market leaders like the chief executive of ExxonMobil, Rex Tillerson, sound convincing when they say the world won't be running out of oil anytime in the near future.

Another important, though hardly comforting, reason why peak oil is not likely to become conventional wisdom in the near future is that, "We won't know that it has happened until we're well past it," as I was told by Tom Petrie, the energy analyst and head of the firm that bears his name, Petrie Parkman. Petrie's own disquieting opinion is that we are within "spitting distance" of peak oil's arrival.

■ ■ ■

Just as Captain Kirk helps to explain the way things are, so too does the
TV series *The Twilight Zone*. In one classic episode (then again, weren't
they all classics?) a middle-aged woman on horseback chases a mysteri-
ous young woman, also on horseback, but never catches her. The mys-
tery rider is actually an apparition. She is the middle-aged woman as she
was many years earlier, before she ruined her life through a bad marriage. The middle-aged woman is doomed to keep riding after her
younger self in a futile attempt to fix the big mistake of her past.

The world is now that middle-aged woman, unable to correct its past
mistake, namely, failing to sufficiently develop substitutes and efficiency
back in the 1980s. So now, for probably the next 10 years or so, the world
is fated to ride as fast as it can, pump and refine as much crude oil as it
can, in order to keep gasoline tanks full so that parking lots at Wal-Mart,
Home Depot, Best Buy, and so on stay full and consumer spending keeps
the overall economy afloat.

The scariest aspect of the rise in crude oil prices in 2006 was that the
$70-a-barrel plateau was crossed because of fear of something going
wrong, not because of something *actually* going wrong. In 2005 it had
taken Hurricane Katrina's impact on production facilities in the Gulf of
Mexico to push prices above $70. In 2006 it took only fear of calamities
both natural (hurricanes) and man-made (Iran and terrorism). This fear
outweighed the relative peace of mind the trading community should have
felt based on there being enough oil on hand to meet current demand.

So palpable was the state of fear in the oil market in 2006 that forecasts that had previously seemed irrationally fearful started looking "rationally fearful."

Case in point: CIBC chief economist Jeffrey Rubin's prediction, made
back in his September 2005 "Monthly Indicators" report, that crude
would hit $100 a barrel by the fourth quarter of 2007.[22]

In May 2006 the authoritative *Platts Energy Economist* wrote that "the
prospect of $100 oil is no longer a fantastical pronouncement—it's a real
possibility."[23] In July, *BusinessWeek's* web site ran a story titled, "Would
$100 Oil Slam the Global Economy?" (Probably not, the article con-
cluded, but it could help put the brakes on U.S. growth.)[24] In August an
article on MSN.com began, "Investors, get ready for $100-a-barrel oil."[25]

To be sure, by September the media had done an abrupt about-face in the wake of suddenly falling oil prices. Whatever this may say about the media, the point is that in the first half of 2006 the world was flummoxed about oil even though there wasn't an actual shortage.

This brings us to a prediction that Rubin made in his "Occasional Report #53" back in April 2005, namely, that starting in 2007 and 2008 a significant global shortage of oil will begin to develop.[26] As irrationally fearful as this may sound to some, one indication that Rubin may be right is what has been happening to Mexico's Cantarell oil field, second largest in the world after the Ghawar field in Saudi Arabia. Between 2004 and 2006 Cantarell production reportedly declined 15 percent, and experts have now predicted that the falloff is going to accelerate. "Cantarell is going to fall a lot, and quickly," a former executive with Mexico's state-run oil monopoly was quoted as saying in a July 2006 *Los Angeles Times* story about the fact that "fears that wells that generate 60 percent of (Mexico's) petroleum are in the throes of a major decline."[27]

Did I mention that, as the story points out, Mexico is the second biggest source of the United States' imported oil, after Canada?

Whenever I think that I am being irrationally fearful about the future of energy, I remember something Matt Simmons told me. Matthew R. Simmons, head of a Houston-based energy investment bank that bears his name, is well known in oil circles for his controversial assessment of remaining Saudi oil reserves, which Simmons believes have been overestimated by officials there. Whether Simmons is right about that is not the point. The point is that, as Simmons told me back in 2005, "Few people even in the energy business have any idea how fragile our remaining energy reserves are and how expensive it will be to recover them." Then he made this chilling observation: "There is no ceiling" to oil prices—at least not in the oil industry as it has existed for decades. But what about in the new oil industry?

Energy analyst Wattley believes that the price of oil eventually will settle at whatever level makes oil as expensive as, or a little less expensive than, its alternatives. This is an eminently logical prediction to make for a market that has robust competition, which oil, given its stranglehold on transportation, has not been for many decades. But in the new oil industry, oil will have to compete with substitutes selling for the equivalent of roughly $40 to $60 a barrel (a reasonably conservative range of the estimates that have been made by promoters of various substitute liquid fuels).

Importantly, gains in vehicle efficiency should also serve as competitive pressure on oil's market price (as well as on the price of gas substitutes). Negaoil will be found through such improvements in car and truck efficiency as better design and lighter materials.

Of course, in order to have a competitive market, one must have competitors. Critics of Big Oil argue there are too few major oil companies for there to be genuine competition. Whether or not this is true, in the new oil industry the number of competitors should grow to include automakers, agricultural business companies, unconventional fossil asset holders such as coal companies, and a host of other companies with enabling technologies.

As people think about which investment ideas might pay off in the new oil industry, they should not get hung up on any particular price target or date. Whether oil tops out at $100 a barrel in 2009, or maybe at $90 a barrel in 2010, is not that important in the scheme of things.

Indeed, the whole way in which the market—and the media—uses numbers can be misleading. Great emphasis is placed on the amount of oil that is in storage even though, at the rate at which the world consumes oil, what's in storage generally represents only several weeks' worth of supply. Great emphasis also is placed on oil consumption in the United States, with insufficient attention paid to China, India, and the oil-producing countries themselves, in part because of the difficulty of obtaining statistics that are reliable.

Another point to remember about numbers is that there is no direct correlation between the price of crude and the retail price of gasoline. While crude costs represented roughly 55 percent of the retail price of a gallon of gas in 2006, refining, marketing, oil company profits, and so on also were significant factors.

Simply put, for the next few years gas will sell pretty much at whatever price is needed to squeeze enough demand out of the global market to maintain a delicate balance between supply and demand. The actual price will be up to you, to all of us, and it will depend on how badly governments want to develop their economies, as well as on how badly we want to keep living our lives the way we have come to believe is our right as Americans, Chinese, and so on.

Some Americans have locked themselves into workday lives that require them to drive more than 90 minutes, one way, to work. These so-called extreme commuters reportedly now total 3.4 million, double their number in 1990. "Even $3-a-gallon gas and growing gridlock aren't slowing the rise of this group," *Newsweek* reported in 2006.[28]

What is particularly important about the trend toward extreme commuting is that it highlights how, in addition to many of us wanting to drive, many of us *need* to drive, sometimes long distances. According to energy economist Copulos, more of the miles we Americans travel are for need versus want. It's nature versus nurture in a new guise. Nature is the inbred call of the open road. Nurture is the clear and present need to put food on the table. Both are powerful motivators to getting behind the wheel.

None of this, it should be added, takes into account the growing amount of gasoline that nurturing is going to cause us to waste in the coming years. University of North Carolina at Charlotte professor David Hartgen wrote in his newspaper op-ed piece that four U.S. cities (Los Angeles, Chicago, Washington, and San Francisco–Oakland) presently have so much traffic that peak-hour commuting trips require 50 percent more time. In another 25 years, he wrote, 30 cities will be added to the list, and in 12 cities peak-hour commutes will take at least 75 percent longer than traveling the same distance in non-peak periods.[29]

When I interviewed Michelle Foss, head of the Center for Energy Economics at the University of Texas, I asked her how high gasoline prices might go in the United States. We don't really know, was her answer. Why not? Because of factors that are very difficult to measure, she said. She noted that as gasoline prices have been going up in recent years, these rises have been partially offset by declining prices for other things Americans buy with their disposable income.

Foss also alerted me to a phenomenon that makes a lot of sense from a cultural point of view, namely, the more fuel-efficient a car is, the more miles it tends to be driven. My translation: The automobile will remain the ultimate freedom machine, and freedom tastes even better when driving does not ruin the environment.

So here is the ambitious task the new oil industry faces: Come up with enough fuel to keep everyone who wants or needs to be behind the wheel of a car able to do so without it costing an arm and a leg, ruining the environment, or putting the nation's security at risk.

"This is way too complicated for Adam Smith's invisible hand," independent energy analyst Glenn Wattley emphasized to me. "Government must get intimately involved in planning and setting policy for the energy industry over the next several decades.

"If government does not get involved, we will see more dramatic boom-and-bust cycles in energy prices that will threaten global economic stability."

CHAPTER 2

Terrorists, Nationalists, and Shock Absorbers

There are moments when economic subjects are expressed in terms everyone can understand.

Such a moment occurred in 2006 during a meeting of the U.S. Senate Foreign Relations Committee when the executive director of the Energy Modeling Center at Stanford University discussed the likelihood of a major disruption in the global flow of oil. "Your odds of drawing a club, diamond or heart from a shuffled deck of cards are three out of four," Hillard Huntington said, according to his prepared testimony, while "the odds of a foreign oil disruption happening over the next 10 years are slightly higher at 80 percent."[1]

That's four out of five—odds nobody should ignore when the pot on the table is their retirement savings, college savings, or rainy-day fund for when there is a medical emergency or they unexpectedly lose their job.

To absorb an oil price shock, investors should consider having "shock absorbers" in their portfolios. Shock absorbers will not enable investors to beat the odds. For the next 5 to 10 years, no amount of cushioning will prevent investors from taking a hit should the global flow of oil be interrupted for any length of time. But as the prices of one's other investments are going down, shock absorbers should be able to hold their own.

Importantly, some shock absorbers have two-way potential. Just like football players used to play both offense and defense, some shock absorbers could pay off not just when it's time to play defense but also when it is time to play offense in the new oil industry.

There is no way to know how much of one's portfolio should be in shock-absorbing investments. It all depends on the unknowable, namely, the exact nature of and response to the event that causes the disruption. It further depends on when the disruption occurs. The weaker the economy at the time of a disruption, the more likely the disruption will lead to a recession that damages one's other investments, and vice versa.

Experts disagree on how much damage a major disruption that, say, doubled oil prices would inflict on the U.S. economy as a whole. Huntington noted in his testimony that many researchers think the level of real gross domestic product (GDP) would decline by 2 percent, while others believe it would decline by 5 percent, more than twice as much. He said in his prepared testimony that his personal view is that a 5 percent decline "may be closer to what would actually happen." He added, "That would mean a recession."

It doesn't take an economist to figure out that the closer one is to retirement or to having to write a big check for, say, a kid's college tuition, the more shock absorbers may make sense.

■ ■ ■

At a recent World Economic Forum in Davos, Switzerland, experts played a war game in which they acted out what would happen to the price of oil if there were a three-prong terrorist attack involving the sinking of a tanker ship that blocked access to Central Asian oilfields, a successful attack on the Alaskan oil port of Valdez, and a rebuffed attack on the Saudi oil complex at Ras Tanura which resulted in a months-long loss of about 5 percent of the world's oil supply. The players decided that oil would spike overnight to $120 a barrel and gasoline in the United States would hit $5 a gallon.[2]

Alas, this is only one of many geopolitical scenarios that would probably cause an oil price shock. Simply put, never have so many people been so dependent on so many politically unstable oil-producing countries. The world is increasingly vulnerable to severe oil supply disruptions, the International Energy Agency said in November 2006.[3] Such is the resulting psychological strain on global oil markets that even pugnacious countries that aren't oil producers can strike fear in the hearts of traders when they do something provocative. Indeed, while the one missile probably capable of reaching the United States test-fired by North Korea on July 4, 2006 was, not surprisingly, a dud, the price of oil still rose to a then-record high for the year.

Oil traders won't have reason to breathe easier for several years. As previously discussed, even after substitutes and efficiency start making their presence felt, the world will still need lots of oil. Most investors should probably just get used to the idea that for the foreseeable future their portfolios are going to be at risk from the effects of a major supply disruption. Today, tomorrow, or five years from now, you could wake up to discover you are worth considerably less on paper than you were the night before.

■ ■ ■

The three countries that should cause investors to lose the most sleep are Iraq, Iran, and Saudi Arabia.

While it is no longer a "shock" when some subversive group blows up an Iraqi oil pipeline, what would be a shock to the global oil market would be if the United States lost Iraq to Islamic extremists or to bring-the-troops-home-now advocates in America. Whatever one's opinion about whether American soldiers should have gone into Iraq in the first place, if they leave Iraq in a chaotic state, the oil market will react badly.

This is because the U.S. military is the only thing preventing Iraq's unpredictable neighbor, Iran, from establishing at least partial political dominance over oil-rich Iraq. The Bush administration unintentionally rekindled Iran's centuries-old dream of a Shiite Muslim empire ruled from Tehran when it created a political vacuum in Iraq, freeing Iraq's long-repressed Shiite majority. As the world's fourth largest oil producer, Iran's incessant saber rattling against the United States generates continuous upside price pressure. But what would really give the oil market a jolt would be if Iran got its hands on Iraq's oil reserves, much of which lie in Shiite-dominated territory.

Tehran is doubly dangerous because it doesn't just *want* Iraq's oil; it *needs* Iraq's oil. Indeed, despite Iran's current preeminence in the oil world, its future as a global oil power is shaky.

Iran's problem is that, due to steadily rising domestic demand and a plateau in production, the amount of oil the country has available for export is expected to start dropping sharply. CIBC's Jeff Rubin has written that by 2010 Iran may have only about 1.4 million barrels a day available for export, down from about 2.5 million barrels in 2006. Due to a lack of refining capacity, Iran already is the world's second largest importer of refined gasoline, Rubin also noted in CIBC's June 2006 "Monthly Indicators" report.[4]

Goldman Sachs's vice chairman Bob Hormats also sees Iran headed for trouble. "The country is basically a welfare state that's dependent on its oil revenue," he told me. Hormats has seen research showing that Iran's oil production should continue to decline as its domestic demand continues to grow, with the two lines converging only a few years out.

The thought of losing its oil-based political power in a few short years must have the Tehran regime in a panic. How far would the mullahs go to save their collective asses? How about as far as Iraq? Texas-based independent petroleum geologist Jeffrey Brown told me that Iraq has "the best remaining potential oil reserves."

Without the oil revenue Tehran now depends on to keep its economy afloat, unless Iran can get its hands on Iraq's oil, the government in Tehran could find itself the victim of a popular uprising—which, of course, would be deliciously ironic from an American point of view, given how the mullahs came to power in the first place.

In short, then, the Tehran regime is as likely to roil things out of fear of losing power as out of a desire to extend that power beyond its own borders. Tehran's push to develop nuclear technology despite worldwide condemnation illustrates the government's split personality. Tehran wants nuclear technology in the form of a bomb in order to cement its role as a global power broker. At the same time, Tehran needs nuclear technology in the form of electricity to help offset the plateau in oil production and to keep its own people from casting too longing an eye on the bounteous economies of the West. It should come as no surprise that the regime in Tehran confiscates the equipment that enables the Iranian people to watch foreign TV.

There may be no bigger geopolitical oil problem in the world today than Iran's nuclear program. Will the United States decide that it can't live with a nuclear Iran and bomb Iranian installations? If attacked, would Iran retaliate by cutting off its oil exports?

Given Iran's dependence on imported gasoline, the mullahs likely would not cut off their nose to spite their face. More likely Iran might do something like fire a shot or two across the bow of some oil supertanker, an act that would not by itself stop the global flow of oil but could precipitate a psychological crisis that produced a price spike.

Of all the Bush administration officials, the one you might expect would be the most committed to protecting the global flow of oil is the energy secretary. And yet, according to news reports, Samuel Bodman has said that stopping Iranian nuclear enrichment is more important than the price of oil.[5]

One can well understand how Washington might want to slow down Iran's nuclear program with some sort of precision missile strike. By the time Iran recovered, its petro-power might be spent and its turn on the global stage all but over.

From Washington's perspective, the stakes probably seem the highest they have been since World War II. Writing in the *Washington Post* in September 2006, former U.S. Secretary of State Henry Kissinger warned of nothing less than a "war of civilizations" against the backdrop of a nuclear-armed Middle East. According to Kissinger, at the center of this potential "global catastrophe," to use his words, is Iran.[6]

Indeed, if the United States did attack Iranian nuclear facilities, Tehran might easily do something incredibly provocative like loose its dogs of war (Hezbollah) in an all-out assault on Israel. Having been in Iran as a reporter nearly 30 years ago, during the period when Ayatollah Khomeini successfully deposed the U.S.-supported Shah of Iran, I strongly believe that if both sides were to start seeing their differences in terms of a "war of civilizations," the spiritual descendants of Khomeini would not for a moment hesitate to ignite a regional conflagration that could spread far beyond the Middle East. It should be noted that on the fifth anniversary of 9/11, President Bush, in a solemn prime-time address to the nation, said the war on terror "has been called a clash of civilizations. In truth, it is a struggle for civilization."[7]

Then, too, there is this disturbing possibility: an unholy war within the Muslim civilization between Shiites and Sunnis. The escalation in Shiite-Sunni violence in Iraq in 2006 indicates how brutal a Muslim-versus-Muslim war could become, with global oil supplies held hostage. Hezbollah versus al-Qaeda: now there's a conflict nobody wants to see.

Hopefully, all this will remain the stuff of war games. Unfortunately, oil traders have to think like players in a war game.

■ ■ ■

Five years from now, if Iran is not still the most likely launching pad for an oil price spike, then that dubious distinction probably will fall to nearby Saudi Arabia.

To be sure, Saudi Arabia's oil facilities are among the best defended pieces of real estate on the planet, thanks in no small part to the United States military. Nevertheless, a couple of years ago terrorists were able to detonate explosive-laden cars at Abqaiq, the massive Saudi oil processing facility, during an attack that ultimately, though barely, failed. If there is one thing the oil market is sure of, it is that it cannot be sure there won't be another attack on Saudi oil installations. In a *fatwa*, or edict, issued in 2004, Osama bin Laden urged his supporters to target oil supplies in the Middle East that "do not serve the Islamic nation but the enemies of this nation." Can anybody guess who he meant by "enemies?"

Because al-Qaeda and its sympathizers have managed to infiltrate all levels of Saudi society, it is only a matter time before terrorists succeed in plunging a dagger into the heart of the Saudi oil industry. So says Milton Copulos of the National Defense Council Foundation. Copulos, who appears frequently before Congressional committees on energy security matters, described for me an all-too-believable scenario in which he said 10 percent of the world's oil supply would be taken off the world market for several months. Such an event, he said, would cause oil to spike to $125 a barrel, gasoline to hit $6 to $7 a gallon, and the stock market to crash. And here's the fun part: "It would all happen before the U.S. military and Saudi security forces had time to respond," he said.

Copulos detailed how three or four al-Qaeda fanatics with excellent computer skills could, in his opinion, knock out the computer system at Ras Tanura. When asked why the Saudis wouldn't switch to a backup system, Copulos said the computer system in question was one of a kind. When asked why security forces would not have time to respond, Copulos said it is almost certain that these fanatics are already in place, just waiting for the right moment, and that it would literally take them only seconds to run around with hammers smashing everything to smithereens.

In October 2006, "Top world oil exporter Saudi Arabia said . . . it was taking measures to protect its oil and economic installations from a 'terrorist threat,'" Reuters reported. The Reuters article quoted a Saudi Interior Ministry spokesman as saying, "The terrorist threat to the kingdom's economic installation exists and it is a declared goal of the straying faction to affect the interests of the Saudi citizen."[8] Not to mention the rest of the world.

Sleeping pill, anyone?

And if Saudi Arabia, Iran, and Iraq were not enough to worry about, oil traders have lots of other scenarios to haunt them. One could be called the *choke point* scenario.

While a third of young Americans reportedly can't find Louisiana on a map even after Hurricane Katrina, every investor needs to know where the Strait of Hormuz and the Strait of Malacca are. Each is a narrow shipping channel through which much of the world's oil travels via tanker on its way to the big oil-consuming nations in Europe, North America, and Asia.

Located off the southern tip of Iran, the Strait of Hormuz is part of the bigger Iran-Iraq problem. (Isn't it funny how we keep getting back to Iran?) In April 2006 it was reported in the media that the chap with the title Supreme Commander of Iran's Islamic Revolution Guards Corps had suggested that Iran might blockade the Strait of Hormuz as a way of punishing what he called "the aggressive powers from beyond the continent that want to endanger the security of the region."[9]

Meanwhile, thousands of miles away, the Strait of Malacca represents China's primary oil-import corridor. With Indonesia and other al-Qaeda–infested countries located nearby, the Strait of Malacca is a tasty target for the bin Laden crowd. Adding to the Asian danger are bands of pirates, any one of which presumably could be financially enticed by terrorists to strike.

Pirates, it should be noted, are not just an Asian phenomenon. After my stint in Iran, I wrote a story about pygmies who were paid to guard against pirate attacks on Western-owned ships when they were docked in the Nigerian capital of Lagos. Pirates are but one of many dangers faced by oil companies trying to do business in Nigeria, a place where bad guys always seem to be blowing up pipelines and kidnapping Western oil workers. Without its oil, Nigeria's internal problems would be ignored by the West. While one certainly can make a human rights case against one country being more important than another because of oil, the damnable fact is that the world is addicted to Nigerian crude, which is that sweet (low-sulfur) kind that goes great through a refinery. When a pin drops in Nigeria, it can be heard on the global oil market.

Meanwhile, some have speculated about the possibility of a terrorist attack against oil installations on U.S. soil. While striking directly at the U.S. oil industry probably would not cause as much physical disruption as an attack on Saudi installations, the shock of it happening in America might give the global oil market a heart attack.

In the wake of the Oklahoma City bombing, it is no longer out of the question that an attack on American oil installations might be carried out, not by Islamic terrorists or agents of Iran-backed Hezbollah, but by angry Americans. As wrong as I believe they are in their thinking, the fact remains that a majority of Americans believe that oil companies are ripping them off. News reports of record profits and record high gasoline prices fuel the public's distrust. It is hard to refute a perception that "good ole Texas boys" are ripping off the rest of us.

Logically, either homegrown or foreign terrorists might want to attack a big, visible symbol of America's energy might. Viewers of the TV series *The Sopranos* are probably familiar with the storage tanks in New Jersey across the river from where the World Trade Center towers once stood. Attacking them would serve a diabolical propagandistic purpose. One shudders at the thought of aerial shots of thick smoke once again darkening the New York City skyline running nonstop on every TV news program around the world, not to mention every jihadist web site.

■ ■ ■

As much as America's energy interests are at risk from the tactical threats posed by Iran and terrorism, they are at almost as much strategic risk from anti–U.S. nationalism emanating from countries like Venezuela, Russia, and China. The danger here is not a war of civilizations. Rather, it is the potential of a new cold war over energy supplies.

In 2006 American Secretary of State Condoleezza Rice alluded to these nationalistic threats when she told a Senate committee that the world's "energy problem" was "warping" diplomacy. Said the secretary:

> I can tell you that nothing has really taken me aback more as Secretary of State than the way that the politics of energy is—I will use the word warping—diplomacy around the world. It has given

extraordinary power to some states that are using that power in not very good ways for the international system, states that would otherwise have very little power.

Secretary Rice further said that "some states that are growing very rapidly (are undertaking) an all-out search for energy—states like China, states like India—that is really sending them into parts of the world where they've not been before, and challenging, I think, for our diplomacy."[10]

One country that Rice did not mention by name but which is most deserving of the Secretary's ire is Venezuela and its stridently anti–U.S. leader Hugo Chavez. Already a key supplier of oil to the United States—a point which Chavez makes sure Washington does not forget—Venezuela sits on a vast source of tar sands, one of the solid unconventional fossil fuel sources. Located along the Orinoco River, this sticky strip of tar-laden land—known as the Orinoco Belt—may hold hundreds of billions of barrels of oil. Until the recent multiyear rise in crude prices, Venezuela's tar sands deposits were pretty much of an afterthought in the oil world, a resource considered too expensive to exploit fully. Now, however, the Orinoco Belt is seen as a key asset, a bountiful source of hydrocarbons that can help keep global demand from getting away from supply. The media has reported that Venezuela, which already has the most proven oil reserves outside of the Middle East, hopes to quadruple its proven reserves total to 315 billion barrels by counting its Orinoco reserves by the end of 2008.

Chavez keeps itching to throw his oil weight around. He has harangued foreign oil companies operating in Venezuela. He has made friends with Iran's petulant president. He has gone to China to do business. He is trying to convince his neighbors to join him in an anti–U.S. campaign.

Yet, while the threat posed by Venezuela is not insignificant, it is not nearly as serious as the respective threats posed by Russia and China. Russia *really* wants to throw its weight around. Not only has Moscow been harassing Western oil companies that are supposed to be its partners in different energy projects, but Moscow also has designs on forming a brand new kind of OPEC, an energy cartel that would control the global supply and price of natural gas. To be sure, the logistics of natural gas are less conducive to the formation of cartels than are those of oil. Still, the sheer magnitude of Russian energy production (natural gas and oil combined) could be enough for Moscow to succeed in developing an "energy weapon" that it could use to influence global energy markets, and with it global politics. If Russia's energy weapon became a *fait accompli*, it would permanently raise the geopolitical risk—and, hence, the risk premium—traders put on energy prices.

Russian president Vladimir Putin left little doubt as to his intention to try and develop an energy weapon when he temporarily cut off Russian natural gas to neighboring Ukraine in January 2006, after first raising the price by 400 percent. In November 2006, London's *Financial Times* reported that "NATO advisers have warned the military alliance that it needs to guard against any attempt by Russia to set up an 'OPEC for gas' that would strengthen Moscow's leverage over Europe."[11] Global energy traders know all too well how thoroughly dependent Europe currently is on Russian natural gas.

The threat Moscow poses globally can only grow in the coming years as the world becomes increasingly dependent on liquefied natural gas (LNG), which is natural gas cooled to a liquid state so that it can be shipped in tankers anywhere in the world and then regasified upon reaching its destination. It is an important way for the world to tap so-called "stranded" natural gas found in isolated reservoirs. Like Russia, other potential members of an LNG-based OPEC are no friends of the United States. They include Turkmenistan, Kazakhstan, Uzbekistan, Libya, Algeria, and—here we go again—Iran, for which LNG could help offset its loss of oil revenue. Just imagine an energy cartel controlled not by America's seeming friend, Saudi Arabia, but by an opportunistic Russia in league with America's sworn enemy, Iran.

Washington has. In May 2006 President Bush sent Vice President Dick Cheney to Lithuania to declare that, as one news magazine put it, Russia "should stop using its oil and gas supplies to keep customer countries in line."[12] For the most part, however, this vitally important energy security issue has so far been camouflaged in America by raging local political battles along the East and West Coasts over whether LNG terminals should be constructed. Many Americans are vehemently opposed to having an LNG terminal in their backyard because LNG can cause serious accidents—as in ka-boom! Whether or not LNG terminals can be safely operated near populated areas, however, the fact is an LNG industry is quietly starting to take shape out of sight in the Gulf of Mexico, where an estimated $50 billion or so of LNG facilities are being constructed.

One can seriously question the wisdom of putting more of America's critical energy infrastructure in the Gulf of Mexico after the damage caused by Hurricane Katrina, some of which still had not been fixed more than a year later. In point of fact, Hurricane Ivan, which was a category 3 hurricane in September 2004, took out a dozen or so oil and natural gas platforms in the Gulf that were supposed to be able withstand a category 5 storm.

Think about the potential for energy markets to be roiled in the future every time it even looks like a hurricane might enter the Gulf of Mexico. These things go in cycles, so for the next several years there could be a lot of hurricane activity. (Let's not get into the question of whether global warming is making storms more intense.) Given that America has no choice but to rely more in the future on oil and gas production from the Gulf of Mexico, concentrating an LNG industry there as well seems off the wall. Talk about putting all of your eggs in one basket.

Energy insiders basically throw up their hands and say there are few other places that will accept LNG infrastructure and that, given projected demand for natural gas, America has got to have an LNG industry sooner rather than later. Thus, unless Washington can somehow convince more Americans to accept the safety risk that an LNG terminal poses in the name of national security, America will have Mother Nature as well as Russia to worry about.

As Kevin Petak, the natural gas analyst, observed, "We're going to run the risk of having a large portion of our national energy industry knocked out of service for a prolonged period of time as a result of a major hurricane."

■ ■ ■

While this is a discussion about risks to America's energy security, it makes sense at this point to look at companies that could do well, thanks in part to the birth of America's LNG industry.

While he doesn't like to stock-pick, successful Denver-based energy analyst Tom Petrie thinks Chicago Bridge & Iron, an engineering and construction company, could be a winner because it is building tanks that are integral to these LNG facilities. Other experts believe that another winner could be Houston-based Cheniere Energy, whose stock symbol, appropriately enough, is LNG. Cheniere is building regasification facilities and is also engaged in oil and gas exploration in the shallow waters of the Gulf of Mexico. Petrie further forecasts that the South Korean shipyards building many of the new LNG tankers could do well, specifically Daewoo Shipbuilding and Marine Engineering, Hyundai Heavy Industries, and Samsung Heavy Industries.

This brings us to the second category on the list of companies to watch. The first, introduced in Chapter 1, was called "Automotive Efficiency." It ranked 4th out of 15 in terms of having the potential to shape the future direction of the oil industry. The first two inductees into that category were Toyota and Honda. The title of this next category is "Infrastructure Providers," and it comes in ninth, after primarily groups of new technology providers. All five of the previously mentioned companies—Chicago Bridge & Iron, Cheniere, Daewoo, Hyundai, and Samsung—are included, as will be a number of other global engineering and construction firms still to be discussed.

In the new oil industry, infrastructure providers will have their hands full. They will be counted on to help extract and bring to market every last drop of conventional energy, not just crude oil but also natural gas. They will be counted on to build the facilities for extracting the solid hydrocarbons (tar sands, coal, and maybe shale). They will further be counted on to construct the facilities for processing both solid hydrocarbons and biomass sources such as corn and soybeans into substitute liquid fuels. They will have to do all this while somehow also repairing America's (and the world's) rapidly aging energy infrastructure, as well as the rigs, platforms, and so on that could get slammed every time a hurricane roars through the Gulf of Mexico.

While other categories on the list of companies to watch are going to be more important in determining the actual direction of the new oil industry, this category will be darn important to its realization. Globally, trillions of dollars will have to be spent on new and old energy infrastructure over the next two to three decades.

■ ■ ■

If the global energy business were a game of Monopoly, which it often seems to be, then China would be the player trying to buy up every available property on the board. As Secretary Rice alluded, China has been busy cutting deals with most of Africa's energy-producing countries, including Nigeria, Angola, Sudan, and Chad. It has struck major deals with Iran, Kazakhstan, and Saudi Arabia, the latter supposedly America's special friend. With the United States preoccupied with violence on the streets of Baghdad, China has started making oil deals with the very government American troops are protecting. China has even been trying to make deals with America's energy-rich neighbor Canada, presumably its most politically secure source of energy other than what is found in the United States itself. If China continues its acquisitive ways, the United States could find itself cut off in the future from important sources of energy around the world.

To be sure, any war, cold or hot, is a scary proposition. But when you think about it, an energy cold war with Beijing would have a silver lining, namely, it could turbocharge the development of the new oil industry's alternative fuels and efficiency.

On the fuels front, a cold war would spur efforts to develop fuels that could be safely grown on American soil or extracted from America's fossil fuel deposits. On the efficiency front, the United States would want to expand efforts to literally plug vehicular transportation into America's safe and secure electric power grid. Conventional oil production might also benefit as the United States expanded high-tech efforts to recover every last drop of oil from its existing fields, while at the same time opening up for exploration potentially valuable fields that lie just offshore in areas currently off-limits to drillers due to the combined opposition of environmental, tourist, and other interests.

Indeed, a cold war over energy might do as much to develop a safe and sustainable U.S. energy program as the launch of the Russian satellite *Sputnik* did to launch the U.S. space program.

Without a doubt, however, the far saner approach would be for Washington and Beijing to work together. Aside from the obvious risk of a cold war turning hot, a partnership between the United States and China would take a lot of the sting out of the threats posed by Russia, Mother Nature, Iran, terrorism, and so on.

Furthermore, a U.S.–China partnership could give the new oil industry an even stronger turbocharge than a cold war.

Consider the following: Some of the most innovative work being done in the areas of substitutes and efficiency is being done outside the United States. A lot of it is being done in China, often with technology from other countries. Especially in the areas of biofuel and coal, China and the United

States appear to be going down parallel paths, developing on their own technology that could be developed faster if they were in partnership.

Such a partnership would create a vast common market for new technologies, some of which are already proving their worth, but only to the extent that they can be supported locally in isolated countries around the world. With a U.S.–China partnership, there would be a global exchange of ideas and constant pressure on companies on both sides of the Pacific Ocean to raise productivity and increase efficiency across the board. As much as they sometimes are a national security threat to one another, through an energy partnership Washington and Beijing would help one another's national security.

Building on such a partnership, eventually countries everywhere might become linked in a drive to end the world's addiction to oil. Such a partnership would go a long way toward meeting the challenge set forth in Chapter 1 regarding governments finding a way to foster competition among the different sectors of the new oil industry within a spirit of co-operation.

From an investor's point of view, a U.S.–China partnership could be huge. It could make the payoff of the energy technology revolution at the heart of the new oil industry bigger and better, not to mention quicker.

Sadly, to date the China–U.S. energy relationship has on occasion looked more like a cold war. Witness the way Congress vehemently opposed the proposed acquisition of Unocal by China National Offshore Oil, eventually causing the unsolicited bid to be withdrawn. However, in September 2006 there was a spark of hope when Chinese and U.S. energy officials reportedly agreed to cooperate more on developing new and renewable energy sources. According to an article in *China Daily*, the two countries "agreed to intensify their partnership" in new and renewable energy.[13]

■ ■ ■

While China, Russia, and Venezuela can't be forgotten, investors need to stay focused on the danger to their portfolios posed by Iran and terrorism. So what are the best shock-absorbing investments to own?

Many investors may think that the best way to be prepared for an oil price shock is to own shares of well-known U.S. oil companies like ExxonMobil and Chevron. They are, after all, *oil* companies, and they are familiar—if not beloved—corporate entities. But, as previously indicated, big-name oil companies could be the next victims of a terrorist attack, maybe on U.S. soil.

It is also logical to think that one way to be prepared for an oil price shock would be to own shares in companies that drill for oil, especially those active in the United States and other stable parts of the world. But while oil drillers should definitely be among the new oil industry's long-term winners, it is possible that they could get dumped by investors in the illogical aftermath of a price shock. Anyone old enough to have been sitting in front of a stock terminal in October 1987 knows that when fear strikes Wall Street, investors head for the exits, and it doesn't always matter whether it makes sense to sell a particular stock or group of stocks.

For the same reason, a similar fate might befall alternative energy stocks, including even the companies well positioned to make money from substitute fuels and efficiency. To be sure, the period right after an oil price shock might be exactly the right time to buy (or buy more) stock in potential long-term winners like oil drillers and alternative companies. They just should not be thought of as shock absorbers.

So what's left? Are there any bulletproof investments that would buffer the effects of an oil price shock heard 'round the world?

One seemingly bulletproof investment would be defense stocks. When I asked defense expert Milton Copulos which defense companies he would own to brace himself against a price shock, he mentioned two by name, Lockheed Martin and Raytheon. He explained that as giant contractors to both the Pentagon and the Department of Homeland Security, Lockheed and Raytheon make money on everything from jet planes and missiles to surveillance systems and biometric identity cards.

Copulos, however, quickly added that probably "almost any" defense company would be a good hedge against an oil price shock. That makes sense. As Copulos has told Congress, in 2006 the United States spent roughly $2.70 per gallon—*nearly as much as the actual summertime price of gasoline*—to make sure that its imported oil safely reached Americans' gas tanks. Think of this as the hidden cost of America's gasoline, the price we all pay to protect shipping lanes and countries, many of whom hate us, on whom we are increasingly dependent for our black gold. When a country is already spending billions of dollars a year to keep its oil flowing, chances are it is going to pay extra to its defense companies to get that oil moving again if there is a sudden disruption.

By the way, if Copulos's $2.70 a gallon shocks you, join the crowd. Ready to be shocked even more? Copulos, who is on the leading edge of this sort of economic analysis and whose research, I suspect, will become increasingly pivotal in America's energy planning, says that defense-related expenditures represent only about a third of the hidden cost of America's gasoline. He has calculated that the total hidden cost in 2006 came to about $8.35 a gallon, of which about $2.70 was defense related. Copulos told me that the rest of the money represented lost economic activity due to the huge outflow of dollars from the United States into the bank accounts of oil-producing countries. In this broad category he has included such things as jobs lost (or never created in the first place). This in turn has done things like reduce payroll and sales taxes, thereby also reducing the amount of money available for important things like education. By Copulos's calculation, *the true cost of a gallon of gasoline bought in America in 2006 was over $11*, after factoring in the only part of it we could actually see—the $3-a-gallon pump price.

Try to keep this in mind, because it shows that there is an absolutely huge financial incentive to radically restructuring the oil industry so that America no longer has a single-source transportation system but, rather, a multisource system that is more dependent on domestic energy sources. Put another way, as much as it could cost Washington (through a variety of financial incentives) to develop substitute fuels and efficiency, the current cost of not developing them is probably far greater. While many Americans value a free market that doesn't subsidize new technologies, it is impossible to think of oil as being a free market when every American driver is subsidizing it. As much as the United States, by itself or in partnership with China and other nations, might spend on spurring the energy technology revolution, it will wind up saving a lot more if the hidden cost of gasoline can be made to really disappear.

Eliminate gasoline's huge hidden cost and keep those billions upon billions of dollars out of OPEC bank accounts, and it should be possible to construct the new oil industry without going against cultural norms or penalizing low-income Americans by raising gasoline taxes.

Regarding Copulos's idea that almost any defense company would be good to own if there was an oil price shock, it should be noted that if the shock were caused not by some military flare-up but, rather, by a weather-related disaster like a hurricane, defense companies would not be the center of attention. Then again, if another major hurricane did hit the Gulf, presumably the United States would be even more reliant on imported oil from the Middle East and defense spending might benefit anyway.

Until the day oil traders are breathing easier because America has licked its addiction to imported oil, defense companies warrant a spot on the list of companies to watch, although, viewed in terms of their importance to the development of substitute fuels and efficiency, defense companies must rank at the bottom of the list, in 15th position. Because Copulos said that almost any defense company could benefit, there are no individual companies in this category, just "defense companies" as a whole.

■ ■ ■

What should be apparent by now is that defense companies have decent two-way potential. They aren't just good shock absorbers if and when trouble strikes. They also are prospects for long-term growth as long as we live in a terror-crazed world where every drop of available oil needs to reach its destination.

Defense companies are not the only shock absorbers that appear to have two-way potential. Another is oil tanker operators.

Some investors may not be familiar with the major companies in this group, such as Overseas Shipholding Group, Teekay Shipping, General Maritime, Frontline, and OMI Corporation. In part this is because these companies are seldom in the news. (Other than stories about rising pump prices, how many oil-related stories do you remember reading or seeing in 2006?) So when these oil tanker operators appear on TV, as they did in June 2006 on the always-insightful CNBC program *Kudlow & Company*, it's worth tuning in.

To a man, the tanker executives who appeared on that program were upbeat about their industry's prospects, citing rising demand for their services, especially out of Asia. This self-assessment was supported by more than one bullish assessment from Wall Street. As for being a shock absorber, as the British newspaper the *Guardian* reported the day after the World Trade Center was attacked, "tanker freight rates are expected to rocket upwards today as oil companies and traders grab all available vessels for fear of a shortage."[14]

To be sure, if a terror attack were to slow the global economy to a crawl, oil tanker operators' fortunes would be hurt like everyone else's. But in general, tanker operators benefit in a world of pervasive geopolitical risk, in part because their ships can be used as floating storage terminals that enable refiners generally to build inventory at less expense than on land. Rates also rise when new shipping routes must be found that require more time and, hence, more money. For example, if Venezuela's Chavez were to cut off shipments to the United States, refiners would have to go farther afield to replace that lost crude.

Oil tanker operators are part of a category on the list of companies to watch titled "Transportation Providers." This category comes in 10th, just behind "Infrastructure Providers." The aforementioned tanker operators and the other firms in this category make up what might be called "moving" infrastructure. Without these transportation companies, not just the oil but also the coal, corn, and other energy feedstock would not get to where it needed to go. As with the infrastructure providers, transportation companies will not be strategically important to the development of the new oil industry. But, like infrastructure firms, nothing will be possible without them.

■　■　■

Being prepared for an oil price shock doesn't just mean owning the right investments. It also means not owning the wrong investments.

No corporate executive is ever going to come right out and say, "Don't own me." But sometimes the media reports stuff in a way that should raise a big red flag. As a reporter, I know there have been stories I have written where I would have loved to have been able to scream at the reader: *Read this one!*

In 2006 a story that had all the signs of being a "read this one" story quoted the chief economist for the International Air Transport Association (IATA)—in other words, a guy who should know a thing or two about the financial condition of his industry. When one does a Google search on the organization's name, one finds that it is an international trade group that sets airfares and cargo rates between the United States and Europe. What was particularly intriguing about this story was that it was based on something the IATA exec told the reporter on the sidelines of the association's annual general assembly. It doesn't take formal journalistic experience to sense that comments made on the sidelines tend to more accurately reflect what an interviewee really thinks than what he may say in a prepared speech.

The story, from the French news agency, began: "Oil prices of 100 dollars a barrel or more are a possibility that would seriously threaten airlines, IATA chief economist Brian Pearce told AFP."[15]

Seriously threaten? Uh-oh.

The story went on to say that the exec had told the AFP reporter "on the sidelines" that airlines had been able to cope with $70 oil through cost cuts and gains in efficiency. But if oil were to climb to $100 a barrel, this would pose a "real danger" for the aviation industry.

Enough said.

Another "read me" occurrence was the coverage given to a conference call conducted by economists at Standard & Poor's, the highly respected ratings agency, during which these acknowledged experts gave their take on the effects of high oil prices on the economy as a whole and on certain sectors of the economy.[16]

The main point was that if oil hit $100 a barrel (which they were not predicting), the U.S. economy would stay out of recession but its GDP would be trimmed by about 1.5 percent. Such a prediction, of course, has broad implications for the overall direction of the stock and bond markets and for interest rates, unemployment rates, inflation, wages, and more.

The economists reportedly discussed the potential impact of $100 oil on specific sectors, finding that, for example, low-end consumer sectors such as discount stores and fast-food chains would be in trouble, but not high-end retailers. This, of course, dovetails with the idea that people who have money buy a disproportionately large amount of gasoline. It further suggests that even if the U.S. economy did fall into a recession because of oil, there would be pockets of relative prosperity, which in turn suggests that any recession might hit harder in the heartland than in higher-salaried areas on either coast.

The economists also reportedly noted that neither supermarkets nor drug stores should be in trouble. This would seem to reflect the age-old notion that investors generally need to think defensively in times of economic difficulty. America has a consumer-driven economy, so the question is: What can the consumer *not* do without? Food, obviously—and, given the rising ages of Americans, their medications. By extension, of course, companies whose products are sold in supermarkets and drug stores also might avoid serious trouble.

One industry whose products are found throughout the economy is the chemicals industry. The economists reportedly said chemical companies ought to be able to cope with $100 oil by raising their prices, but that they could get hurt by an economic slowdown. Since people have got to eat no matter what, price increases by chemical companies presumably could increase the cost of food through such things as the cost of fertilizers and packaging.

Economists in general have a term that describes the situation when prices are rising as economic growth is slowing. It is called *stagflation*. It was coined in the 1970s, which, not coincidentally, is the last time oil prices went through the roof. During a period of stagflation, it can be tough to assess which direction the economy is going. In turn, the Federal Reserve Board has a tough time guiding the overall economy as it tries to figure out whether to stimulate the economy in order to fight a recession or to restrain the economy in order to fight inflation.

The S&P economists reportedly said two industries that would take a big hit from $100 oil were the airline and automobile industries. One thing this suggests is that people would hold on to their cars longer than usual, which of course would make it harder to popularize the more fuel-efficient vehicles that are now being developed that will generally carry fairly high sticker prices.

■ ■ ■

It is also useful to consider which companies might get some positive publicity in the wake of an oil price shock. While many could, some may find themselves permanently thrust into the spotlight.

One company that might stay in the spotlight is California-based ZAP, a company that specializes in fuel-efficient forms of transportation such as electric cars and battery-powered bicycles. In the immediate aftermath of an oil price shock, reporters might zero in on ZAP for an uplifting story, a kind of "how to fight back" story. As any public relations professional will attest, this is the sort of positive publicity that money can't buy.

Another company that could score with the media—that is, more than it already has—is Tesla Motors. Starting in 2007, California-based Tesla plans to sell an electric sports car. Actors George Clooney and Dennis Haysbert (the latter the star of CBS's *The Unit*, after having portrayed the President of the United States on Fox's *24*) reportedly have written $100,000 checks in order to be among first 100 to drive this sexy new two-seater roadster, which is being built in England by Lotus. With

Clooney and Haysbert, Tesla has what the mass media craves most—celebrities! Can't you just see it? After a day when oil prices have surged past $100 a barrel because Iran fired a missile at a U.S. Navy warship, on comes one of those TV entertainment news programs with a story about how celebrities are doing their part to cut down on imported oil and protect the environment. How? By zipping around Hollywood Hills in their sports cars like George Clooney.

Somebody roll the videotape.

ZAP and Tesla have two-way potential, Tesla especially so. Indeed, Tesla may just have a product that hits a sweet spot in the new oil industry in terms of being able to protect the environment by not using gasoline, which in turn helps national security. The price tag is steep, though the company has said it plans to make lower-priced models. But here is where Tesla is really on to something: the company has emphasized that it is building a car for people who love to drive. The Tesla roadster reportedly will be able to go from 0 to 60 in four seconds and will have a top speed of 130 miles per hour, which definitely ought to appeal to freedom-loving cowboys.

Tesla and ZAP are part of a category on the list of companies to watch called "Alternative Transportation Providers." This category ranks 12th on the list and is for companies that have the potential to popularize new options in personal transportation.

A third company in this category is Massachusetts-based Zipcar, a so-called "car-sharing" company. To understand the potential importance of the concept of car-sharing in changing how Americans think about personal transportation, it is useful to look at a study that was done by Sustainlane, an online source of information about healthy and sustainable living.

SustainLane did a study[17] of which American cities are in the best shape to handle super-high energy prices. Here are the results, starting with the best prepared:

1. New York
2. Boston
3. San Francisco
4. Chicago
5. Philadelphia
6. Portland (Oregon)
7. Honolulu

8. Seattle
9. Baltimore
10. Oakland (California)

Sustainlane explained on its web site that it looked at areas most directly impacted, such as "how people get around, where their food comes from, and how they worked." The top 10 cities "combine strong public transportation with access to locally grown fresh food." Most also have "significant access to local wireless networks for telecommuting."

The common thread here can be summed up in one word—mobility. Sustainlane's study measured how well people could get around while avoiding the cost of owning a car.

Car-sharing has been described as an "always-on" personal mobility service where reservation, pickup, and return are self-service; where insurance and gas are included in the rates; where cars can be rented by the hour as well as the day; and where users are members who have been preapproved.

Zipcar is one of a number of car-sharing companies to be found in cities around the world. Started in 1999, by 2006 Zipcar was operating in a number of metropolitan areas in the United States and Canada. In May 2006 the company reportedly had 55,000 active members in 11 states and provinces. That same month, the media reported that General Electric Company's Commercial Finance group had given Zipcar $20 million in lease line financing.

The service provided by a car-sharing company like Zipcar is intended to appeal to urban dwellers who normally get around on public transit or on foot. For these people, especially younger drivers, owning a car doesn't really make financial sense and car-sharing makes it easier to rely on public transportation except when a car is truly needed. The *Washington Post* has written more than once about car-sharing. In June 2005 the *Post* ran a story flattering to Zipcar about a 24-year-old new arrival to D.C. who said she uses Zipcar instead of owning her own car. In September 2006 the *Post* ran a story about how car-sharing is moving into the mainstream as more businesses and universities turn to it as a way to avoid not only the high price of gas but other costs associated with owning a car, such as insurance and maintenance. "The mainstream person is thinking about car-sharing as a transportation solution," the CEO of another car-sharing company, Flexcar, told the *Post* reporter.[18]

Flexcar, too, makes the list of companies to watch. Like Zipcar, it has recently increased its number of available vehicles. Though not in the same league as Tesla, Flexcar has some star power of its own with America Online co-founder Steve Case owning a controlling interest in the company through an investment firm he owns. On its web site (www.flexcar.com) Flexcar describes car-sharing as "transportation, simplified," which you've got to admit has a nice ring to it. The company makes a pitch for environmentally minded consumers, noting that it has a "modern fleet of Ultra Low Emission Vehicles and fuel-efficient hybrids." Not to be overlooked is the sense of community that Zipcar and Flexcar are trying to foster, a community of people who may not be able to afford high gas prices and who are concerned about the environment and America's dependence on imported oil.

In short, what a company like Tesla may do for people who want to drive, companies like Zipcar and Flexcar may do for people who need to drive, though only occasionally, and especially for those who need to save money and who want to protect the environment.

■　■　■

The Sustainlane study is also a useful illustration of the advantage that certain other industries, such as telecommunications, could have in the new oil industry. If, as Sustainlane has concluded, the ability to telecommute will be important, then presumably companies that build and operate wireless networks could benefit, as could companies that build the networks and companies that produce the metals and electronic devices that go into the networks.

Of course, one can't telecommute unless one has a top-notch computer system, so another beneficiary might be computer manufacturers and their parts suppliers. Also, as more people start working from home, it's possible that digital entertainment providers could see a rise in business. (Nobody works *all* the time.) And since no one is going to know whether you and your laptop are working at home or at the Starbucks with the wireless network just down the street, retailers that have places for people to congregate—Barnes & Noble comes to mind—might see foot traffic and sales rise. Retailers with established reputations for making it easy for their customers to shop online also might benefit. (Which web sites do you use the most for online shopping?)

The more dots one connects, the more it looks as if the digital economy as a whole could be a beneficiary of the new oil industry—and for more reasons than I've just laid out. This is why I'm holding off on adding digital types to the companies to watch list until later on.

While Sustainlane considered only one aspect of commercial transportation, their study raises questions about commercial transportation generally. Whether the item being transported is a turnip or a television, clearly the cost of transporting that item to market is impacted by high gas prices.

This ought to help the railroad industry but may hurt the trucking industry.

According to a July 2006 article in the online edition of the *St. Petersburg Times*,[19] the railroad industry already is getting a big boost from high oil prices. The article indicates that railroads' advantage over trucks is that they can haul three times the freight for the same amount of fuel. The article quotes an independent railroad analyst as believing that the railroad industry is in the midst of a renaissance and that the industry as a whole is hauling 40 percent more containers than it did five years ago.

Morningstar, the respected provider of independent investment research, reported in 2006 that the current situation is perhaps the best operating environment for railroads in a half-century. Not coincidentally, the trucking industry is facing a host of challenges that have threatened its competitive advantage over railroads, according to Morningstar. To be sure, Morningstar hedges its bets, citing a number of reasons why this rosy outlook might not last, but concludes, "the party should continue for at least a while."[20]

According to Morningstar, four railroads in particular—Burlington Northern Santa Fe, Union Pacific, Canadian National, and Canadian Pacific—should benefit from what it described as "one of today's hottest industries," namely, ethanol.

Since the same four railroads, plus two others—CSX and Norfolk Southern—should also do well hauling coal, all six join the oil tanker operators on the watch list in the category of "Transportation Providers."

CHAPTER 3

Substitute Liquid Fuels, Part One: Biofuel

Okay, so it isn't a catchy chapter title.

When writing or talking about energy, one inevitably winds up using a fair amount of jargon. It is important for a person, as an investor and as a participant in the global discussion about the future of energy, to understand this jargon, which is why, by the end of this chapter, you will know about things like *cellulosic ethanol* and *biobutanol*. (I've provided a glossary in the back of the book.)

Let's review: There are liquid transportation fuels that can substitute for gasoline made from crude oil. These substitute liquid fuels (SLFs) can be grouped into two broad categories. The first is biofuel, which is fuel made from things that grow, including plants such as corn and soybeans. The second is unconventional fossil fuel, which is fuel made from hydrocarbon sources other than crude oil. Unconventional hydrocarbon sources include natural gas and the three solid alternative fossil fuels—tar sands, coal, and oil shale—all of which can be processed into a liquid.

Biofuel is really solar power in disguise, because if the sun doesn't shine, there's no "bio" in biofuel. Think of biofuel as stored solar power, and think of solar power as a common denominator between mobile energy (cars and trucks) and stationary energy (homes and businesses). With the latter, the sun's rays are converted into electricity through solar panels and solar roofing shingles.

Because of all the news coverage it has been receiving, you are most likely aware that the main biofuel in the United States today is ethanol. (See Figure 3.1.) You are probably also aware that America makes most of its ethanol from corn—more specifically, corn kernels, the same stuff we put on our dinner tables. What you may not be aware of is that corn ethanol is but a part of the first step—that is, the first technological step—in the development of what should be a global biofuel industry that greatly relieves the strain on crude oil supplies while still allowing people to exercise their right to drive (as well as their right to sit in traffic), without doing as much environmental damage as driving on straight gasoline.

What's old is new again, meaning that biofuel was America's first transportation fuel. (A horse has to eat.)

Experts say that in 2012 the leading biofuel in the United States will still be corn ethanol. To be sure, corn is not the only grain that can be used to make ethanol—wheat is another. Again thanks to all the news coverage, you are probably aware that in Brazil they make ethanol from sugarcane. In 2005 the United States and Brazil were the world's two leading ethanol fuel producers, each producing about 45 percent of global supply. By 2012 China should also be a major producer, which is important to keep in mind because it points up one of the key potential areas of cooperation in a U.S.–China energy partnership.

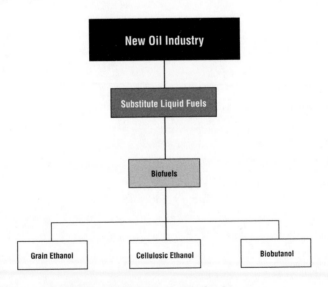

FIGURE 3.1   Substitute Liquid Fuels: Biofuels

Ethanol's track record in Brazil is strong evidence that ethanol can play a crucial role in quenching the world's thirst for transportation fuel. Alone among countries, Brazil turned to ethanol after the oil price shocks of the 1970s. Today Brazil is considered energy independent thanks in large part to its homegrown ethanol. Indeed, Brazil is now frequently cited by U.S. advocates of biofuel as a way to enhance America's own national security.

Ethanol, also known as ethyl alcohol or grain alcohol, is a tasteless, colorless chemical compound that has gone into alcoholic beverages for thousands of years. When blended with unleaded gasoline, ethanol increases the fuel's performance while decreasing harmful emissions.

In 2006 all vehicles in the United States could run on a blend of 90 percent gasoline to 10 percent ethanol. About 5 percent of vehicles could run on a blend of 15 percent gasoline to 85 percent ethanol. This latter fuel is commonly called E85. (Brazil is an E85 country. Europe is at E5 but is pushing for E10.) Vehicles that can run on E85 are called *flex-fuel* vehicles. In 2004 about one-third of America's gasoline was blended with ethanol, mostly in a 90-10 mix. U.S. automakers have publicly stated that they are committed to putting more E85-ready vehicles on the road.

Also in Europe, in 2012 another biofuel called biodiesel, which is made from edible oils like soy and palm, is expected to be the primary biofuel, just as it was in 2006, owing to the high percentage of diesel-powered vehicles on European highways. (Diesels reportedly accounted for about half of 2005 European new car sales.) Biodiesel sales in the United States should also significantly increase between 2006 and 2012 even though some experts believe that, because of the American consumer's concern about the performance of diesel-powered vehicles, in America biodiesel may remain primarily a truck and fleet fuel. In that other huge consumer market—China and the rest of Asia—there is expected to be a growing market for both ethanol and biodiesel. Due to rising European demand, by 2012 a number of Asian countries are expected to be important biodiesel exporters. Indeed, in 2006 Malaysia said that it and Indonesia, the world's leading palm-oil producers, would begin setting aside nearly 40 percent of their crude palm oil output for biodiesel production.

■ ■ ■

By some estimates, sales of corn ethanol in the United States are about to surge. By 2012 corn ethanol sales in the United States could be as much as 10 times higher than they were in 2006—roughly $45 billion to $60 billion versus 2006's $6 billion, according to a forecast done for this book by Michael Millikin of Green Car Congress, the authoritative alternative energy information web site, based on his analysis of information in the public domain. (Millikin's complete forecast is provided in Appendix A at the back of this book.)

As bright as corn ethanol's five-year outlook appears to be, however, because technologically it is only a first-generation biofuel, its longer-term outlook is more guarded. Indeed, by 2012 or sooner, two other bio-fuels that were still in the development stage at the beginning of 2007 could be taking aim on corn ethanol's market dominance in the United States. One of these challengers has the unwieldy name of *cellulosic ethanol*. The other goes by the odd name of *biobutanol*.

Cellulosic ethanol is ethanol made from the hard fibrous parts of plant matter. It can be made from wild grasses and from agricultural, wood, even municipal solid waste. Key to cellulosic ethanol's attractiveness as a second-generation biofuel is that, unlike corn ethanol, which is made from a food crop, cellulosic ethanol can be made from stuff that doesn't currently have much economic value—like switchgrass and other wild grasses, corn stalks, wood chips, even garbage.

Biobutanol is alcohol with a different chemical composition than ethanol that can be made from both grains and cellulose. (For the chemists in the audience, butanol is a four-carbon alcohol while ethanol is a two-carbon alcohol.)

Millikin's forecast was not the only bullish prediction for biofuel de-velopment issued in 2006. Another eye-popper came from Clean Edge Inc., the respected California-based energy research and consulting firm. Clean Edge forecast that the worldwide market for ethanol and biodiesel (global manufacturing and wholesale pricing) will grow some 234 per-cent over the 10-year period 2005 to 2015, reaching $52.5 billion com-pared with $15.7 billion.[1]

Also in 2006, an official of the United Nations Food and Agriculture Organization (FAO) said publicly, "The gradual move away from oil has begun. Over the next 15 to 20 years we may see biofuels providing a full 25 percent of the world's energy needs."[2]

In addition, the U.S. Energy Information Administration forecast that production of unconventional fossil fuels (including tar sands, coal-to-liquids, and gas-to-liquids) plus biofuels will increase by 9.7 million barrels a day between 2003 and 2030, representing 25 percent of the total world liquids supply increase.[3]

To be sure, predictions of big impending growth in biofuel come with an equally big caveat that should come as no surprise, namely, politics will be a major factor in how the biofuel business develops. Everyone, including investors, should understand that there are political crosswinds blowing that could buffet biofuel's growth in America and elsewhere.

One problem is that the oil industry, not unexpectedly, sees biofuel as an unwelcome addition. It does not help that car manufacturers in Detroit are keen on E85 vehicles, or that some U.S. legislators seem to be trying to force E85 down the oil industry's throat through proposed legislation. Because very politically connected oil companies dominate the distribution and marketing of transportation fuel, their lack of enthusiasm for biofuel could spell trouble for the newcomer.

Outside of corn-rich Iowa and a handful of other Midwestern states, there are few E85 pumps. Indeed, their number can be measured in the hundreds, while the total number of gasoline service stations in the United States is roughly 180,000. As is discussed later in this book, it is hard to see much of a future for flex-fuel vehicles in the United States, and not just because of oil industry opposition. The idea of buying a brand-new car, or retrofitting an existing one, just to be able to burn more ethanol (which, by the way, does not make a car more fuel-efficient) seems unlikely to move many people to open their wallets. This could be especially true if another biofuel comes along that oil companies feel more kindly toward because it can be burned in ordinary vehicles in greater concentrations than 10 percent biofuel to 90 percent gasoline.

A looming problem for both ethanol and biodiesel is the growing number of environmentalists who fear that these biofuels could make a number of environmental problems worse, such as forest destruction (which reduces carbon dioxide sinks), freshwater depletion, and excessive use of ground- and water-damaging fertilizers and pesticides. "There are big opportunities with biofuels, but there are big problems too. It's not a free lunch," the director of Britain's Royal Botanic Gardens, Sir Peter Crane, told a reporter on the eve of his retirement in 2006.[4]

Sir Peter's quote perfectly captures the inherent dilemma of biofuels for environmentalists. On the one hand, by helping reduce airborne emissions caused by gasoline, biofuel can help impede the progress of global warming. On the other hand, biofuel development may accelerate other serious environmental problems.

Environmentalists and others might not be so worried if governments, especially the one in Washington, had gone about developing their biofuel programs differently. The U.S. Congress effectively gave birth to the American biofuels business when it passed the Renewable Fuel Standard program. Part of the Energy Policy Act of 2005, this program calls for a doubling of biofuel production by 2012 over 2004's level as a way to supplement the nation's supply of transportation fuel with domestically available renewable energy sources. As praiseworthy as Congress's action was, however, when it came to deciding how this increase in biofuel production should be implemented, America's legislative branch allowed politics to get in the way of good science.

Naz Karim is chairman of the Department of Chemical Engineering at Texas Tech University. An expert in how to convert biomass into fuel, he told me that the best—meaning the most scientific—way to develop a biofuel program in the United States would be to use feedstocks that are best suited to the country's different climates. "There's a feedstock for everyone," he said, explaining that while corn would be appropriate in the Midwest, forest waste and paper would be more appropriate in the Northeast, Northwest, and Georgia. Sugarcane would be Karim's first choice in the deep South, agricultural waste in California, rice in east Texas, forests in Arizona, and wild grasses in west Texas and Hawaii.

In an unintended homage to the movie *Back to the Future*, Karim said that garbage should be used as a feedstock in and around all urban centers. This is an extremely important point once you realize that in 2007 more than half of all the people in the world will live in cities for the first time in history, that there will be over 400 cities of 1 million or more people, and that there will be 20 "megacities" with 10 million or more residents. Tokyo alone will have more people than in all of Canada.[5]

Overall, what Karim was effectively saying is that science dictates that there ought *not* to be a one-size-fits-all approach to ethanol production in a multiclimate country like the United States. Yet this essentially is the path Congress put America on when it all but anointed corn as the national ethanol feedstock.

The biggest reason for corn's ascension appears to have been political pressure applied by lobbyists and political representatives of corn-producing states. Indeed, even when it became apparent in 2006 that America could have difficulty producing enough corn ethanol to meet market needs, these interests worked to keep imports of Brazilian ethanol at bay by maintaining the U.S. tariff on imported ethanol.

Corn ethanol's scientific shortcomings are readily apparent. One of its biggest drawbacks is that it does not provide much more energy per gallon than is required for its production after factoring in all of the fuel needed to grow and harvest the corn and transport it to market by truck or rail. In a world taking steps to fight global warming such as by reducing the amount of carbon dioxide released into the atmosphere, ethanol producers could be penalized for "CO_2 liberation," as energy analyst Glenn Wattley put it. What an incredible irony that would be.

Another drawback is that corn ethanol is too corrosive to be transported in the most cost-effective manner, namely, via America's existing petroleum pipeline system. Instead, it must be moved by truck or rail. Still another problem that could prove the most serious of all is that trying to meet ethanol production goals with corn ethanol could require the diversion of so much farmland that food prices could increase significantly. Ron Pernick, co-founder and principal of Clean Edge, told me that by 2010 the United States will have reached the optimal amount of corn that can be grown for ethanol, after which there could develop a food versus fuel land battle.

The food versus fuel conundrum was put in stark perspective in 2006 by well-known environmental leader Lester Brown of the Earth Policy Institute, who wrote, "Cars, not people, will claim most of the increase in world grain consumption this year. The U.S. Department of Agriculture projects that world grain use will grow by 20 million tons in 2006. Of this, 14 million tons will be used to produce fuel for cars in the United States, leaving only 6 million tons to satisfy the world's growing food needs."

Brown sees a disaster in the making, writing that, "In agricultural terms, the world appetite for automotive fuel is insatiable. The grain required to fill a 25-gallon SUV gas tank with ethanol will feed one person for a year. The grain it takes to fill the tank every two weeks over a year will feed 26 people."[6]

Given corn ethanol's clear-cut shortcomings, one would have thought that Congress would not have been so quick to jump on the corn ethanol bandwagon, notwithstanding the political pressure. But Congress—and the public, too—apparently was under the impression that only corn had near-term commercial viability as an ethanol feedstock. I know I was, until Karim told me, "I can build a cellulosic ethanol plant today." He mentioned that a private company, Iogen Corporation of Canada, already operates a cellulosic ethanol plant.

Iogen is one of several companies on the list of companies to watch in the category of "Ethanol and Biodiesel Technology." This category ranks second, behind only a related category, "Biobutanol Technology."

I believe that the category of "Ethanol and Biodiesel Technology" is extremely important because there are going to be a great number of vehicles on global highways, so many, in fact, that even with major improvements in vehicle efficiency, for probably at least the next 10 to 20 years it is unlikely that gasoline and diesel made from crude oil will have the legs to meet this huge demand. Moreover, when you combine the environmental damage caused by making gasoline from tar sands and coal with the damage that would be caused if every vehicle were to continue running just on hydrocarbons, ethanol and biodiesel will be needed to keep the environment from imploding and, just as importantly, to keep environmentalists from exploding.

Iogen's prominent investors include Royal Dutch/Shell Group and Goldman Sachs, the latter being "the first major Wall Street firm to make a commitment to cellulose ethanol," according to Iogen CEO Brian Foody, as quoted in an Iogen press release. In addition to its plans for cellulosic ethanol production in Canada, in January 2006 Iogen announced that it was teaming with Shell and Volkswagen to study the feasibility of making cellulosic ethanol in Germany.[7]

To be sure, nobody would have said in 2006 that cellulosic ethanol was anywhere near as commercially viable as corn ethanol. There are two main problems with cellulosic ethanol. The first is to find (through genetic engineering) the best enzymes for breaking down the cellulose. This so-called enzyme pretreatment process is not necessary with corn ethanol. The second is the ability to ferment the two different kinds of sugars contained in cellulose.

Much work remains to be done in perfecting cellulosic ethanol. Thus from a scientific point of view, it would have been better for Congress not to push for corn ethanol production but, rather, to push for a Manhattan Project–style program for the development of cellulosic ethanol technology. (The Manhattan Project was a crash U.S. government program during World War II to develop the first nuclear bomb.)

If Congress had taken this far-sighted course of action, there would not now be a "staggering," to use Lester Brown's word for it, 55 ethanol plants operating or proposed just in the corn-rich state of Iowa. While so many biorefineries in one location makes financial sense in a world where corn ethanol is king, it does not make sense in a scientifically justified world where ethanol refineries are located throughout the United States, positioned to take advantage of the many different cellulosic feedstocks found in a multiclimate country.

Now that the U.S. government has belatedly announced a Manhattan-style initiative for cellulosic ethanol development over the next 10 to 20 years, investors need to think about the way the ethanol industry is developing today versus how it may look in the future. They should keep in mind that President Bush, in a 2006 Earth Day speech, sang cellulosic ethanol's praises and indicated that technological breakthroughs are not far off. President Bush told his audience that "the idea is to be able to use your money to figure out how to use other materials to be able to manufacture ethanol. And we're close to some interesting breakthroughs; we're close to breakthroughs to be able to make ethanol from wood chips and stalks and switch grass, and other natural materials. And it makes a lot of sense if we're trying to get off oil, and it makes sense to use taxpayers' money to research ways to use switch grass, for example, to become a fuel for your automobile."[8]

Overall, investors should remember that the best prospects in biofuel are going to be those found at the intersection of politics and science. Washington's push for corn ethanol production, notwithstanding the obvious scientific limitations, has demonstrated the importance of a biofuel company having political pull. Washington's new program to develop cellulosic technology, which has the president's backing, demonstrates what should be the increasing importance of a company with scientific expertise.

Most of all, investors should remember that, as a biofuels research manager for a major corporation put it, the biofuel market "is ripe for innovation."[9]

■ ■ ■

The company to be found smack dab in the middle of the intersection of politics and science is Archer Daniels Midland Company (ADM). The political prowess of ADM has been well documented over the years. Already the biggest ethanol producer in the United States, ADM is making what *Ethanol Producer* magazine called "bold moves" to advance its leadership status through a significant expansion of its ethanol-production capacity. The scientific prowess of this agricultural business giant is no less formidable. According to Karim, ADM has the scientific "upper hand," thanks in part to its many years in the corn syrup business.

ADM's strong ethanol prospects are hardly a secret. *Fortune* magazine, in an article back in January 2006, was already describing how ADM's "growth is being turbocharged by its ethanol business."[10] By midyear, shares of ADM were hitting an all-time high, "partly because (ADM) is the leading U.S. ethanol producer," Reuters reported.[11] The word *safe* frequently seems to be used to describe ADM as an investment option. The *Fortune* article called ADM "probably the safest choice" among ethanol investments, and Millikin of Green Car Congress called ADM "a safe buy." To be sure, no company is without risk. But thanks to the head start Congress gave it, in 2012 the U.S. corn ethanol business likely will be many times the size it was in 2006, and ADM thus should prosper.

ADM makes the list of companies to watch primarily for its production prowess in the category of "Biofuel Production." This category ranks eighth on the list.

To be sure, it remains to be seen how well ADM makes the eventual transition from a corn-based to a cellulose-based ethanol industry. The same is true for the growing roster of smaller ethanol producers led by VeraSun Energy, Aventine Renewable Energy Holdings, and Pacific Ethanol. On Wall Street in 2006, these companies were hot one minute and cold the next, reflecting in part the general tendency of the financial community to run hot and cold on a given industry. Still, given the probable strong growth in the corn ethanol industry up through 2012, everyone ought to be able to prosper, which is why each of these three other companies has been included in the "Biofuel Production" category.

Needless to say, some companies may do better than others. Texas Tech's Karim told me basically that not all corn ethanol refineries are created equal. He explained that the best corn ethanol refineries are those built close to sources of corn that use very efficient enzyme systems for getting the sugar out from the starch. In addition, they optimize the fermentation process by using highly efficient yeast that can tolerate a high concentration of ethanol as well as enable the plant to minimize energy and time while maximizing productivity in terms of volume per hour of ethanol produced. It's all very complicated and, as Karim noted, can include proprietary information.

Meanwhile, there is this related point for investors to chew on. (Corn, chew—get it? . . . Forget it.) In an article from the magazine *BusinessWeek* that ran on the MSNBC.com web site in June 2006, one investment strategist was reported as thinking that "oil companies should be looking toward ethanol outfits with an eye for acquisition."[12] To be sure, major oil companies have their own in-house biofuels programs. But in terms of positive public relations value alone, it could at some point make sense for a major oil company to buy an ethanol producer. I have absolutely no idea whether such a transaction will ever take place. But there is an underlying point here that needs to be emphasized—*strongly*.

As everyone knows, as oil prices have risen, oil companies' profits have, too. Indeed, some of the quarterly earnings recently reported by the major oil outfits have seemed otherworldly. Some politicians would now like essentially to punish major oil companies for making so much money by forcing them to give a chunk of it back to the public. Does anybody out there really expect this to happen? It seems far more likely that oil companies will hold on to their cash stashes. Indeed, even with the increased cost of looking for new oil and natural gas deposits, major oil companies would seem destined to join the ranks of Wall Street's elite investment bankers, at least as far as energy is concerned.

The concept of a company like ExxonMobil one day being not all that different from a company like Goldman Sachs may sound pretty strange. But as a 2006 *Fortune* article that ran on CNNMoney.com noted, oil companies' massive profits may not last. "Weak production gains and an inability to refill reserves may put big oil in a pinch in coming years," the article noted, adding that, "if the oil giants can't find new fields, going forward they'll essentially be liquidating the source of future profits."[13] Or, to use a metaphor more appropriate to biofuels, the big oil companies will start eating their seed corn.

By then, however, the major oil companies each should have accumulated umpteen billion dollars by performing their fiduciary duty of charging as much for their gasoline as the market will bear. This should be true even if one or more companies "pulls a Microsoft" and gives shareholders a big one-time special dividend.

This is why I have taken the perhaps unusual step of putting the really big oil boys—ExxonMobil, British Petroleum, Shell, and Chevron—in a category titled "Investment Bankers." (I deal with the traditional investment bankers in this category later on.) This category ranks way up there in fifth position, behind only the various groups of companies whose technologies could determine the direction of the new oil industry. It's simple, really. Technology's great, but without adequate financial support, it won't make a difference. While oil companies will continue to make money directly from oil for quite a while, in terms of how major oil companies are going to influence the direction of the new oil industry, they are likely to have more impact as very deep-pocketed, very politically connected energy investment bankers.

Indeed, oil companies likely will have a huge impact on the shape of the new oil industry. As is discussed in the Chapter 4, some oil giants are already investing heavily in solid alternative fuel development, basically propelling this other SLF industry forward over the strenuous objections of environmentalists. Some have started getting into biofuels.

Where big oil companies choose to invest the bulk of their billions likely will become the source of intense speculation on Wall Street. If oil companies are mindful of the mess that electric utilities made when they tried to diversify beyond their core competencies (only to later adopt a back-to-basics business strategy), oil companies may stick close to home with their investments. In the new oil industry, however, staying close to home may mean investing not only in solid fossil fuels but also in areas such as advanced battery technologies. To be sure, these are oil guys first and foremost, and it is probably going to take some convincing by Wall Street before they think to diversify. Even then, they will still be at the helms of some of the biggest companies in the world, which will make it hard for each captain to reposition his ship. Still, oil companies' investment agility—and their big bucks—should not be underestimated. We're not talking the *Titanic* here. In general, expect major oil companies not just to survive but to thrive *after* technology has ended the world's oil addiction.

Another related point that needs to be emphasized strongly is that, in order for ethanol production to grow anywhere near tenfold, it is going to take a lot of new construction. A March 2006 press release put out by an investment bank ran on Yahoo! Finance under the headline "Over $5 Billion Needed for Construction of Ethanol Plants to Meet 2012 Energy Act Deadline."[14]

Five billion dollars is a fair piece of change. And that figure presumably does not include the many billions of dollars that China and other countries will spend on ethanol plants of their own. We have already discussed some companies included in the category "Infrastructure Providers"—Chicago Bridge & Iron, Cheniere, Daewoo, Hyundai, and Samsung. Now here are some more: Fluor, Jacobs Engineering, Halliburton, Shaw, Foster Wheeler, ABB, and McDermott International. Each provides multiple infrastructure services for the energy and other industries, services such as engineering, construction, operations, and maintenance.

Really infrastructure providers could be discussed at almost any point in this book, so omnipresent is the need for their services. Building the multibillion-dollar foundation of a global biofuel industry sounds like a daunting task, but on this industry's list of things to do, it borders on being an afterthought. Somehow, the big boys in this category are going to have to build the foundation of a biofuel and an unconventional fossil fuel industry, while at the same time expanding and, very importantly, repairing the aging foundation of the global oil and gas industry.

On this last point: remember how a unit of British Petroleum had to shut down crude production operations at Alaska's Prudhoe Bay in the summer of 2006 due to pipeline corrosion? "(I)f this incident is just a hint of future problems for U.S. energy infrastructure," it means "there are several names in the infrastructure space that could benefit from this additional spending," wrote a guy I have met whose work I respect a lot—Christopher Edmonds, on the TheStreet.com.[15]

Just as the sporty electric car company Tesla may have found a sweet spot in terms of its environmental appeal to people who love to drive, infrastructure providers would seem to be sitting in the middle of a very large sweet spot of their own in terms of being both an absolute necessity to maintaining the present-day oil industry and an absolute necessity to the construction of the new oil industry. (Here's hoping Mother Nature doesn't throw another Katrina at this industry anytime soon.)

■ ■ ■

Before getting back to ethanol it should emphasized that, as important as oil has long been to transportation, it has also long been an important source of industrial fuel and home heating oil. Curing America's addiction to oil means also finding substitute fuels for these important uses of refined crude.

Milton Copulos, the defense expert, mentioned a company that he said is trying to do just that, essentially making biofuel oil that can substitute for crude-derived industrial boiler fuel and home heating oil. The company is working with cellulosic feedstocks. Unlike with ethanol, he said, it is not necessary to first break down the cellulose before producing the biofuel oil.

The company is Dynamotive Energy Systems. It is in Canada. In August 2006 the company said in a press release on its web site that it was transitioning to operating status, so obviously it still is just getting going.[16] As with so many other companies working on potential substitutes for oil, only time will tell if Dynamotive is successful. But it is worth putting it on the list of companies to watch in the category of "Biofuel Production" to highlight the fact that there's more out there than just gasoline—that biofuel should also be looked upon as a way to run factories and heat homes without relying on fuel made from crude.

■ ■ ■

Now back to ethanol—specifically, the reasons why corn ethanol should at some point get overtaken by cellulosic ethanol and some possible investment ideas that could grow out of this turn of events.

In Professor Karim's scientific blueprint for how best to develop an ethanol business in a multiclimate country like the United States, nearly all of the recommended feedstocks—grasses, agricultural waste, municipal solid waste, and so on—are cellulosic sources. As the Bush administration also seems to have decided, based on its blueprint for biofuel development issued in 2006, eventually cellulosic ethanol is going to have to supplant corn ethanol, whatever the politics of the situation. (It will interesting to watch the 2008 presidential candidates try to dance around corn versus cellulose questions as they woo Iowans during primary season.)

The advantages of cellulosic ethanol are many, starting with the aforementioned fact that it can be made from waste, a fuel source that presumably will never run out. Using already-existing waste products instead of food crops could help alleviate the environmental quandary posed by biofuel that so worries leading environmentalists like Sir Peter Crane.

Another advantage of cellulosic ethanol is that the net energy produced is greater than it is for corn ethanol. Still another is that cellulosic ethanol would help avoid the problem spotlighted by Clean Edge's Pernick, namely, the diversion of so much farmland into crops grown for energy that nations are faced with a food versus fuel dilemma.

There is, however, one key problem that cellulosic ethanol does not solve: It cannot be transported through the United States' existing petroleum pipeline system any more than corn ethanol can. It is this fact, among others, that would appear to give that other biofuel, biobutanol, which should be transportable in the existing petroleum pipeline system, the opportunity to wind up center stage in the energy universe.

By Millikin's assessment, cellulosic ethanol will be a $1 billion or so annual business by 2012—definitely not chump change, but still only a fraction of the revenue expected to be derived from corn ethanol. But the scientific push to develop cellulosic ethanol should be far along by then, and so companies that are in the category of "Ethanol and Biodiesel Technology" because of their potential in cellulosic ethanol deserve to be watched now.

In addition to the aforementioned Iogen, there are a number of companies that could be key to the technological development of cellulosic ethanol. One is SunOpta of Canada. SunOpta is an organic and natural food company whose BioProcess Group in 2006 represented a very small percentage of corporate revenue. In June 2006 SunOpta made an intriguing announcement. As reported by the business technology web site *Red Herring*, SunOpta announced that its BioProcess Group would develop China's first cellulosic ethanol plant. According to *Red Herring*, "the news could help position the company as a technology leader in the world's fastest-growing large economy."[17] Of course, no foreign company waltzes into China; it usually takes a lengthy period of relationship building, a fact that makes SunOpta's announcement even more intriguing. Only time will tell whether and to what extent this is a genuinely significant development in the area of cellulosic ethanol technology. But the announcement itself is interesting, coming as it did around the same time as another announcement by the company that it had entered into an agreement with a large European ethanol producer.[18]

Another potential contributor is Dyadic International, a Florida-based biotech firm. In July 2006 Dyadic's chief science officer reportedly said "we are making rapid progress in the development of potent enzyme mixtures that work well in the cellulosic ethanol application."[19] Dyadic sells more than 45 liquid and dry enzyme products to more than 200 industrial customers in approximately 50 countries for the textile, pulp and paper, animal feed, alcohol, and other industries.[20]

Yet another firm with potential is Novozymes, a Danish biotech firm which in 2005 earned the Technology Leadership of the Year Award in the area of alternative energy technologies from the well-known research firm Frost & Sullivan. The award followed Novozymes' announcement that it had achieved a thirtyfold reduction in enzyme cost of converting a certain kind of cellulosic feedstock.

In June 2006 Novozymes made a China announcement of its own. The company said it was entering into a three-year cooperation agreement with China Resources Alcohol Corporation on research into processes for producing cellulosic-based ethanol. Included in this announcement were some intriguing observations from Novozymes on how the company expects biofuel development in China to differ from that in the United States. "In the long term Novozymes expects China to become an important market with regard to biofuel." However, "Novozymes envisages that the production of ethanol based on corn—first-generation biofuel—will not grow as strongly in China in the coming years because, to a large extent, China imports corn and other cereals as foodstuffs. On the other hand it expects China to focus keenly on the development of second-generation biofuel or cellulose-based ethanol."[21]

If this is true, it is further evidence that a U.S.–China partnership might benefit both countries—and the entire world. It also is a disturbing piece of evidence that if it goes it alone, China, instead of the United States, could become the world leader in cellulosic ethanol technology.

Still another company with intriguing prospects is Genencor, a unit of another Danish company, Danisco, one of the world's largest producers of food ingredients. Genencor is active on several fronts. For example, it reportedly is working with the French forest products industry to develop cellulosic ethanol from paper pulp.[22] Also, like Novozymes, Genencor has made significant breakthroughs in reducing the cost of enzymes for cellulosic ethanol production.

If you are keeping score, we now have five companies—Iogen, SunOpta, Dyadic, Novozymes, and Genencor—whose potential seems sufficient to include them on the list of companies to watch in the category of "Ethanol and Biodiesel Technology." Take note: This is a wide-open category in terms of not knowing where the big technological breakthroughs might come from. As with important biotech breakthroughs in human medicine, biotech breakthroughs in biofuel could happen at any time from a company anywhere on the map.

One more company to add to this list is Ceres, Inc., a California-based plant genetics company. Ceres has gotten a fair amount of media attention for its work with switchgrass, a cellulosic source mentioned by President Bush in his 2006 State of the Union address. In July 2006 Ceres completed a detailed analysis of more than 12,000 switchgrass genes. The company has been working with a foundation whose ability to breed switchgrass could, given how switchgrass has drawn the attention of Washington, put this native grass at the forefront of cellulosic ethanol sources.[23]

Still another company that would have been listed in this category if it wasn't already listed in another category is Honda, which in September 2006 was reported by Reuters to have co-developed the world's first "practical" process for producing ethanol out of cellulosic biomass. The story said that Honda's partner, the Research Institute of Innovative Technology for the Earth (RITE), described in the story as a nonprofit entity set up by the Japanese government and private enterprises, had developed a new microorganism.[24]

While it remains to be seen how big a deal this really is, the fact that a car company would be on the leading edge of biofuel technology shows how wide open the field is. It is so wide open, in fact, that when I asked Green Car Congress's Millikin to pick the most likely winners, he said it was impossible at this stage. Texas Tech's Narim doesn't pick winners but he provided what could turn out to be an important clue when he happened to mention that Novozymes and Genencor "are at the top."

Whether it is thanks to one or more of these companies or to some other company not yet on the radar screen, whenever cellulosic ethanol takes center stage, this should give rise to a number of other *indirect* investment possibilities.

For example, waste disposal companies presumably should benefit when municipal solid waste becomes feedstock. Candy companies could find their gooey sugary waste in demand. Paper and packaging companies also should benefit. While it is too soon to put any of these in a category, it's not too early to start thinking about them.

"Wasting" no time, in 2006 the Georgia Forestry Commission appointed its first forest energy and development director, his duties to include "analyzing the viability of marketing the forest energy source, biomass, which is used to make ethanol." The new director "will serve as a liaison between energy investors, commercial and public entities and the Forestry community as the state's biomass industry grows."[25] (Don't forget what Texas Tech's Karim said about Georgia being a great place for cellulosic ethanol made from wood waste.)

It would seem that waste is waste—until it is transportation fuel.

■ ■ ■

This brings us to the wild card of biofuels: biobutanol.

By Millikin's estimate, biobutanol could be a $10 billion-a-year business in the United States by 2012. Europe and Asia conceivably might add billions more to the pot.

Then again, he told me, by 2012 biobutanol might be only a $1 billion business in the U.S.

How and when will the world know if biobutanol is going to be a $10 billion business in 2012, a $1 billion business, or something in between?

The "when" could be as early as 2007. The "how" could come from a project scheduled to be conducted in Great Britain by DuPont and British Petroleum (BP).

As described to me by Millikin, DuPont and BP will be attempting to raise the yield for that part of the biobutanol production process in which the sugars are fermented into alcohol. If they succeed, this could get biobutanol's production costs down to the point where, given this biofuel's many favorable attributes, a global biobutanol development and production program could take off.

Biobutanol's attributes would appear to give this biofuel the potential to become nothing less than the world's foremost biofuel. According to published information:[26]

- Unlike ethanol, it is expected that biobutanol will be transportable through a petroleum pipeline system and sellable through existing station pumps. (My comment: This should make biobutanol easier and cheaper to distribute than ethanol. It should also mean that it will take less energy to bring biobutanol to market.)

- Biobutanol has a higher energy density than ethanol. (My comment: This should give biobutanol better engine performance that translates into more miles per gallon than for ethanol.)
- Ordinary vehicles should, without modifications, be able to run on a higher concentration of biobutanol to gasoline than ethanol to gasoline. (My comment: According to BP's web site, the potential maximum is 16 percent biobutanol to 84 percent gasoline; however, other observers believe that eventually the percentage of biobutanol could be much higher. Even at 16 percent, biobutanol could be used in a higher concentration than ethanol in unmodified vehicles.)
- It will be possible to make biobutanol either from grain or cellulose. (My comment: It will thus be possible to use food crops like corn up to their optimal point in terms of land use, while at the same time using wild grasses grown on suboptimal farmland, plus all of the world's organic waste.)
- Existing corn ethanol refineries can be retrofitted to make them biobutanol refineries. (My comment: The best of all those biorefineries now being built in the Midwest to process corn ethanol would stay in business.)
- Biobutanol is an oxygenate, which means that it increases the level of oxygen in gasoline. (My comment: Higher levels of oxygen improve combustion, which is a plus for the environment.)

It is worth emphasizing that biobutanol's promise must be borne out in the real world. Still, it is not as if DuPont and BP are starting from scratch. Butanol made from oil has been a fuel for a long time. It is just that the cost to produce it was never competitive with gasoline.

DuPont believes biobutanol can be competitive with gasoline even if the price of oil were to drop to $30 to $40 a barrel.[27] If this is true, biobutanol could be a very important factor not only in the development of biofuel but also in the development of unconventional fossil fuels like coal, oil shale, and tar sands. Indeed, based on the theory espoused in Chapter 1 by energy analyst Glenn Wattley that oil prices ultimately will settle at levels that make oil about as expensive as or a little less expensive than its alternatives, global use of biobutanol might force down the price of oil below where it would need to be to support full-scale development of tar sands and coal.

If DuPont succeeds, the politics surrounding biobutanol could be fascinating to watch. A lot of people have a lot of money invested in corn ethanol, and biobutanol could hasten the end of corn ethanol's reign by being a flat-out superior fuel. As discussed, biobutanol can be made from cellulose, so if biobutanol were on the horizon, the drive to develop cellulosic technology presumably would get a tremendous push.

Meanwhile, major oil companies will have something to think about. It is hard to imagine major oil companies liking the idea of the billions they are sinking into tar sands development possibly being at risk. But while their knee-jerk reaction may be to use their political muscle to try and stifle biobutanol, one or more oil companies may see things quite differently.

Think about it: What really is biobutanol to a major oil company? Is it a threat? Or is it, just maybe, *one of the biggest opportunities ever to come down the road?*

Biobutanol strikes me as the biofuel an oil company could learn to love, a biofuel which, unlike ethanol, is complementary to the oil industry in that it can be transported through the industry's pipeline network. For any oil company smart enough to figure it out, biobutanol could turn out to be one of the biggest gushers of all time—an elephantine oil field that never dries up and is never in danger of being nationalized by some radical ruler like Venezuela's Chavez. Embracing biobutanol, moreover, could give an oil company a reputation for caring about the environment that could be money in the bank. (Ask yourself: If given a choice between filling up at the station that sells gasoline and the one that sells a blend of gasoline and biobutanol, which one are you going to pick?)

All of this, of course, takes us right back to the importance major oil companies will have in their added role as investment bankers. Right now, DuPont is working with BP, but experts say that whether it is BP or one or more of the other major oil companies that ultimately embrace biobutanol remains to be seen. It is conceivable that they all somehow will, or that none will, the latter under the theory of (oil) boys will be (oil) boys.

As big a deal as biobutanol could turn out to be, it is not the only aspect of DuPont's plan for growth in alternative energy technologies. The company discussed its multifaceted strategy at a "clean tech" conference in May 2006. This strategy, subsequently described in a company press release, includes photovoltaics (solar power), fuel cells, and crop genetics, in addition to biofuels. The company emphasized in that press release that it owns one of the world's largest patent estates in biotechnology, covering both the rapidly growing agricultural sector and the emerging industrial sectors.[28]

None of this should go unnoticed. In mapping out a strategy that seems based to a significant extent on innovations in biofuel developed with its own crop genetics expertise, DuPont appears to be going for an extreme makeover. It could be goodbye image of DuPont as a chemicals company and hello image of DuPont as a cutting-edge science company, a biotech company—in short, a company in the "sustainability" business.

Sustainability, which refers generally to the use of the planet's natural resources in ways that can be sustained over time, is becoming a big deal on Wall Street. Financial analysts increasingly are judging companies on whether they have sustainable business models. Companies such as DuPont appear to be going after business based on their abilities to provide sustainable products and solutions. Due in part to pressure from large institutional investors led by the managers of public pension funds, many companies now issue environmental annual reports just like they issue financial annual reports.

To reiterate, biobutanol's long-term prospects won't be discernible until the results are in from the DuPont-BP project, and even then it may take several more years to know for sure whether biobutanol will be an important biofuel. DuPont has indicated that it doesn't expect to introduce biobutanol in the United States until the company has developed what it calls "Gen 2," which has been described as a biocatalyst that will improve the fermentation process, increasing both the yield and concentration of biobutanol. DuPont has said it hopes Gen 2 will be ready by 2010.[29]

Whatever the future holds, however, it is hard not to like "newcomer" DuPont's apparent scientific and technology potential in the area of energy. Whether it is biobutanol (for which the company could wind up not only licensing the technology but also designing and building biorefineries), genetically improved varieties of feedstocks, or any of a number of other sustainability products, DuPont would seem to be positioned to become a scientific and technological leader in the new oil industry.

But it is mostly because DuPont may deliver on, and benefit from, biobutanol technology that it is up there all by itself in the top spot on the list of companies to watch in a category titled—duh—"Biobutanol Technology." Investors should not in any way take this category's top ranking as an endorsement of the company's chances of making money. Yes, biobutanol could well be the proverbial next big thing. But just as drivers are looking over the horizon, so also are technology firms. Just as technology always seems to be improving in the telecom and medical industries, DuPont's Gen 2 organism could turn out to be but one in a succession of biotech advances from a host of companies, all of which ends up in the creation of a biofuel even better than biobutanol.

Such advances might appear first in the work being done by the U.S. Energy Department's Joint Genome Institute (JGI), which unites the expertise of several national laboratories—Lawrence Berkeley, Lawrence Livermore, Los Alamos, Oak Ridge, and Pacific Northwest—along with the Stanford Human Genome Center. JGI's mission is to advance genomics "in support of clean energy production and environmental characterization and clean-up."[30] In sum, looking out to 2015, while biobutanol and DuPont could be on everybody's radar screen, by then another company whose technology is still in some scientist's head may have come to the fore.

Where might some of these still-undiscovered technological breakthroughs come from?

How about termites? Termites reportedly have attracted the interest of federal researchers because they have microbes that may help with cellulosic ethanol. How about elephant feces? Seriously. In 2006 a European university claimed that it had achieved a scientific breakthrough in the production of cellulosic ethanol by genetically modifying a fungus found in elephant excrement.

If and when any fantastic new breakthroughs come, hopefully they will come from something less disgusting than elephant poop.

■ ■ ■

Biobutanol isn't the only second-generation biofuel under development that could one day help reshape the global market for biofuels. Other fuels, such as NExBTL, also have that potential.

Yeah, I know. Here we go again—another convoluted word that is not easy to pronounce, much less remember. What, exactly, is NExBTL? It is short for "Next Biomass to Liquids."

Big help, right?

The proprietary NExBTL process technically doesn't produce biodiesel. Rather, it turns out a high-quality bio-based fuel which, according to its developer, Neste Oil of Finland, "outperforms conventional biodiesel and diesel grades currently on the market, according to recent tests by leading heavy-duty engine manufacturers." This bio-based diesel fuel can be produced and blended with regular diesel at the same refinery where the diesel is made, thus facilitating large-scale production. It can be made from waste animal fat as well as vegetable oil (soy, palm, etc.), which should come as a relief to environmentalists worried about forest loss.[31]

On its web site (www.nesteoil.com), Neste describes itself as "a refining and marketing company focusing on advanced, cleaner traffic fuels." Millikin told me that Neste "could make out like a bandit"—a sentiment the Green Car Congress guru did not express often during our numerous discussions over many months.

While only time will tell whether NExBTL or some other biodiesel makes out like a bandit, Millikin's assessment carries a lot of weight with me, and so Finland's Neste Oil goes on the watch list in "Ethanol and Biodiesel Technology" category.

(If anyone at Neste is listening, it would help if you gave your fuel a more consumer-friendly name, something as appealing as the phrase "cleaner traffic.")

■ ■ ■

While Europe is known for diesel-powered vehicles, there are a lot of gasoline-powered vehicles there, too, and the European market for ethanol is growing.

The leading ethanol supplier in Europe as of 2006 reportedly was Abengoa, a Spanish conglomerate that describes itself as a technology company that applies innovative solutions for sustainable development in the infrastructures, environment, and energy sectors. (Sounds like another sustainability company.) Through a subsidiary, Abengoa Bioenergy, which is headquartered in St. Louis, Missouri, Abengoa is also heavily involved in the U.S. ethanol market. Abengoa Bioenergy also reportedly is working with technology providers including Novozymes on cellulosic ethanol.[32] All of this would seem to justify putting Abengoa on the watch list in the category of "Biofuel Production." Indeed, I would not be surprised if Abengoa became as much of a household name in the United States as ADM.

Meanwhile, just as ethanol production is growing in Europe, so is biodiesel production in the United States, due in no small part to federal regulations that started kicking in in June 2006 requiring the removal of most sulfur from highway diesel fuel, though it should be noted that mixing biodiesel with diesel isn't the only approach. Refinery operators can take the sulfur out themselves at the refinery. Both approaches were being used in 2006.

In talking with Clean Edge's Pernick about biodiesel in the United States, one name kept coming up: Imperium Renewables. In May 2006, Seattle-based Imperium announced plans to build the United States' largest biodiesel manufacturing facility, a plant capable of producing 100 million gallons per year primarily from soybean, canola oil, and other extracts. In its press release the company said, "The demand for biodiesel has risen sharply in recent months due to the combined surge in the price of petroleum products and increases in concern for the environment."

While any company can predict a rosy future, when one reads the last paragraph of Imperium's press release as it appeared on the Clean Edge web site, something jumps out—at least it did to me. The paragraph reads: "Imperium Renewables is the first biodiesel focused company in the United States to be funded by Venture Capital and has received venture funding from Nth Power, Technology Partners and Vulcan Capital."[33]

Pernick emphasized, as energy analyst Tom Petrie had, that "a shift is happening" in the U.S. venture capital community, with biofuel starting to come on strong. While important, what has struck me as being particularly important is the interest in biofuel being shown by the San Francisco–based energy-technology venture capital firm Nth Power. I have known about and spoken with folks at San Francisco–based Nth Power for a long time, and so I know Nth Power was a key provider of venture capital to alternative energy companies long before it became fashionable in Silicon Valley.

Nth Power's backing of Imperium Renewables was enough to cinch the company's inclusion in the "Ethanol and Biodiesel Technology" category.

If you are still keeping score, the total number of companies in this wide-open category is eight, in alphabetical order: Ceres, Dyadic, Genencor, Iogen, Imperium, Neste, Novozymes, and SunOpta. Once again, do not think of this as a final list. Rather, think of this category—indeed, of the entire new oil industry—as a work in progress.

CHAPTER 4

Substitute Liquid Fuels, Part Two: Unconventional Fossil Fuels

Unconventional fossil fuels get their name from the fact that while gasoline can be made the conventional way, from the refining of crude oil, it also can be made unconventionally from other fossil fuel sources. Tar sands, coal, and oil shale all have hydrocarbons, just in solid form (see Figure 4.1). All three, and also natural gas, can be turned into what may be called synthetic oil through processes that have long been considered too expensive to compete with crude oil. But when the price at the pump is pushing $3 and higher around the world, some oil-producing countries are as unstable as nitroglycerine, and there is growing unease that conventional oil production has peaked or soon could, unconventional oil sources start to look pretty good.

Two points of clarification: First, while some describe the oil produced in the deep waters of the Gulf of Mexico and similar locales as unconventional oil, it is still liquid hydrocarbons. Thus I have chosen not to characterize deepwater oil as unconventional oil but, rather, as an extension of the conventional oil universe—indeed, a very logical extension given the overall situation on land. Second, while some forecasts include tar

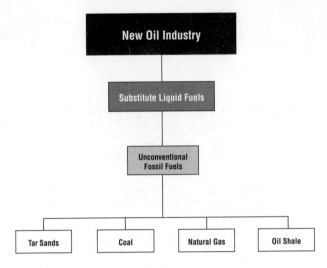

FIGURE 4.1   Substitute Liquid Fuels: Unconventional Fossil Fuels

sands when calculating how much oil the earth has left, I think tar sands oil should be kept separate from crude oil in part because the extraction process involves digging, not drilling. Also, tar sands exploitation is inherently more expensive and more destructive to the environment. Thus the cost-benefit relationship of tar sands is different than for crude oil, and to view tar sands and crude as essentially one and the same is to muddy the waters of public debate on the future direction of the global oil industry.

Once again, a little review is in order.

The new oil industry consists of three basic parts: substitutes (biofuel and unconventional fossil fuels), efficiency, and conventional oil (crude). As much as these three complement each other, they also compete with one another. Thus it seems only logical that the amount of gasoline from unconventional fossil fuels that the world is going to need will depend on how much biofuel gets produced, on how much more efficient vehicles become, and on how much more crude oil gets extracted from the earth.

It takes really big bucks (hundreds of millions to billions of dollars per project) and really long lead times (5 to 10 years or longer) to build the infrastructure needed for a new unconventional oil industry such as tar sands. To justify the time and expense, tar sands and the other unconventional oils must be considered economically viable not just for a few years but for a few decades or longer. Indeed, if the financial backers of unconventional fossil fuels were to decide that increases in biofuel production plus improvements in vehicle efficiency were going to be enough of a supplement to conventional oil to satisfy rising gasoline demand, then unconventional fossil fuels would have a hard time getting out of the ground.

No, wait—scratch that. As logical as all this sounds, it does not reflect the way things really are. The fact of the matter is that at least two out of the three solid fossil fuels—tar sands and coal—definitely have a future in the world, and the third, oil shale, eventually may, too. What remains unclear is how big a future.

Why do these solid fossil fuels *definitely* have a future?

Because when it comes to a nation's energy security, no price is too high. Well, is it? How much would you as an American (or Chinese or Indian) be willing to pay for a big new domestic oil source, albeit one that was hell on the environment and expensive to exploit, but a source nonetheless that reduced your dependence on imported oil and could be protected from terrorists? Throw in the possibility that conventional oil production really may be in the process of peaking, and then ask: *What price energy security?*

To be sure, energy security also is one of biofuel's selling points. But at least until scientists figure out things like how to genetically engineer microbes to increase productivity, synthetic gasoline will trump biogasoline as a "secure" transportation fuel—and rightly so. Indeed, a case can be made that if a nation were to rely too heavily on biofuel, the nation would put itself in danger of using so much of its agricultural land to grow crops for energy that it would have to import a lot more food, thereby risking becoming food insecure in order to become energy secure. No politician is going to be willing to take that risk, whereas the debate over whether the extraction of unconventional fossil fuels is worth the environmental damage it causes is really just another round in the long-running fight over environment versus national security—a drama in which every politician knows his or her lines by heart.

Let's look at the script for the 2008 U.S. presidential campaign. Democrats, in an effort to look "green," think about calling for a moratorium on unconventional fossil fuel development on government land, only to realize that to do so would give Republicans another reason to call Democrats soft on national security in an election where national security should again be a game-changing issue. Meanwhile, Republicans realize they face opposition to unconventional fossil fuel development from within their own ranks from those who don't cotton to the idea of digging up wide swathes of pristine Western land in quest of coal. Party leaders move to nip things in the bud by stressing repeatedly that America needs to lick its addiction to imported oil.

Frankly, no matter how the 2008 U.S. presidential election turns out, now that the Pentagon has decided that synthetic fuel from domestic sources should be a top priority, and there are several big government-backed coal-to-liquid (CTL) projects planned in China, and deep-pocketed and politically connected oil companies have tar sands projects in Canada, the political momentum globally for unconventional fossil fuels is damn near unstoppable.

Lest we forget—not that anyone could, given how environmentalists are always bringing it up—increased fuel efficiency, too, can make a nation more energy secure by reducing the need for imported oil. But as important as increased automotive efficiency is in the scheme of things, in terms of national security, a case can be made that it would be unwise for America to put all its eggs in that basket when the automobile industry is dominated by foreign companies. It would be nice to think that General Motors and Ford might again dominate the global automobile industry but, sadly, that ship has sailed. It's the age of Toyota and Honda and, at best, Detroit is going to be one of a number of others in the mix. Sorry, environmentalists, but viewed in terms of national security—which every government has the responsibility to make its first priority—it does not make sense to exchange dependence on one foreign-controlled industry (conventional oil) for dependence on another, albeit less malevolent, one.

■ ■ ■

As was mentioned in Chapter 2, it has been estimated that the United States spent upwards of $3 per gallon of gasoline in 2006 to insure that the oil it imported safely reached its shores. These defense-related expenditures were on top of the actual pump price. When many other economic dampening effects of high oil prices were also factored in, estimates are that the true cost of a gallon of gasoline in 2006 exceeded $11 a gallon.

Viewed this way, gasoline made from American coal or oil shale reserves—or from tar sands found in America's friendly neighbor to the north, Canada—is not just an important way to boost the national security of the United States. Relatively speaking, it is also a financial bargain. To be sure, gasoline made from North America's unconventional fossil fuels might not be looked upon as any sort of bargain if it looked like peace was going to break out in the world sometime soon. But Washington assumes the global war on terror is going to last many years. A U.S. State Department fact sheet on terrorism concludes that "Terrorists' proven ability to adapt means it is likely that we will face a resilient enemy for years to come."[1]

Given this situation, the U.S. Department of Defense (DoD) is primed to spur the development of domestically available unconventional fossil fuels. The military brass are said to be emphasizing alternatives that utilize so-called Fischer-Tropsch (FT) technology. In 2006 an aide to one U.S. Congressman told a reporter that DoD is going to become a major FT customer in the future.[2]

Fischer-Tropsch technology has been around for many decades. Its roots can be traced to Nazi Germany and to South Africa during the latter's apartheid era. Both countries turned to FT technology in order to utilize large domestic coal reserves after the world cut off their sources of imported oil.

Without getting too technical—like most investors, I'm no scientist—Fischer-Tropsch technology uses a chemical reaction to convert carbon monoxide and hydrogen into liquid hydrocarbons after the gasses have been generated by partial oxidation of coal or wood-based fuels. The same process can be used to directly convert natural gas into liquid hydrocarbons. When they invented the process in the 1920s, Messrs. Fischer and Tropsch were researchers at the Kaiser Wilhelm Institute.

One especially active area of military research is synthetic jet fuel. The air force's ambitious goal is to have 50 percent of its aviation fuel come from alternative sources by 2016. Of special importance to investors is the fact that the air force is conducting its research "in a visible and transparent way so that our partners in the commercial aviation industry will be able to see our testing. By working together we can expand the market for synthetic jet fuel and make it more economical to produce by increasing volume."[3] The air carriers of the world no doubt hope so, what with every penny-a-gallon increase in fuel prices said to add nearly $200 million per year to industry operating costs.

The air force is interested in acquiring 100 million gallons of synthetic fuel by 2008. The air force is working initially with natural gas, but has said that long-term it will use coal. This makes a great deal of sense given America's probable future dependence on imported natural gas (LNG) versus its abundant supply of mined-in-the-U.S.A. coal.

A point that investors should definitely remember is that DoD could end up using this sort of fuel in all branches of the military. In other words, it could be the air force today, army tomorrow, and navy and marines the day after that. However, any such decision probably is several years off.

The air force took a big step toward achieving its long-term goal in September 2006 when it conducted a successful test of a 50-50 blend of jet fuel and synthetic fuel made with FT technology. The air force called it the first step in opening up new horizons for sourcing fuel for military purposes. The company that made the synthetic fuel, Syntroleum, called it a historic flight and used the occasion to reiterate that it believes its synthetic fuel can be made from America's vast domestic coal reserves.

Should the air force succeed in establishing a synthetic jet fuel industry based on coal, this obviously would be a big boost both for providers of FT technology and for U.S. coal-mining companies. In the case of the coal companies, it would represent an added boost; coal is already in the process of becoming an even bigger source of fuel for America's electric utility industry. Currently, coal accounts for roughly 50 percent of America's electrical generation, and U.S. utilities have plans to build as many as 150 new coal-fired power plants over the next several years. This has led some to ask whether there will there be enough domestic coal to go around. Yes, experts say, noting that the United States is often called "the Saudi Arabia of coal." Experts further say that while it is commonly believed that the U.S. is sitting on 250 years' worth of coal, a more realistic number would be 100 to 125 years. That's still *beaucoup* coal.

According to energy analyst Glenn Wattley, if gasoline were made from coal, it could compete with petroleum-derived gasoline if oil were selling for roughly $45 to $50 a barrel. This is considerably less than what oil was selling for in 2006. Nevertheless, Wattley says that plans for a CTL industry in the United States are mostly still just that—plans.

"There are lots of plans," he told me, but apparently pump prices are still not quite high enough for anyone to pull the trigger. Wattley said a number of CTL plants will be built in the United States when pump prices "go north of $3.50 a gallon." At $4 a gallon CTL "looks exciting," he added, and at $5 a gallon, "It's a no-brainer." What would also no doubt spur CTL development in the United States would be passage of legislation that would extend the $0.50 a gallon CTL excise tax credit to 2023 from 2009, which would build on the interest of governors of a number of coal-producing states to have a CTL facility built in their state.

One company that would appear to have long-term potential thanks to its FT technology is Syntroleum, which made the synthetic fuel for the air force to test and presumably could significantly benefit if the air force achieves its long-term goal. Syntroleum has provided synthetic fuel for testing purposes not just to the defense department but also the energy and transportation departments for several years. In 2006 the company entered into an agreement with a private Swiss firm to convert coal and other materials into "ultra-clean fuels."[4]

Another company that appears to have potential is Colorado-based Rentech, which in 2006 announced that it would use its technology to develop two CTL plants in association with Peabody Energy, the coal company. The project is seen as an important early step in establishing a U.S. CTL industry. On its web site Rentech describes itself as one of the world's leading developers of Fischer-Tropsch coal-to-liquids and gas-to-liquids technologies. In testimony before a Senate committee, Rentech's president said, "I think the great potential of CTL is using American resources, American know-how, and American innovation to create both energy independence and jobs."[5]

A third company—this one seemingly with lots of potential—is the granddaddy of Fischer-Tropsch: Sasol Ltd., the South African firm born out of that country's apartheid-era need to replace imported oil. Sasol's potential lies more outside the United States, especially in China, where the government seems to be pulling out all the stops in an effort to bring a CTL industry on line as early as 2012.

In early 2006 China reportedly had over two dozen CTL projects in different stages of planning. The government subsequently took steps designed to cut back on smaller projects, reportedly to "ensure a healthy development of the coal liquefaction industry across the country."[6] Also in 2006, the Chinese government said it plans to spend the equivalent of $5 billion by 2020 to explore for new coal reserves, the apparent goal being to increase the nation's coal reserves by a whopping 60 percent or so. Even then, China will have a long way to go before fully exploiting its coal resources, which have been estimated at over 5 trillion tons.

Sasol should be in the thick of China's CTL development. In 2006 Sasol signed major agreements (two as of midyear) with Chinese coal interests to study the feasibility of building CTL facilities. Each facility could be in operation as early as 2012, Sasol said, adding that it would be an investor in the plants as well as a technology provider. In the company's press release announcing the agreements, a Sasol executive was quoted as saying, "Sasol offers China commercially proven and world-class experience in converting abundant coal reserves into valuable synthetic liquid fuels. Our proprietary and proven Fischer-Tropsch technology offers China a compelling and competitive fast-forward to meeting its future energy requirements in an efficient, reliable and sustainable manner."[7]

To be sure, China is not the only major market where Sasol is advancing. The company has held discussions that could lead to it building a CTL facility in India. Importantly, the company also is moving on a related front, natural gas-to-liquids (GTL), having announced a deal with Qatar Petroleum, a state-owned concern, for the first commercial GTL facility outside South Africa.

It should be noted that GTL could give Russia and the other would-be members of a natural gas cartel even more influence over global energy markets. Whereas LNG is still gas, just in liquid form, GTL is basically the same stuff that is being carried by all those gasoline-carrying tanker ships crossing the Atlantic from Europe to the United States as the latter becomes increasingly dependent on imported gasoline (on top of imported crude oil) in order to meet growing demand without having to build new oil refineries. Imported gasoline dependence is a problem that keeps getting worse as Americans exercise their not-in-my-backyard veto power over new refinery construction.

While only time will tell how well Sasol does, Wattley sees Sasol as "an economic powerhouse" for reasons that go beyond the potential demand for CTL and GTL in China and other countries including the United States—where Sasol also has significant prospects.

"Sasol," Wattley told me, "really is a chemicals company, not an energy company." He explained that Sasol's technology can be used to turn coal into some 130 different chemicals (profitable by-products), any one of which could, in the future, be made more from coal in order to reduce a company's (and a country's) dependence on imported oil.

Because of Sasol's global long-term potential in these various areas—each of which could experience explosive growth over the next decade or so—the South African company makes the list of companies to watch in a category titled "Coal Technology." Given how much weight I have been putting on technology companies to direct the growth of the new oil industry, it should come as no surprise that this latest category also is near the top of the list. "Coal Technology" comes in sixth, behind only the biofuel and automotive efficiency technology categories and the also-very-important investment banker category.

Though not in the same global league as Sasol—at least not yet—both Syntroleum and Rentech also make it. By the end of this chapter, they will be joined by a much, much smaller company with intriguing technological prospects called GreatPoint Energy.

As important as technology will be in tapping coal's potential as a liquid transportation fuel, investors should not lose sight of the fact that coal companies, too, should prosper as coal increasingly becomes a global source of liquid fuel to go along with its expanding role as a fuel source for electricity. There also is the potential for coal to benefit when more people start using electricity as an alternative transportation fuel in plug-in vehicles.

Which coal-mining companies should investors be thinking about? Well, as Credit Suisse, the investment banking firm, noted in a 2005 issue of its e-magazine, "It is not easy to invest directly in pure coal producers. Some coal producers are government-owned . . . while others are unlisted parts of large groups. . . . Other big international mining conglomerates . . . own coal mines, but these account for only (a small percentage of the) conglomerates' operating profits." But as the Credit Suisse report further noted, the situation is different in the United States, where there are "numerous suppliers, most of which are listed."[8]

Among the largest U.S. producers in terms of market capitalization are Peabody Energy, CONSOL Energy, and Arch Coal, and while it is impossible at this point to say which member of this group ultimately might perform the best, obviously all three would seem to have pretty fair prospects. Energy analyst Wattley notes that all three have "low-cost" coal reserves. All three thus have been included in a category titled "Synthetic Oil and LNG Providers," which ranks seventh on the list, the highest position occupied by companies that are primarily producers of energy as opposed to technology providers for energy. (Right after them come the biofuel producers.) By the end of this chapter, the three coal companies will be joined in the "Synthetic Oil and LNG Providers" category mostly by companies active in that other burgeoning synthetic oil business, tar sands.

■ ■ ■

It's worth taking a moment to reflect on how the world's growing dependence on coal is going to present governments with an incredible challenge.

Coal is rapidly becoming the world's "everyman" fuel, the resource probably best able to compensate for tightening supplies of the conventional oil and natural gas the world has long depended on to keep the wheels turning in many vitally important global industries such as plastics and chemicals.

Extraction from tar sands also will be important, primarily for reasons of national security, but its high financial and environmental costs ultimately will likely limit its development. Biofuel also has a bright future, but how bright will depend on whether there are biotech breakthroughs that significantly enhance productivity. Even if one accepts environmentalists' demand that efficiency should go at the top of the world's energy agenda, any stupendous breakthrough in automotive efficiency (and there are at least a couple on the horizon) will take years to hit the road in a meaningful way. Realistically speaking—and remembering coal's ubiquitous role as a source of both mobile and stationary energy—it is probably going to take an awful lot of coal to satisfy the incredible increase in total worldwide energy demand that has been forecast.

Indeed, as mentioned in Chapter 1, the Paris-based IEA has predicted that by 2030 the world will need a tremendous amount of additional energy. The agency has forecast that even with significant growth in biofuels, nearly all of that increase—85 percent of it—will have to be met by oil, natural gas, and coal.[9]

Many seriously question whether oil and natural gas will be up to the task. Some have emphasized that no matter how much oil is still in the ground, it won't be possible to expand the infrastructure necessary to keep pace with this monstrous demand growth. All this would seem to suggest that coal is going to have a very big job on its hands—almost as big a job as the infrastructure providers.

But if the world tries to consume coal in the same old ways, the game of life may have to be called on account of pollution and global warming.

Okay, that's an exaggeration. But it is no exaggeration that the world could experience a health care nightmare unless government policies, market mechanisms, or both are put into place that cause coal to be used in a far more environmentally friendly fashion.

One has only to look at China's horrendous environmental problems stemming from coal to see that coal-caused pollution could wind up killing not just tens of millions of Chinese but also, thanks to prevailing wind currents, a lot of Americans as well. As the *New York Times* noted, "Unless China finds a way to clean up its coal plants and the thousands of factories that burn coal, pollution will soar both at home and abroad. The increase in global-warming gasses from China's coal use will probably exceed that for all industrialized countries combined over the next 25 years, surpassing by five times the reduction in such emissions that the Kyoto Protocol seeks."[10]

Globally today, fossil-fuel power generation accounts for roughly 40 percent of man-made carbon dioxide emissions. When a Chinese-led global CTL industry kicks into gear sometime in the next decade, CO_2 emissions from coal could get even worse.

This is why I believe that one of the greatest governmental challenges of the next half century will be figuring out how to use coal without poisoning the environment. It's a challenge that includes tar sands and oil shale.

Given the urgency of the situation, it is hard to believe how slowly Washington is proceeding on a project to demonstrate that coal can be used cleanly to generate electricity. But while Washington moves at a snail's pace, private companies are picking up speed, sensing the long-term payoff of being a "clean" technology provider.

Enter General Electric.

In 2006 General Electric (GE) announced plans to build as many as 15 clean power plants over the next 10 years in partnership with British Petroleum. Plans call for at least one plant to be built in California and another in Scotland. Each will take a fossil fuel—either natural gas or petroleum coke, the latter a synthetic form of coal—and convert it into hydrogen and carbon dioxide. The hydrogen will be used as fuel to cleanly run the power plant, while the carbon dioxide will be captured, transported, and permanently stored underground—a process commonly called carbon sequestration.

At present, the United States has no requirements for controlling carbon emissions from fossil fuel sources, the Bush administration having opted for a voluntary approach that environmentalists say will be devastating because it will permit an entire new generation of coal-fired power plants to be built without carbon capture technology (which isn't cheap). Hopefully, the GE project will demonstrate that an economically viable market-based solution already exists. In turn, this could put enough public pressure on power plant owners that they would be socially if not legally obligated to utilize carbon capture and sequestration technology in all of their planned new generating facilities.

Needless to say, if GE's clean power project succeeds, the company might make a penny or two. Among other things, the CO_2 that GE plans to sequester might get used by companies engaged in "enhanced oil recovery" (EOR). While EOR is discussed later in Chapter 6, suffice it to say that the more oil that can be pushed to the surface by carbon dioxide gas, the better. (Jed Clampett of *Beverly Hillbillies* fame notwithstanding, the phrase "up from the ground came a bubbling crude" applies to only a portion of the oil that lies beneath the surface.)

Obviously, GE is a very big company with numerous lines of business so that no one new business opportunity is likely to make that much of a difference to its overall profit prospects. Still, GE has been busy recently getting into a number of so-called clean businesses, basically getting into the sustainability business. Wind power is one. Nuclear power plants are another (although I realize that some do not think of nuclear power plants as being "clean"—even though they don't give off any global-warming emissions—because of the toxic waste fuel they produce). It's all part of a corporate strategy you may have heard of that GE calls "ecomagination." Given the probable role that solid fossil fuels, which are as "dirty," if not more so, as crude oil, are likely to play in the new oil industry, it's enough to add GE to the watch list in the category of "Infrastructure Providers."

Now now let's talk about GreatPoint Energy.

I had never heard of the company until Wattley brought it to my attention. Basically, GreatPoint is a small, privately held outfit headquartered in Cambridge, Massachusetts, and started by folks from the

Massachusetts Institute of Technology, which is no slouch school. The best source of information on what GreatPoint does can be found on the company's web site, www.greatpointenergy.com. Basically, GreatPoint has a technology for converting coal into hydrogen and carbon dioxide through a proprietary catalytic process that the company says is less expensive and more efficient than other coal gasification processes. The hydrogen can be used to run a power plant cleanly, while half of the carbon dioxide can be captured and sold to oil companies to be used for getting more oil out of older oil fields through the process mentioned earlier called enhanced oil recovery.[11]

In essence, GreatPoint may have a way to make it cheaper and, very importantly, less environmentally harmful to use coal. That would be cool, and it will be very interesting to see if GreatPoint's technology catches on. GreatPoint was scheduled to begin pilot-plant tests in autumn 2006. The company could be big, Wattley believes. Thus Great-Point gets added to the watch list in the category "Coal Technology," joining Sasol, Syntroleum, and Rentech.

■ ■ ■

Let's move on to tar sands.

Yes, I know that tar sands have built-in importance as a politically secure source of oil. I get why national security all but dictates that tar sands have a role in the new oil industry. I realize that tar sands are being counted on—literally—to raise the total supply of oil to meet future demand. But I've still got to ask: Is a tar sands industry *really* necessary?

The way I see it, tar sands development has the potential to be a financial, environmental, and energy disaster—a triple threat!

Tar sands are pretty much what the name suggests. They are a mixture of sand, water, and clay containing deposits of thick, sticky oil called *bitumen* that can be extracted through a heating process.

Financially, tar sands development is extraordinarily expensive. (Think billions of dollars per mining project). It is extremely vulnerable to cost overruns due to such things as materiel and labor shortages. Nor is tar sands' high cost limited to the mining side of things. It is also going to cost a lot of money to retool a number of refineries so that they can handle this kind of oil.

While any estimate is just that, some experts would not be surprised if synthetic gasoline made from tar sands wound up being cost competitive with gasoline made from crude oil only if the price of crude were somewhere around $60 to $70 a barrel. This is higher than estimates for either coal or biofuel, which tend to be down in the $30 to $40 range.

Environmentally, tar sands production seems like a fifth horseman of the apocalypse. It can foul the water and spew into the air large amounts of gasses linked to global warming. It also can force one to tear down whatever is aboveground (like a carbon-sequestering forest) in order to get at what is belowground.

But it is from an energy perspective that things really start to look cockeyed. So much natural gas can be required during the extraction process that, when coupled with increases in Canada's domestic natural gas demand, "the amount of Canadian gas available for export to the U.S. is likely to diminish considerably over time," according to Raymond James & Associates, the brokerage firm.[12]

The United States, it should be noted, is heavily dependent on imports of natural gas from Canada. As those imports decline, and given the stagnant natural gas production in the United States itself and the fact that a U.S. LNG industry is still a ways away, America could find itself with a supply gap representing 9 percent of total U.S. gas consumption sometime over the next 15 years, according to Raymond James.[13]

Did you catch that? To solve one shortage we may create another.

To be sure, experts say there are methods that in the future may lessen the amount of natural gas required by the tar sands industry. Still, Ronald Barone, the well-known natural gas analyst at UBS Securities Inc. in New York, has issued a warning similar to the one Raymond James issued. "A ramp up in Canada's gas intensive oil sands industry, specifically in the province of Alberta, has significant implications for U.S. gas imports," Barone wrote in a September 2006 report.

Barone further wrote:

> A study by the Canadian Energy Research Institute (CERI) titled, "Spreading the Wealth Around: The Economic Impact of Alberta's Oil Sands Industry," estimates that the amount of natural gas required by the province to tap into its oil reserves over the next 15 years would be . . . close to half of the . . . established reserves in Alberta. Consequently, as Canada's oil sands industry shifts into higher gears, imports to the U.S. should continue to experience a marked decline . . . EIA, which is projecting a 1.9

percent annual growth rate in Canadian domestic gas consumption, predicts that by 2010 Canada's falling exports will be overtaken by LNG as the main source of U.S. gas imports. Put into perspective, as recently as 2003 Canada supplied almost 90 percent of U.S. net natural gas imports.[14]

In other words, instead of relying on good old politically reliable Canada for its natural gas, the United States is going to bet its economy—its future—on the new LNG industry that will come with serious political and weather-related risks.

Does this make sense?

For more on why this does not make sense, let's bring back Kevin Petak, the natural gas analyst. According to Petak, natural gas production continues to "tread water. For every bright spot, there's an area that's declining." While some drillers have had good success in the deepwater Gulf of Mexico, drilling there continues to run up against a shortage of available equipment. While there was a lot of natural gas in storage in 2006, to use Petak's words, "Storage can only go so far."

Storage can only go so far.

This point needs to be trotted out every time energy prices—both oil and natural gas—go down, seemingly giving some journalists and analysts cause to all but declare that the world's energy problems are over and happy days are here again. It is an understandable tendency in today's minute-by-minute, second-by-second financial marketplace where web sites enable investors to track their net worth in real time. Looking at things the way they should be looked at—on a year-to-year basis—just doesn't have enough pizzazz to keep everyone glued to their TVs or computer screens (especially when junior wants to pop in an awesome new video game).

In answer to the question, "Does tar sands development make sense?" the answer, all evidence to the contrary, apparently is that it does. Witness the many billions of dollars oil companies have been pouring into Canadian tar sands development over the last several years, with more injected every day. By 2020, according to a Canadian oil industry lobbying group, Canada's oil production could roughly double, despite declining conventional oil production, thanks to tar sands.[15]

Actually, if one thinks like an oilman, tar sands development makes perfect sense. Unlike coal and natural gas, which can be *converted* into oil, tar sands *are* oil. In one important way, tar sands are even better than crude oil. When exploring for crude, a company can drill a dry hole even with the best technology. With tar sands, every hole is a winner.

To an oil company, Canada's tar sands are extremely attractive, in part because they contain so darn much oil. Indeed, outside of Saudi Arabia, Canada's tar sands are said to be the world's biggest source of oil. Just as importantly, unlike the crude found in many oil-producing countries, Canada's tar sands are still open to private investment.

Once upon a time, before there was an OPEC, Big Oil owned the global oil industry lock, stock, and oil barrel. But now that 80 percent or so of the world's conventional oil reserves are effectively off-limits to private investment, Big Oil's influence is waning. As it looks into the future, Big Oil can see new players from the coal, agricultural, automotive, biotech, and other industries who, collectively, threaten to take away much of its remaining control over the industry that it literally built from the ground up. Canada's tar sands—along with deepwater oil drilling—represent Big Oil's last best chance to stay in control. Is it any wonder, then, that oil companies have come to the Canadian province of Alberta, where oil sands cover an area said to be larger than the state of Florida?

Whether or not tar sands should be an industry, look for tar sands to join coal at center stage in the new oil industry.

While many oil companies are working in Canada, probably the three that were most frequently mentioned by analysts interviewed for this book were EnCana Corporation, Canadian Natural Resources, and Suncor Energy. EnCana has been described generally as an oil and natural gas exploration, production, and marketing company. Canadian Natural Resources is said to be involved in all aspects of oil and natural gas. Suncor breaks out its operations into segments including tar sands, natural gas, and energy marketing and refining.

The "tar sands three," as we shall call them, join the watch list in the category of "Synthetic Oil and LNG Providers."

■ ■ ■

Compared with tar sands development, oil shale development is nowhere—yet. As a June 2006 article in *USA Today* noted, "Pushed by the Bush administration and legislation from Congress last year, and spurred by oil prices above $70 a barrel, the energy industry is mobilizing to unlock the secret of oil shale. As it has before, oil shale holds out the hope of a USA no longer dependent on foreign oil."[16]

Notice the word *pushed?* Apparently there is no stampede to Colorado, Wyoming, and Utah—despite the possibility that as much as two trillion barrels of oil could be underground—as there has been to Alberta's tar sands. This may be because, as a 2005 Rand Corporation Research Brief noted, crude oil would likely have to cost $70 to $95 per barrel (in 2005 dollars) in order for the first commercial oil shale extraction facility to be profitable over the operating life of the plant.[17]

It really is hard to see crude oil costing *that* much after biofuel, CTL, and efficiency—not to mention deepwater oil drilling, enhanced oil recovery, and even tar sands—went to work in the new oil industry. Still, the political push from Washington is not to be underestimated. The *USA Today* story quoted the then-head of the Senate Energy and Natural Resources Committee, New Mexico Republican Pete Domenici, as saying, "This is not pie in the sky. It's real this time."

Specifically what Senator Domenici thinks is "real" is a new oil shale recovery process that uses heaters to cook the oil-containing rock while it is still deep below ground, recovering what is then liquid oil and natural gas. But according to the company whose process this is, Shell Oil, not until 2010 will it be known whether the process is "commercially sustainable." (The Shell statement was reported in the same *USA Today* story.)

Colorado's state geologist, Vincent Matthews, told me he has "always been skeptical" about oil shale development, and from the sound of his voice, he still is. But Matthews has a lot of respect for Shell and its process. Shell is "one of the most scientific, long-range companies in the world," he said. Furthermore, "the beauty of their process" is that it produces only highly marketable light hydrocarbons.

While prospects for oil shale as a source of synthetic gasoline seem pretty much to be what they have been for a long time—uncertain—this is an opportunity to do what I should have done before: Add Shell to the watch list. Shell is right up there with Sasol in terms of coal-to-liquids technology. (Shell is another player in China.) Though shale is its baby, I've put Shell into the category with a far more likely payoff for investors, "Coal Technology."

No, wait. Shell already made the list in the category of "Investment

Bankers." Think of Shell's work in oil shale as part of the company's investment banking strategy.

■ ■ ■

Given that, for various reasons, there is going to have to be a global LNG industry in the United States, I asked Petak which companies he thought would prosper from being an LNG provider. One in particular came to mind: Woodside Petroleum Ltd. Woodside is "kind of interesting," he said, explaining that the company is "potentially sitting on a lot of reserves" that could go into Asia, India, and the west coast of Mexico.

Headquartered in the western Australian city of Perth, Woodside describes itself on its web site as "Australia's largest publicly traded oil and gas exploration and production company," with assets of more than (US) $21 billion. Further, "The company sells liquefied natural gas, natural gas, crude oil, condensate and liquid petroleum gas around the world."

As part of a May 2006 presentation to North American investors in New York entitled "LNG Growth," Woodside showed a chart indicating that, excluding national oil companies, in 2010 it expects to have the second most "potential operated LNG capacity," behind Shell. The chart further showed that between 2010 and 2015, Woodside's potential operated LNG capacity will grow significantly. Interestingly, another chart that was part of the presentation forecast that, even with a nearly 100 percent increase in the supply of LNG between 2007 and 2015, in 2015 global supply will exceed global demand by only a little bit.[18]

Thus does Woodside Petroleum become the final company on the watch list in the category of "Synthetic Oil and LNG Providers."

■ ■ ■

Taking a step back again, the global LNG industry has put the new oil industry "on the clock."

Let me explain. It appears as if LNG is going to be priced based on a basket of *oil* prices. In other words, whenever the United States wants to buy LNG, it may have to pay prices that are comparable to what the price of oil is at the time. If in 2015 the price of oil is still $70 to $80 a barrel instead of $40 to $50 a barrel, the price Americans will pay for natural gas will be higher, too, because by 2015 the United States could need imported LNG to satisfy as much as 20 percent of the nation's demand for natural gas.

By tightening the existing link between the price of oil and the price of natural gas, the coming emergence of a global LNG industry makes it that much more important for the United States (and the world) to get the price of oil down as far and as quickly as possible. In short, the more *competitive* pressure that can be brought to bear, the better it will be for everyone's pocketbook.

Competitive pressure should come from substitute liquid fuels, although if tar sands are used extensively—which seems likely—the price of gasoline will be higher than if CTL and biofuel were relied upon. As Chapter 5 describes, additional competitive pressure in the form of negaoil will come from efficiency-oriented automakers.

When and to what extent American politicians and consumers understand all this remains to be seen. They have got to start connecting the dots. The point for investors to remember is that the more Washington understands the growing natural gas problem it's got on its hands (e.g., potential shortages from stagnating domestic production and cutbacks in Canadian imports offset by imports of LNG priced comparably with oil), the more it may politically and financially support the creation of the new oil industry.

CHAPTER 5

The Power of Efficiency

The year is 2012. Time to replace that car you bought right after the turn of the century.

Let's go car shopping. We will need a guide. Much has changed since the last time you were in the market for a new car.

Meet Felix Kramer. He knows a lot about a new kind of car called a plug-in hybrid electric vehicle.

Kramer is the founder of a group called the California Cars Initiative. CalCars.org, as the group is commonly known, is made up of entrepreneurs, environmentalists, engineers, and others interested in efficient, nonpolluting automotive technologies—the "Efficiency" part of the new oil industry (see Figure 5.1).

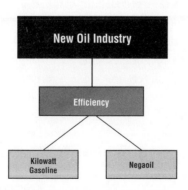

FIGURE 5.1 Efficiency

Back in 2006 CalCars.org was among the leaders of a consumer cru-
sade to get car manufacturers to build plug-in hybrid vehicles. That year
the group was involved in an Internet petition drive that asked people to
urge carmakers to build plug-in hybrids.

It is worth recalling the language of that petition. The petition read: "If
I could buy a vehicle that was cheaper to operate, cleaner, and ran on domestic electricity, and I could buy it from you for a few thousand dollars
more, yes I would positively WANT to plug it in to a 120-volt outlet."[1]

It sounds like plug-in hybrid vehicles were in the process of being
recognized as a great way to help solve at least two of the three energy
problems vexing the world. To be specific, they could help solve environmental anxiety by running cleaner, and they could help solve a nation's
addiction to imported oil by enabling cars and trucks to fuel up on electricity made from domestic fuel sources. As for the third problem, sky-
high prices, the picture appears to have been mixed. While its supporters
were stressing that plug-ins were "cheaper to operate," they had to admit
that it took "a few thousand dollars more" to purchase one.

In 2006 none of the hybrids on the road had plug-in capability, except
for a handful that had been converted by people like Kramer. "I'm the
first consumer-owner of a (Toyota) Prius converted to a plug-in," he told
a reporter that year.

Back then, hybrids had batteries that were "charge sustaining," which
basically meant that the vehicle produced its own electricity when the
brakes were applied and this electricity was stored in the vehicle's battery
until needed.

By contrast, batteries for plug-in hybrids are said to be "charge depleting." They require periodic recharging from an outside power source. As
the name suggests, a plug-in hybrid vehicle can be recharged literally by
plugging the vehicle into an ordinary 120-volt wall socket. (A plug-in, it
should be noted, also recaptures energy through braking.) When the
charge has been fully depleted, the vehicle can run on liquid fuel the way
any vehicle can.

So here we are at the car dealership with plug-in pioneer Felix
Kramer. Whose dealership? It could be anyone's, according to Kramer.
This being 2012, plug-in hybrids are available from every manufacturer.

What can we expect to get for our money? According to Kramer, we
will get a vehicle that can go up to 1,000 miles on a single tank of gas.

How is that possible?

According to our guide, the battery of a 2012 plug-in vehicle has a range "north of 30."

Translated, this means that for the first 30-plus miles that the vehicle is driven after its battery has been charged, the fuel used is electricity. After those first 30-plus miles, the vehicle's other fuel—its liquid fuel—takes over until the car is plugged in, its battery is recharged, and the process repeats itself.

Still, as we discovered when we did some preliminary research, how many miles a plug-in hybrid vehicle goes on electricity depends on how the vehicle is routinely operated. If the vehicle is used mostly on daily trips of 40 miles or less—like to the office and back—and then is plugged in every night, it will go a lot farther between liquid fill-ups than plug-ins driven longer distances and/or recharged less frequently.

How much does it cost to fill a plug-in's electric tank?

According to the CalCars.org web site, in 2006 it was possible to fill the electric tank of a (converted) plug-in hybrid for the equivalent of less than $1 a gallon of gas, using the average U.S. electricity rate of 9 cents per kilowatt-hour (kWh). So if that plug-in were able to go, say, 20 to 25 miles on that electricity, a plug-in owner presumably could eliminate the need for roughly one gallon of gasoline costing somewhere between $2 and $3.

Not bad.

■ ■ ■

The advantages of plug-in hybrids seem so numerous that it is easy to see Kramer's vision of plug-in hybrids showing up in car dealers' showrooms by 2012 coming true.

Then again, it is also possible to imagine plug-ins *not* arriving in showrooms until well after 2012 due to efforts by the new oil industry's biofuel and conventional oil sectors to delay their arrival out of fear that the third sector, efficiency—made up of car manufacturers and their natural allies, electric utilities and alternative energy firms—could gain too much of a competitive edge.

Think about the position oil companies could be in by 2012. Reserves of crude oil are mostly beyond their direct control, in the hands of state-owned oil companies. There are more signs that conventional oil production has peaked or could soon, which has politicians in an even greater tizzy than they were in 2006 over the need to reduce dependence on imported oil. The industry's attempts to persuade the world that no country can ever be energy "independent" have fallen on deaf ears.

Meanwhile, biofuel is continuing to make inroads. While first-generation ethanol made from corn was easy to attack on the basis of cost, how much farmland it diverts from growing food, and the amount of energy it takes to produce, cellulosic ethanol has been much harder to fend off. In part this is because the public really likes the idea of being able to make transportation fuel from garbage. It makes them feel as if they can enjoy their freedom to drive without feeling guilty about what they are doing to the environment. It hasn't helped that Wall Street has discovered that companies in control of cellulosic waste sources—such as forestry and waste disposal companies—have a growing new source of revenue. Moreover, after being introduced in America by DuPont in 2010, biobutanol is starting to look like it could be a real headache. Some oilmen are actually thinking about jumping on the biobutanol bandwagon, which could prove a serious public relations and maybe financial problem for those left standing at the station.

Now think about the position backers of biofuel could be in by 2012. Remember the old Abbott and Costello routine "Who's on First?" Well, who's on first in biofuel in 2012? Is it corn ethanol? Maybe—but probably not as much as in the good old days of 2007 and 2008. Is it cellulosic ethanol? Maybe—though more work may still need to be done to enhance productivity. Is it biobutanol? Possibly. Is it something even better than biobutanol that has popped out of some biotech laboratory? You never know. With so much uncertainty that could surround biofuel's future in 2012, the last thing its backers will probably want to see is a technology that could permanently reduce the need for liquid fuel in cars and trucks.

■ ■ ■

It is important to draw a very clear distinction between the advantages of plug-in and non-plug-in hybrid vehicles.

Both enable a vehicle to go farther between liquid fill-ups. Both help reduce the emissions a vehicle generates. But while a non-plug-in vehicle is still at the mercy of whatever liquid fuel is being sold at the corner gas station, plug-in capability frees that vehicle from its involuntary servitude.

Basically, plug-in capability makes it possible for America's transportation system to tap into virtually all of America's domestic energy resources by utilizing the full range of energy sources that are used to make electricity.

Remember what I said in Chapter 1 about how the revolutions in mobile and stationary energy consumption will increasingly be seen as two sides of the same coin? Plug-in hybrids are the main reason why. Plug-in capability is the connector, the bridge between our two energy universes, the one we inhabit when we are moving and the one we inhabit when we are standing still.

With plug-in capability, it becomes possible to keep a vehicle fueled by:

- Coal, both indirectly in the form of electricity and directly in the form of synthetic gasoline.
- Natural gas, again both indirectly and directly.
- Solar power.
- Wind power.
- Geothermal power.
- Nuclear power.
- Garbage power.
- Synthetic gasoline made from tar sands or oil shale.
- Gasoline made the conventional way from crude oil.

Just as diversity through electricity was the key to America's industrial sector being able to increase productivity without increasing oil consumption, so too is it one of two keys (the other being diversity through biofuel) to fueling the growing number of vehicles expected on global highways without adding to the strain on global oil supplies and without everyone choking on their own exhaust.

If that doesn't sound like advantage enough, consider this: By exchanging a single-source (oil) transportation system for a multisource system that makes greater use of the nation's domestically obtainable fuel sources, America automatically enhances its national security, which in turn reduces the financial burden of having to defend America's sources of imported oil, which in turn frees up billions of tax dollars for more worthy endeavors.

Now that's a sweet spot.

Certainly, non-plug-in hybrids have their own sweet spot that makes them a worthy addition to a nation's fleet of cars and trucks. Still, while one of non-plug-in hybrids' celebrated selling points is their environmental friendliness, a case can be made that plug-in hybrids are even friendlier in the sense that the fuel one puts into his car or truck can be the "green" power one makes himself at home. More specifically, it can be the electricity one generates by putting solar panels or solar roofing shingles on top of his house, or by installing a geothermal heat pump or wind turbine in the backyard. (Before long, another option may be small wind turbines that go on top of a house like a weathervane.) Indeed, a case can be made that plug-in hybrids will accelerate peoples' use of environmentally friendly green power sources, which at present are catching on thanks to the revolution in stationary energy.

Not a do-it-yourselfer? More and more utilities have something called *net metering*, which is a process by which a utility buys the power its customers generate. In practice, net metering—or *reverse metering*, as it is also sometimes called—usually provides homeowners with a credit that gets applied to their monthly bill.

To be sure, the power used to fill up a plug-in hybrid that gets generated from coal or natural gas causes its own pollution. Plug-in proponents point to studies showing that even after factoring in the pollution caused by fossil-fueled electrical generating facilities, there is a significant net reduction in greenhouse gas emissions caused by plug-in hybrids vs. gasoline-powered vehicles. Not surprisingly, other studies indicate that plug-ins' relative environmental advantage varies depending on how much fossil fuel generation a region has. Importantly, it is logistically a lot easier to control the pollution coming out of hundreds of power plants than it is the pollution coming out of millions upon millions of tailpipes.

Plug-ins' dual environmental and national security advantages have created a new pair of strange bedfellows: left-leaning environmentalists and right-leaning national security hawks. Among plug-ins' backers is former U.S. Central Intelligence Agency director James Woolsey. At a Washington press conference to announce a nationwide drive for plug-ins, Woolsey borrowed a line from the old comic strip *Pogo*. "We have met the enemy, and he is us," Woolsey reportedly said, adding, "If you want to know who is paying for hate to be taught in those madrasas in Pakistan, the next time you pull up to the pump, look in the mirror."[2]

At the same press conference, influential conservative Republican Orrin Hatch, Senator from Utah, reportedly said he believes the United States should have a policy to make America the world leader in plug-in technology.

As of the fall of 2006, plug-in advocates were still seeking political support, their cause not yet having achieved critical mass. Given that plug-ins might one day provide additional revenue for its members, it was not surprising that the electric utility industry was already a big backer. However, what was surprising was that support was coming from both investor-owned and municipally owned electric utilities. They seldom see eye-to-eye on issues affecting their industry.

Perhaps an even bigger surprise, however, was that plug-ins were getting a push from the Texas oilman in the White House. In the same 2006 Earth Day speech in which he voiced his support for cellulosic ethanol, President Bush talked in glowing terms about the potential for plug-in hybrid vehicles.

After telling his audience that non-plug-in hybrids were a "positive development taking place in America today," President Bush said:

> What's really going to be interesting, however, is what's called plug-in hybrid vehicles. And we're spending $31 million annually to speed up research into these battery technologies. And what this means is, is that we're trying to develop a battery that will power your vehicle, where you plug it in at night and you drive the first 40 miles on electricity alone. Now, think about what that means for big cities. A lot of people don't drive more than 40 miles a day in big cities. So all of a sudden you've now—we're developing a technology that says you'll drive by the use of electricity, and you won't use gasoline at all.[3]

From the preceding, it seems clear that the president, albeit an oilman, sees a lot of potential in plug-in hybrids. It should not be surprising that in September 2006 the federal Energy Department's Climate Change Technology program issued a report that, according to observers, represented a shift in favor of plug-in hybrids as a near-term solution to America's foreign oil dependence.[4]

Indeed, based on his speeches, President Bush really seems to get that the best way to wean America off its deadly dependence on foreign oil is through plug-in hybrids (and other efficiency improvements) together with cellulosic biofuels—in short, a radically restructured oil industry, a new oil industry. But with so little time left in office, unless the president were to put his chips on a new Manhattan Project–style crash program aimed at achieving energy independence through the rapid development of these game-changing technologies, by the time they are ready for market Mr. Bush will probably have retired to Texas without getting credit for having envisioned the promise of the energy technology revolution.

■ ■ ■

Depending on who you asked, in 2006 plug-in hybrid technology either was ready to go right now, close to a breakthrough that would make it ready, or still in need of considerable development.

For supporters like Felix Kramer, the technology was ready to go. Existing batteries were "good enough," he told me, and "can only get better." President Bush, in his Earth Day speech and in another speech to the National Association of Manufacturers, basically said we are close to a breakthrough. (The president talked about plug-in vehicles providing 40 miles of all-electric power without looking like a golf cart.) But there was more than one automotive engineer who publicly said that plug-in technology was still years away.

There was, however, a common thread here, namely, that plug-in hybrids *are coming*.

Keeping in mind what Kramer said about how plug-in batteries can only get better, there would appear to be any number of companies in the running to grab the "holy grail of PHEV40," as Millikin of Green Car Congress put it, *PHEV* being shorthand for *plug-in hybrid electric vehicle*. Translation: a plug-in vehicle that, as President Bush noted, can go the first 40 miles on electricity before having to switch over to a liquid fuel.

Notwithstanding President Bush's characterization of plug-ins as a great vehicle for people who live in cities, plug-in advocates have had to fight the perception that people generally drive long distances on a daily basis. Citing federal and other statistics, plug-in proponents have argued that four out of five personal automobiles on the road travel 50 miles a day or less.

Just on the face of things, however, these statistics would seem to underestimate the number of miles the average car travels on a daily basis in at least some of America's fast-growing cities, like Phoenix and Atlanta. It also may not give sufficient weight to the growing number of commuters who regularly travel 90 minutes each way to get to and from work. Both conditions apply to people who daily crawl their way down Georgia 400 from homes in north Fulton and Cherokee counties to gleaming downtown Atlanta office towers. However, in and around big cities like New York and Philadelphia, the highway administration stats and President Bush's general impression sound reasonable.

Whether or not currently available statistics are accurate, so important are these sorts of calculations to the future of America in every way (financially, environmentally, and in terms of national security), that new studies funded and carried out by federal and state transportation departments are an absolute must.

And they need to be done immediately—if not sooner.

Think about it. In 2006 oil markets resembled a roller-coaster. Prices surged to nearly $80 a barrel, then plunged to below $60 a barrel, during a time when there was no oil shortage, just fear of a possible shortage caused by a natural or manmade disaster. There is every reason to believe that this unprecedented volatility in prices will become a permanent feature of global energy markets. As more of America's critical energy infrastructure—both oil and natural gas—gets concentrated in the hurricane-exposed Gulf of Mexico, and with the memory of Hurricane Katrina unlikely to fade anytime soon, fear of a weather-related energy catastrophe should worsen. With Osama bin Laden and the legion of terrorists he has spawned well-known for their patience in planning an attack, fear of another terrorist attack—this time maybe on U.S. soil—will not abate.

Enter plug-in hybrid vehicles, which, as the president indicated, have the potential to make it possible for people to not use gasoline.

How many vehicles are we talking about? How many people are likely to make the switch and for what reasons? What are the most likely cities, states, and regions of the United States to feel the impact of plug-in technology? How might this impact oil companies' imbedded infrastructure? What could be the impact of that prediction made by the author of the Reason Foundation study on traffic congestion that over the next 25 years the number of cities where congestion causes peak-hour traffic trips to be delayed by more than 50 percent will grow from 4 to 34?

While it isn't known when plug-in hybrids will arrive, it could be before 2012, even without a Manhattan Project–style program. Will the United States be prepared? Will there be a sitting government panel or task force made up of the best minds in energy, transportation, national security, agriculture, and so on? Will that panel have had time to analyze the mega policy issues that plug-in capability (and also biofuel) raise?

Or will there instead be a hodgepodge of competing interests trying to spin the public and the politicians? In the absence of a clear and coherent government policy for incorporating plug-ins (and biofuel) into America's transportation system, there could be more frequent oil price gyrations as traders face the new uncertainty of trying to predict how much gasoline Americans are going to consume in their cars and trucks versus how much electricity and how much cellulose and grains. This planning must extend to global commodities markets, for in the new oil industry there will be unprecedented linkage between agricultural and energy commodities. Perhaps it is time for the White House to merge the departments of energy, agriculture, and transportation. (Don't forget about coal as a jet fuel.) It definitely is time for financial markets to have more reliable energy and agricultural statistics from China, India, Russia, and so on.

As energy analyst Glenn Wattley put it, this stuff is too complicated for Adam Smith.

To be sure, plug-ins may arrive in China without all this planning. When I asked Goldman Sachs vice chairman and China business expert Bob Hormats if he thought China was keen on plug-in hybrids, he said he had not seen any sign of it yet, and then added that if the Chinese government wants to go that way, it will just go ahead and install external wall outlets in convenient places.

China might want to first think things through, lest it wind up roiling global energy markets.

■ ■ ■

So which companies stand to benefit from improving the battery technology that will be the underpinning of plug-in hybrid vehicles?

To begin with, plug-in batteries will need to be made with lithium, the same element already used in batteries for portable devices such as notebook computers and cell phones. As explained in a must-read article by Bradley Berman, editor of the excellent web site HybridCars.com, the current crop of non-plug-in hybrid vehicles use nickel metal hydride, which, while it is "a step up from the lead acid battery most drivers recognize under their hoods," basically is not powerful or cheap enough for a plug-in hybrid. Enter lithium, an "energy carrier" that is "very light, exists as a solid that you can carry around, and it's cheap. The laws of nature and economics have chosen a winner."[5]

This winner, however, has a very temperamental personality. Trying to scale up from cell phone to automobile has proven difficult. As explained by Berman, "Battery companies trying to create larger lithium batteries, which use cobalt in their formula, quickly encounter a problem known as thermal runaway—which means the batteries can easily catch fire or explode. Not a good idea for cars." This is the same basic problem that caused a ruckus in 2006 when a bunch of laptops caught fire and a couple of major computer manufacturers had to issue recalls.

According to Berman's article, two "enterprising" companies working to solve the thermal runway problem by replacing the cobalt with other materials are A123 Systems and Valence Technology. Berman writes that these companies' proprietary technology "is working like magic to produce energy storage and charging power similar to cobalt, while avoiding the safety and longevity issue." Despite the improvement, however, the HybridCars.com editor believes that "the technology still has a way to go—perhaps three to five years—before car-sized lithium batteries are powerful enough, cheap enough, and most importantly, reliable enough to go into mass production vehicles."

Since this three-to-five-year estimate was made around the start of 2006, if HybridCars.com is right, mass production of plug-in hybrid vehicles could start somewhere between 2009 and 2012. (That's not much time to get a government policy in place.)

"If I had to put my money down, I'd put it on A123," said Millikin of Green Car Congress. He explained that he liked the company because it "comes out of MIT, is already in the power tool market, has good science, and is aggressive."

Millikin also is a supporter of Altair Nanotechnologies, which he says also is "making a lot of progress." Altair has high hopes for its lithium-ion battery, it being the company's stated goal to "deliver battery capabilities that could provide a sedan with a 200-plus-mile driving range, no degradation of operation over that entire distance; a recharge time of under 6 minutes (or about the time it takes to fill the tank of a large SUV); a battery that is completely safe from explosion or leakage of hazardous contents, and not least, no carbon dioxide emissions of any kind."[6]

While most investors are probably not familiar with Altair, A123 Systems, or Valence, they likely are familiar with another company working in this area: Johnson Controls, which describes itself as a global leader in interior experience, building efficiency, and power solutions.

In addition to being an established supplier of nickel metal hydride batteries for hybrids, Milwaukee-based Johnson Controls is developing lithium-ion batteries. In 2004 the company contracted with the United States Advanced Battery Consortium (USABC), a group that includes the federal Energy Department, DaimlerChrysler, General Motors, and Ford, to develop an advanced lithium-ion battery. The following year President Bush toured the company's lithium-ion battery research center and, according to media reports, said, "Johnson Controls has been on the cutting edge of technology for more than a century. The people who work here are on the leading edge of change."[7]

Only time will tell if A123 Systems, Valence, Altair, or Johnson Controls gets its hands on the holy grail of PHEV40. Maybe all will. Maybe none will. That's the way it is with emerging technologies, and energy is no different.

There is no better evidence of the unpredictability of new technology than a company in Cedar Park, Texas, called EEStor. This company doesn't say much, but according to an April 2006 press release from Feel Good Cars Corporation, EEStor is working on technology that sounds as if it could be better than a lithium-ion battery. According to the Feel Good Cars press release, EEStor "is developing a new type of battery" called an Energy Storage Unit, which is "projected to store up to 1.5 to 2.5 times the energy of Li-ion batteries at 12 to 25 percent of the cost."[8]

In November 2006 there was a must-read newspaper article in the *Austin American-Statesman* about the "all-or-nothing buzz building around EEStor." As described in the article, EEStor:

> has come up with a new method for making ultracapacitors, battery-like devices that can store huge amounts of electricity. EEStor's energy storage unit can hold enough charge to power a car 300 miles, according to its patent, and it can be recharged in the time it takes to pump a tank of gas. And it can do all that at only a small, if any, premium to the cost of a gas-powered engine."[9]

If EEStor succeeds, serious men and women might start pondering a future where there is little need in transportation for oil (adios OPEC) or even biofuel (which would make some environmentalists very happy). Electricity might become the alpha and the omega of the global energy industry. Just as many developing countries have used cellular technology to leapfrog into the twenty-first century of global communications, so too might they be able to use solar power to instantly and inexpensively create a transportation fueling infrastructure that bypasses gasoline pumps. Every vehicle might become nearly all-electric with a roof that doubles as a solar collector, providing a kind of continuous recharging during the day to go along with plug-in recharging at night. (I imagine that having a liquid fuel tank in reserve might still be advisable, in case of engine problems.)

While the *American-Statesman* article says that EEStor "might" be closer to *all* than to *nothing*, whether or not this particular company ultimately succeeds, while potentially very important, is not the overriding point here. The overriding point is that a new and totally disruptive transportation technology has been imagined by some engineers who are now busy trying to change the world just as engineers changed the world when they invented the computer.

To be sure, given the average length of time a car or truck is on the road, even if this disruptive new technology were ready for prime time, it might still take 10 to 20 years or longer for the need for oil and biofuel to be whittled way down. Oil would still be a critical bridge to biofuel, and biofuel would still be a critical bridge to nearly all-electric vehicles. The future of energy is extremely complicated; however, it does now seem that a solution may be slowly starting to emerge for accommodating the 2 billion or so vehicles expected to be on global roads in 2050. *Like baseball's immortal Tinkers to Evers to Chance, the future of energy is starting to look like it could be crude oil to biofuel to electricity.*

Under-40 investors especially should keep this in mind, as should politicians who, unlike President Bush, can't see 10 minutes, much less 10 years, down the road. As I've tried to emphasize in earlier chapters, mistakes are already being made. Too much emphasis has been placed on corn ethanol, delaying development of far-more-promising cellulosic ethanol and biobutanol. Tar sands development is ramping up, notwithstanding the consequent cost, environmental damage, and potential for natural gas problems in the United States.

All of the previously mentioned companies—A123 Systems, Altair Nanotechnologies, Valence Technology, Johnson Controls, and last but definitely not least, EEStor—make the list of companies to watch in a category I'm calling "Battery Technology." I consider this the third most important category on the list, behind only the two biofuel technology categories, which is simply a reflection of biofuel's potential to make a more immediate difference. Just to reiterate, whether any of these particular companies makes a lot of money is not why I think this category is so important—though, for investors' sake, I hope they all do. Rather, it's because of battery technology's potential to hit that sweetest of sweet spots—the one where national security is enhanced, the environment is protected, and people don't have to spend an arm and a leg to exercise their democratic right, their freedom, to drive as much as they want or need to drive.

■ ■ ■

As much as car manufacturers are accused by plug-ins' promoters of being overly reluctant to mass-produce plug-in hybrids because the technology lacks a proven record, in 2006 the automotive industry seemed to start warming to the idea.

Maybe it was the fact that the current crop of hybrids was flying out of dealers' showrooms on the wings of $3-a-gallon gasoline, with expectations of half a million non-plug-in hybrids being on U.S. roads in 2007. Maybe it was New York State's announcement that it would spend millions of dollars on a program to convert hundreds of state-owned hybrids to plug-in hybrids, after which it would make the program available to selected private car owners. Maybe it was the highly visible political support plug-ins had started receiving in Washington and how this might translate into tax breaks for buyers of plug-ins when the vehicles became available. Maybe it was the announcement by an insurance company that it was going to offer discounts to drivers of hybrid cars, a decision reportedly reached after the company discovered through its research that hybrid drivers "fall into a low-risk category historically rewarded with cheaper premiums." Maybe it was this insurance company's reported finding that the hybrid owners it presently insures typically are in their 40s and 50s and married.[10] (Somebody say "ka-ching.")

Perhaps it was a bit of all of the above, as well as a growing sense that a race might actually develop to be the first to get plug-ins into dealers' showrooms.

Though frequently blasted in the media for being behind the Japanese on giving consumers the more efficient vehicles they want in an era of high gas prices, General Motors (GM) actually was one of those in position to give the world's acknowledged hybrid leader, Toyota, a run for its money. According to Millikin, GM in Europe has a plug-in that it could introduce as early as 2007. (Whether the company was going to do so wasn't clear at the time of this writing.) If introduced, Millikin said, the GM plug-in likely would have an all-electric range of 20 miles, half the distance to the holy grail of PHEV40.

"GM could have a plug-in capable car before Toyota," said Millikin, who seemed a bit amazed by his own statement. Millikin told me that he believes Toyota is "judging" the lithium-ion battery technology currently available, with an eye toward introducing a plug-in with a 20 mile all-electric range in 2008. He said he further believes that Toyota may try to introduce a 40-mile-range PHEV in 2012.

Toyota perhaps was feeling the heat from DaimlerChrysler, which through its partnerships in the United States was gaining on-road test experience for its own plug-in van. The *Christian Science Monitor*'s resident expert on alternative transportation strategies, staff writer Mark Clayton, wrote in 2006 that, "Gas prices were probably the biggest factor in changing Toyota's stance" toward plug-ins from negative to positive. "But," he added, "it also probably helped that DaimlerChrysler has been delivering its first plug-in hybrid vans to companies."[11]

In September 2006 Nissan announced plans to develop hybrid technology on its own, after previously having had an agreement with Toyota, and hopes to introduce a plug-in model in 2010.

Not to be outdone, also in 2006 Honda reportedly said that it would build a plant in Japan to make key components for hybrid cars that would enable Honda to quadruple its annual production capacity for electric motors to 200,000 units.[12] While Honda's plant plans were not directly related to plug-ins, when combined with the company's homogeneous charge compression ignition (HCCI) engine project, it appeared possible that Honda might be able to wrest the crown of reigning hybrid champion away from its Japanese rival. Honda's ongoing project reportedly involves using an HCCI engine, which is super fuel-efficient, in a non-plug-in hybrid, the goal being to squeeze out as much as 65 miles to a gallon of gasoline.

To be sure, HCCI is just one of a number of new technologies in that other area of the efficiency sector of the new oil industry, negaoil, a term coined to encompass all of the ways of *not* using oil other than through plug-in hybrids. HCCI development further highlights the need for the United States (and other nations) to develop new policies that take into account the many changes technology is about to bring to the transportation and energy industries and how these changes will, in one way or another, affect everyone and all goods and services.

Other important fuel-efficiency improvements are occurring with existing automotive engines. A couple of the more important ones that were pointed out to me by Edmunds.com consumer advice editor Phil Reed are *cylinder shutdown* and *continuously variable transmission* (CVT).

Cylinder shutdown basically is where a computer in the car determines that some of the engine's cylinders aren't needed. As a Scientific American.com article put it, cylinder shutdown technology makes it possible for a V-8 gas guzzler to smoothly morph into a V-4 energy miser as conditions permit.[13]

Meanwhile, as an article on Reed's web site put it, a CVT transmission basically operates by varying the working diameters of the two main pulleys of the transmission. Reed explained that with CVT a transmission isn't limited to a set number of gears. Rather, the gears are constantly and automatically changing for maximum efficiency. In the article, entitled "CVT Enters the Mainstream," CVT is described as a "boon to fuel economy and as a low-cost alternative to conventional transmissions."[14]

As much as there are big changes occurring under the hood, Reed believes there is also a big change starting to occur in the size of the automobiles people buy. You will recall that in Chapter 1 Reed said that while people are still driving pretty much as they were before the price of gas surged, they are starting to change their car-buying habits, with more vehicles being sold because of their fuel efficiency. Well, Reed believes we are going to see a steadily growing number of people buying cars that are inherently more fuel-efficient because of their smaller size, and that ultra-small cars will become all the rage.

Ultra-small models available today include the Toyota Yaris and the Honda Fit. Other models "are waiting in the wings," according to Reed, such as the Mercedes Smart car. In Europe, where ultra-smalls are already popular, there is an ultra-small from Ford called the Ka. Renault has a model called the Twingo.

However, Reed is not predicting the demise of the gas-guzzling SUV. Indeed, with HCCI and hybrid technology even an SUV might be able to earn a degree in fuel efficiency—a point people who would like to banish SUVs might want to think about.

Rather, Reed is predicting the rise of what he calls the "commuter car," an ultra-small, ultra-fuel-efficient vehicle costing only about $10,000 to $12,000. Reed believes that had ultra-small cars been sufficiently available, fully 25 percent of the gasoline price rise we've all endured in recent years would not have happened.

If Reed is as good a prognosticator as he is a writer, future government energy and transportation policies are also going to have to account for ultra-smalls. One question that comes to mind: Is there enough room for two different kinds of super fuel-efficient cars (plug-ins and ultra-smalls) that basically are both intended to be driven short distances?

While plug-ins have the great advantage over commuter cars of being close to gasoline-free when driven up to about 40 miles a day, that only works if people take the trouble to plug them in every night. Otherwise, it's back to the corner gas station. While national security is an extremely powerful incentive for plug-ins, the degree to which plug-ins actually would make America more energy secure would depend on what some have called plug-ins' Achilles heel, namely, the people who drive them.

Marie R. Corio is the noted head of her own energy consulting firm in New York. She thinks the success or failure of plug-in hybrid vehicles hinges on how they are marketed. Corio told me she doesn't think most people are going to want the hassle of having to plug in their cars every night. (Ask yourself: How often might you skip plugging in?)

Still, she thinks plug-ins will be very popular if they are marketed on the basis of being important to protecting both the environment and national security. "Security will sell in the 'red' states and the environment will sell in the 'blue' states," she told me. (She added in a subsequent interview that she thought security would sell in the blue states as well.)

Echoing the *New York Times* article that said people with money buy a disproportionately large amount of gasoline,[15] Corio went on to say, "People who drive big gas-guzzling SUVs can afford to pay a lot for gasoline. You've got to give them a reason besides saving money to go through the hassle of plugging in every night. The environment and national security are huge reasons. People will think it's really cool that they can protect their country and the planet just by plugging in an extension cord that's connected to their car."

Nevertheless, Reed believes that ultra-smalls offer an advantage no other vehicle can, namely, they can help reduce the terrible congestion on the highways. His "pet prediction," as he called it, is that, because commuter cars take up so much less space, cities and states will be able to re-stripe their roads, adding a lane. While that may sound kind of crazy, so did $3-a-gallon gasoline not too many years ago.

Perhaps the ideal way to proceed would be with commuter cars made with plug-in capability for city driving (supported by car-sharing companies like Zipcar and Flexcar), and cars (including SUVs) that have HCCI or similar engines and plug-in capability. The latter would serve equally well for people who want, versus need, to drive.

To be sure, the world may be a long way from realizing the full technological potential of commuter cars. At a 2006 vehicle design conference at MIT, a team of students designed and built a prototype of a commuter car capable of getting the equivalent of hundreds of miles per gallon on a combination of vegetable oil (biofuel) and lithium-ion batteries.

As America's energy and transportation planners lay the policy foundation of the new oil industry, they may want to take a look at the innovative policies starting to pop up in cities around the world. In London, for example, since 2003 there has been a traffic congestion charge for cars entering the designated zone between the hours of 7:00 A.M. and 6:30 P.M. It is enforced through the same sort of E-ZPass system that drivers use to pay tolls in the United States. As part of this program, London reportedly has said it may make high-emissions cars pay more.

■ ■ ■

Not generally discussed yet on Wall Street is the financial impact that plug-ins could have on electric utilities and on the green power industry. If plug-ins catch on—and I'm with Corio that they will catch on if they are marketed based on their national security and environmental benefits—then electric utilities could join battery technology providers in the win column. Green power manufacturers could do even better than they already are.

As previously indicated, according to the CalCars web site, a plug-in's electric tank can be filled for the equivalent of less than $1 a gallon of regular gasoline when gasoline is selling for $3 a gallon, assuming an electricity rate of $0.09 per kilowatt-hour. So if you were to fill up your plug-in car's electric tank five days a week, over a month's time you might buy about $20 to $25 of kilowatt gas. How much do you and your family currently spend on electricity each month? Add $20 to that amount and you begin to see plug-ins from the utility point of view.

Of course, no matter how well plug-in cars were to catch on, there would still be people who wouldn't buy one—even with tax breaks—because of its likely higher sticker price. Moreover, if plug-ins are introduced around 2012 or so, it's going to take several years before there are lots of them on the road, given the average time any vehicle is on the road.

While it thus may be too soon for it to matter to most investors, for those with longer-term investment horizons, Corio told me that a number of electric utilities are well positioned to benefit from the new revenue plug-ins could bring in. What makes them well positioned is that they make a lot of their own power from coal and nuclear sources. These are power plants that generally must be kept running 24 hours a day even though the demand for power is extremely low in the middle of the night—which, of course, is when plug-ins would be filled up. Another important factor, Corio said, is having access to a large number of residential customers who live in houses with easy access to an external wall outlet. (Think suburbia.)

Corio thought that four utility companies in particular could do well: Constellation Energy Group, Exelon Corporation, NRG Energy, and Public Service Enterprise Group (PSEG). Constellation, the parent of Baltimore Gas & Electric Company, is the United States' largest wholesale power seller. Exelon also owns and operates a large amount of generating capacity, and it transmits and distributes electricity to over 5 million customers in Illinois and Pennsylvania. NRG owns and operates a diverse portfolio of power-generating facilities, primarily in Texas and in the northeast, south central, and western regions of the United States. New Jersey–based PSEG is the parent of a utility that provided service to over 2 million electric customers as of 2005. (PSEG and Exelon want to merge, a deal that had not yet won regulatory approval at the time this was written.)

The four make the watch list in a category with the admittedly cumbersome (but appropriate) title of "Nonliquid Fuel Providers." Because the potential payoff is probably a ways off, this category ranks near the bottom of the list in 14th position, one up from the category of "Defense Companies."

A point that needs to be emphasized is that before electric utilities can benefit from kilowatt gasoline, something's going to have to be done about the reliability of the nation's electrical grid. The industry is forecasting growing power unreliability unless large amounts of money are spent on transmission infrastructure. Regulations need clarification regarding who's responsible for what before a bad situation gets worse instead of better.

A quicker payoff might come the way of investors in green power manufacturers, many of which are already doing nicely thanks to that other energy technology revolution in stationary energy production and consumption.

There really is no telling how many more people might put solar panels on their homes in order to fill up their plug-ins' electric tanks with electricity made the environmentally friendly way. Chances are, if you are one of those blue-staters for whom protecting the environment is a damn good reason to buy a plug-in vehicle, you may already have solar panels or a geothermal heat pump. But chances also are that there will be a significant number of folks who are not do-it-yourselfers but who think that if they may buy a plug-in hybrid, they might as well go all the way and install a green power system. Likely the big home remodeling retailers Home Depot and Lowe's will try to seize upon this consumer urge by using plug-ins and green power as a way to get more people to remodel.

One firm that is already benefiting from the stationary energy technology revolution and that, longer term, could benefit from the mobile revolution is Suntech Power Holdings, a Chinese company with a U.S. subsidiary. Another solar outfit that could possibly benefit is California-based Nanosolar, a private company as of mid-2006 whose backers included Google's two founders. Nanosolar has excited some in the energy business with a reported major breakthrough in significantly reducing the cost of solar cells through new technology.[16]

Solar technology generally may be on the cusp of a technological revolution that might make solar power a common household feature years before plug-in hybrids are in people's driveways. In 2006 Japan's Sharp Corporation, the world's biggest maker of solar cells, reportedly forecast that by 2010 it will cut in half its cost of generating solar power. Like that airline industry exec, the Sharp exec quoted made his comments to a reporter "on the fringes" of a trade fair, thus lending—in this journalist's opinion—credibility to his pronouncement.[17]

While there are any number of solar firms, based on Suntech's geography, Nanosolar's promising technology, and Sharp's market position and expected cost reductions, all three make the watch list in the category of "Nonliquid Fuel Providers."

■ ■ ■

By now you may be wondering: When is he going to get around to discussing flex-fuel and fuel cell vehicles?

Right now.

The main advantage of a flex-fuel vehicle is that it can run on a mixture of 85 percent ethanol to 15 percent gasoline (E85), as compared with the 10 percent ethanol to 90 percent gasoline mixture that can be pumped into an ordinary car or truck. As a result, flex-fuel vehicles have the potential to significantly cut America's oil imports, thereby increasing the nation's energy security.

That's the good news. Now here's the bad: Contrary to what a number of people apparently think, flex-fuel vehicles do not get more miles to the gallon than vehicles that run on straight gasoline. Because the energy content of a gallon of ethanol is less than that of a gallon of gasoline, it takes more of the 85-15 mix than of straight gasoline to go the same number of miles.

Nearly 70 percent of people polled in 2006 by Harris Interactive said that the (nonexistent) greater fuel efficiency of a flex-fuel vehicle was a reason why they would be interested in a flex-fuel vehicle. (Nearly 90 percent cited reduced dependency on petroleum.)[18] This misperception could soon be fixed, now that *Consumer Reports* has weighed in with its own finding that gas mileage is worse for a flex-fuel vehicle.[19]

A second problem is that while flex-fuel's proponents highlight that it doesn't cost much to convert a regular vehicle into a flex-fuel vehicle, this still requires car owners to be proactive and to spend money that they don't need to spend.

Another problem: convenience. While it seems like there are more service stations in America than Kellogg's has flakes, only several hundred had E85 pumps in 2006. Proponents of E85 seem keen on getting Washington to underwrite the cost of making it widely available, but realistically speaking, how is that going to happen when oil companies control America's transportation fuel infrastructure? If you were the head of a gasoline marketer, wouldn't you do your best to make sure E85 was *not* widely available? (Biobutanol, by contrast, is a biofuel oil companies can control.)

So why, then, are Ford, GM, and DaimlerChrysler so keen on developing flex-fuel vehicles? No doubt the answer has something to do with politics, given how dead set some Midwestern lawmakers seem to be on flex-fuel vehicles. But as Timothy Maxwell, an expert in alternative automotive fuels and a professor of chemical engineering at Texas Tech University, impressed upon me, hybrid technology goes with *everything*. It would seem a better use of their time and money for these car companies to stop pushing *flex-fuel* and concentrate more on hybrid technology

Let's see if you can identify the company whose executive made the following statement to a reporter in 2006. "Hybrid technology can be teamed with every other promising technology to make it even more efficient and fuel stingy."[20]

The answer is Toyota.

As for fuel cell vehicles, it is perhaps illustrative to note that Hyundai reportedly has changed its mind. According to a story in the *Christian Science Monitor* in September 2005, "Last week, Hyundai said it was shifting its focus from hydrogen fuel-cell research to hybrids."[21] To be sure, Hyundai and other car companies are still working on fuel cell vehicles, but they seem to have decided—rightly—that fuel cell vehicles are probably, at best, many years away.

Basically, a fuel cell vehicle is an all-electric vehicle. The electricity that powers the car is made by an onboard fuel cell. The fuel for the fuel cell is hydrogen gas, which is stored in high-pressure tanks. Through a chemical reaction, the fuel cell makes electricity, with water a by-product of the process.

At first glance, a fuel cell vehicle looks tantalizingly like the perfect car. It runs emissions-free and doesn't need gasoline. But as the refs say in football, upon further review fuel cell vehicles aren't perfect, at least not yet. Probably their biggest environmental problem is the fact that, for now at least, natural gas has to be used to make the hydrogen for the fuel cell. While the vehicle itself may be clean-burning, as a 2003 MIT study concluded, enough carbon dioxide emissions would be produced in the production and distribution of the hydrogen to cancel out the vehicle's clean-running characteristics.[22] Remember also that fuel cells may have to compete with 300-mile-to-a-single-charge ultracapacitors.

When the United States' National Public Radio did an upbeat story in November 2005 about a family that was test-driving a fuel cell car, the story still made clear in its opening sentence that, "Hydrogen power may be in the distant future."[23]

■ ■ ■

While much has been said—favorably—about Toyota and Honda, what about the other car companies? Which other ones might do best in this new technology-driven environment where a car manufacturer will have to be not just committed to efficiency, but nimble enough to turn on a dime when one or more of the new fuel-saving technologies start to show signs of staying on top of the heap?

Philip Reed of Edmunds.com put together for me a list of the top eight car manufacturers in the order in which he personally thinks they are positioned for future success. You already know the top two, although you may not know that Toyota and Honda tied for first on Reed's list. Reed said each has a real corporate commitment to efficiency, adding that while Toyota is ahead on hybrid technology, Honda "shines" in other areas of engine efficiency. Reed added that his own favorite is Honda because he believes that its redesigned Civic, which he said will be capable of getting 40 miles to the gallon, will be "huge."

Third place was also a tie, between Nissan and Mazda. Reed said that while neither is near Toyota and Honda in terms of fuel efficiency, their cars are "fuel-efficient enough. Moreover, they enjoy the advantage of being perceived as 'drivers' cars,'" he said. (It should be noted that Nissan's announcement about its plans for having a plug-in in 2010 came after Reed made up his list.)

Anyone hoping for a U.S. company to be next on Reed's list will be disappointed. The Germans came in both fifth and sixth: Volkswagen and BMW, respectively. Based on what Reed said, Volkswagen could be something of a sleeper. He pointed out that VW has both hybrid and diesel technology, the latter being inherently more efficient than gasoline-based technology, as well as having a reputation for reliability. "I think Americans are going to reintroduce themselves to VW," Reed predicted, especially with the United States' new regulations requiring diesel to burn cleaner.

Reed put BMW at number six not so much for efficiency as for performance. Still, he said BMW's got good engineering, which supports efficiency.

Coming in—finally—at number seven was an American car manufacturer, General Motors. Reed said GM benefits through its partnerships and use of new materials. He further said that GM's power trains are "fairly fuel-efficient." Interestingly, Reed thought that perhaps the most iconic symbol of the freedom of the open road in America—the Chevrolet Corvette—actually could be marketed in terms of its fuel efficiency, noting that the Corvette gets 25-plus miles to the gallon on the open road.

For number eight on Reed's list, we go back to Asia, to South Korea's Hyundai. Even though Hyundai is not a standout in terms of efficiency, according to Reed, its engineering is a whole lot better than it was a decade ago. Hyundai "is rising rapidly," he said, noting that it has beaten out Honda in comparison tests conducted by Edmunds.

To be sure, one can quibble with Reed for not including Daimler-Chrysler on his list, given its work with plug-in hybrids. And devotees of Ford may quibble with Reed's pronouncement that Ford "seems like the worst of the American manufacturers." But given what Reed said about how Volkswagen could be a sleeper with its combination of hybrid and diesel technology, it's the one car company that gets added to the watch list in the category of "Automotive Efficiency."

As has been discussed, diesel is an extremely important transportation fuel in Europe. Thanks in part to biodiesel, diesel vehicles also have the potential to make a greater impact in the United States and Asia, a point reflected in Reed's assessment of VW. By one estimate, China is planning a huge increase in biodiesel production between 2005 and 2020, though whether that actually happens remains to be seen.

■ ■ ■

An extremely upbeat forecast specifically of hybrid technology's overall potential was offered in a June 2006 research report from Alliance-Bernstein L.P., the global investment banking firm.[24] The firm predicted that the world is "on the cusp of a major transition to hybrid-power vehicles," basically because of hybrids' fundamental superiority over gasoline-powered vehicles. The report described hybrids as a game-changing technology that will significantly reduce oil demand by making electricity the primary energy source for transportation. The report went so far as to say the advent of plug-ins could reshape the foreign policies of the United States, China, Japan, and other major oil-consuming countries.

Importantly for investors, the report concluded that technology and utility companies will gain the most from hybrid technology, oil-related companies will lose the most, and leadership in the auto industry will depend on leadership in hybrid technology. While the report concluded that all automakers will produce hybrids, it echoed others' feelings toward Toyota and Honda, noting that the other car companies "will have to act fast since Toyota and Honda will soon be on their third-generation hybrid systems."

The report said that plug-ins will become popular on the heels of development of batteries that offer significant electric driving range. It also broke down the investment potential along sector lines, not surprisingly finding that the sector with the best combined near-, medium-, and long-term prospects is hybrid battery manufacturers. Importantly, the report concluded that electric utilities also have excellent long-term prospects, as do electronic automotive suppliers and power-semiconductor suppliers.

■ ■ ■

While no American car company made my watch list, one American car *model* did—the Chevrolet Corvette. The Corvette made the list not in any category—although its miles per gallon is not all that bad. Rather, it made the list as a symbol of the spirit that I feel must guide the new oil industry.

Like so many Willie Lomans, attention must be paid to the men and women whose feelings were captured by the Internet blogger who wrote, "We love our cars, our pickup trucks, and our SUVs. They present us with the possible. Freedom of movement. Personal mobility. We are no longer confined by the boundaries of local geography. The open road calls. Owning a car has become a rite of passage to personal independence. We have arrived.

"[W]e have built our national culture around this concept of personal mobility. It sets the parameters of our space and time, enables the range of daily activity, and expands the universe of opportunity."[25]

CHAPTER 6

Every Drop of Oil We Can Get Is Important

"The U.S. is out of oil."

Now that's a rather startling statement. But when noted energy analyst Tom Petrie, chairman and CEO of Petrie Parkman in Denver, uttered it as he relaxed one Sunday afternoon on his sprawling Colorado ranch, he was dead serious.

"There may be some oil," he amended, "but nowhere near enough compared to what is needed."

You won't get an argument from Charley Maxwell, the energy investment analyst and 50-year oil industry veteran. Talking about the world as a whole, Maxwell told me, "We're drawing from the past." He then cited some truly depressing numbers.

In 2005 the world used 30 billion barrels of oil and 5 billion new barrels were found. Compare that with 1964, when 48 billion barrels were found and only 15 billion barrels were used. According to Maxwell, 1964 was the best year in terms of the ratio of oil discovered versus oil consumed. The two lines crossed in 1988 at 23 billion barrels, and ever since then the world has been using more oil per year than it has replaced through new discoveries.

"Things have really gotten twisted," he said.

So twisted that oil companies have become mining companies, digging up vast stretches of tar sands in a hugely expensive effort to recover the sort of gooey oil they once would have turned up their noses at. No more. Now, in addition to tar sands, oil companies are exploring deep under the sea—which, if not the final frontier, as Captain Kirk might say, is pretty darn close to it. They are also shooting more carbon dioxide gas down into existing oil fields, hoping to force to the surface as much of what is still down there as they can.

But even with what are called deepwater drilling and enhanced oil recovery (EOR) (see Figure 6.1), experts say we are going to keep falling further behind in terms of oil discovered versus oil consumed.

James Day is chief executive of Noble Corporation,[1] a company whose drilling rigs penetrate the ocean floor miles beneath the surface. On an Australian public affairs television program in July 2006, Day, according to the program's written transcript, said, "The people that I trust and believe—geophysicists, geologists—say the days of the big fields are gone." The program's correspondent then said, "Only a tiny proportion of the deep ocean floors are thought to cover substantial reservoirs of oil—mainly on the fringes of the South Atlantic, and in the Gulf of Mexico." After which Day said, "While we can drill off West Africa, and they have significant reserves, or Brazil, or the deepwater U.S. Gulf, they're just going to be replacing what we're currently consuming. But that's just treading water. That assumes that we're not increasing consumption."[2]

The same situation applies to natural gas. "These new supplies coming in from isolated areas do nothing more than replace natural gas supplies from more mature areas that are likely to become heavily depleted over time," natural gas analyst Kevin Petak told me.

FIGURE 6.1   Conventional Oil

The world has reached the point where "we are virtually 100 percent utilized," according to Maxwell, who added that the 2 million barrels a day of supposedly surplus production that the world enjoyed in 2006 was really 2 million barrels that the Saudis could not sell because of the oil's unfavorable characteristics.

"I'm worried about the next 10 years, the transitional decade" to when, it is hoped, the world will be able to rely far more on a combination of substitute liquid fuels and efficiency technologies, Vincent Matthews, Colorado's state geologist, told me. Until then, he said, "Every drop of oil we can get is important to have."

"We're trying to buy time," Petrie told me.

■ ■ ■

It needs to be emphasized that nothing that is happening today is new. Indeed, this is the second incarnation of the "new" oil industry. What happened to the home heating industry back in the 18th century also needs to be highlighted.

First, oil. History teaches that back in the 1800s *supply* meant whale oil and *demand* referred not to cars and trucks but to oil lamps. The more people said, "Let there be light," the more Captain Ahab and his brethren set sail in search of whales to kill. Eventually, too many lookouts shouted, "Thar she blows!" Whale populations declined and demand for whale oil began to exceed supply. Prices rose. Sensing opportunity, many companies and individuals started to search for alternative sources that would be longer lasting. This search utilized new technology. It led to the creation of a new oil industry based on crude oil that came from wells drilled in the ground.

The similarities between what happened then and what is happening now are striking. The impetus for change was the realization that the supply of oil from current sources was finite. Change was *necessary*. Meanwhile, it looked like the demand for oil would continue to grow as more people sought to put away their candles, not unlike how more people today want to get behind the wheel of their own car.

Eventually, of course, gas supplanted oil as a source of artificial light, only to be itself supplanted by electricity. While oil got a brand-new gig as a transportation fuel, a point not to be overlooked is that even after outgrowing whale oil, lighting technology continued to evolve as more people sought a better life, to exercise their right not only to light their homes but also to partake in such pleasurable pursuits as listening to the phonograph without the hassle of having to crank it up.

Another point of similarity: Whereas whaling had been the province of a single industry, the search for alternative sources suddenly threw open the oil industry to other companies and individuals. This is not unlike how biotech, automotive, and other companies, plus scientists in universities around the world, are now involved in the twenty-first-century search for alternatives to crude oil.

As those nineteenth-century companies and individuals looked around for a new and more stable source of oil to replace whale oil, they were aided in their search by advanced technology. (Oil drilling may not seem so "advanced" by today's standards, but it certainly was compared with what Quequeg and the actual harpooners of the nineteenth century did for a living.) While land drilling came first, as technology continued to advance, drillers started moving offshore, a development which, if this had been a novel like *Moby Dick*, might have been seen as the "foreshadowing" of events such as the coming switch from corn to cellulosic ethanol.

Many times in the past, as demand has started to catch up with supply, the oil industry that has essentially been in place since the nineteenth century has been able to dig into its bag of technological tricks to push enough additional crude to the surface. But the industry's all-out deployment in the tar sands of Canada is a tacit admission that it does not have enough technological tricks left up its sleeve as far as crude oil is concerned. It is a tacit admission that demand has grown beyond the ability of the industry to meet it the same way it has for the past 100-plus years.

Now, about that eighteenth century home heating crisis. History teaches that homes in the eighteenth century were heated by firewood in open fireplaces that were both extremely inefficient and a health and fire hazard. A firewood shortage inspired none other than Benjamin Franklin to invent what was called the Pennsylvania Fireplace. The Franklin stove, as it came to be known, was a marvel of what was then modern technology—an efficient, freestanding fireplace that provided heat and smoke control. Simply put, the Franklin stove was the advanced technological solution to an energy fuel shortage (as well as an environmental crisis). Its inventor wasn't a "firewood man." Rather, he was simply a scientific genius drawn to a problem who was able to come up with a great solution.

Who will be the Benjamin Franklin of the second incarnation of the new oil industry? Likely there will be several. In addition to the technological geniuses who perfect biofuels, plug-in hybrids, and so on, there (hopefully) will be the wise men and women who sit at the table where policy is made to guide the development of the new oil industry so that a balance is achieved between science, politics, and finance, with the end result being changes that lower energy prices while increasing and securing available supplies so that people feel they can still go over the horizon whenever they want to.

■ ■ ■

Oil companies continue to dig into their bags of technological tricks in the hope of coaxing every possible drop of crude out of the ground. According to Tom Petrie, there is "enormous pressure" on the industry to drill more wells and to drill them "smarter." He explained that instead of drilling one well per 40 acres of land, companies now drill 5 and 10 wells per 40 acres. They also are doing more "horizontal drilling," which is kind of like drilling sideways in order to follow a meandering reservoir of oil. Horizontal drilling can be 50 percent more expensive than vertical drilling, but it can result in as much as 8 to 10 times more production, Petrie said.

To a certain extent, the pressure the industry is under is its own fault. Maxwell told me that back in 1994 and 1995, oil companies could see the coming growth in worldwide oil demand and should have gotten ready for it. He acknowledged that before 2000 the industry did not have the cash flow to increase exploration and drilling. But after 2000 it did, and still nothing happened. The industry got "caught flatfooted," Maxwell said. How did that happen? "Wall Street turned their heads," he said, explaining that the investment banking community wanted oil companies to raise their dividends and buy back their stock, which led to oil firms not paying enough attention to new exploration and production activities.

Inattentiveness has vexed the world's national oil companies for even longer. As was explained (by Maxwell) in Chapter 1, the technocrats in charge of the big Middle Eastern oil fields effectively lost direct control of the spending back in the late 1970s and early 1980s. Over the years billions and billions of dollars may (probably?) have been diverted into other areas. Ironically, the politicians in these oil-producing countries have tried to justify what they did by arguing that it should be the job of the private oil companies in the West to spend money on exploration, production, and field maintenance.

Inattentiveness—and age—also appears to be catching up with the world's oil infrastructure. British Petroleum's shutdown of a huge Alaskan oil field due to pipeline corrosion in 2006 wasn't an isolated situation. Similar sorts of problems have hit other oil-producing countries, according to *Bloomberg News's* August 22, 2006, story headlined "Age and Neglect Meet in Global Pipelines." In the story, one BP official is quoted as saying the company "thought" it had an "adequate" program for catching corrosion problems. An experienced analyst is quoted as saying, "This is an industry problem," one that "people don't like to talk about."[3]

Not very reassuring, is it?

With maybe nobody doing as good a job as they should have been, the world ended up in 2006 with barely enough oil for this huge, but predictable, global increase in demand. If everyone had done their jobs, Maxwell believes the world would have had 4 to 5 percent real surplus capacity in 2006. To be sure, demand eventually would have caught up with supply, he said, but probably not until 2010 or 2011. In other words, the world would have had another four or five years to prepare for what, in 2006, would only have been the "coming" squeeze on global oil supplies.

Don't expect new oil field technology to save the day. As geologist Matthews explained, there have been many major breakthroughs over the last 35 years, but when you add them all up, they have not been enough to keep supply comfortably ahead of demand. Horizontal drilling, which began in the mid-1980s, was one, he said. Another around that same time was *3D seismic*, which is basically a process in which energy waves are used to put together a kind of three-dimensional X-ray of a formation so that scientists can better analyze things like composition, geometry, and fluid content. More recently, Matthews said, there has been a tremendous increase in computer-driven technology that has resulted in a number of advanced drilling techniques.

But while not a salvation, oil field technology could make a difference in how much more oil the world might be able to recover. For example, there could be as much as 20 billion barrels of oil hidden under salt domes and lava flows, according to Maxwell. "We can't see through" either, he said, although in the case of salt domes, "we are learning more about whether it's worthwhile to drill blind." Maxwell estimated that lava flows, an onshore feature, could be hiding 10 to 15 billion barrels, while salt domes, an offshore feature, could be hiding 3 to 5 billion barrels.

That's not that much, relatively speaking, but when every drop counts . . .

The two basic technologies involved in enhanced oil recovery (EOR) have been around for many years. One approach utilizes thermal heat to thin heavy oil so that it flows more easily to the surface. This is used primarily in heavy-oil California. The other, more widely used approach employs primarily carbon dioxide to force "stranded" oil to the surface. According to the U.S. Energy Department, state-of-the-art CO_2-EOR recovery techniques make it technically possible to recover an estimated 89 billion barrels of stranded oil in the United States.

While this is a good amount of oil, it should be noted that we are talking about *potential* reserves. Also, as Reuters noted in its story about all this, "The DOE gave no time frame for when the extra barrels could be added."[4] Moreover, as DOE itself acknowledges, historically EOR has been hampered by its relatively high cost.

Indeed, however much more oil might be pushed up by EOR, according to Maxwell it takes so much energy to do the job that it doesn't take very long before the cost of recovering the oil is equal to the value of the oil itself.

Maxwell, whose knowledge of the history of oil is formidable, predicted that thanks to EOR, in 20 years we should be able to get 41 percent more oil out of the ground than if EOR wasn't used. While this is significantly better than the 25 percent extra oil EOR was responsible for in the 1930s, it is just a little better than the 35 percent additional oil EOR generated in the 1970s, and a miniscule 1 percent better than the 40 percent additional oil he said we are getting from EOR today.

While energy consultant Glenn Wattley does not disagree with any of this, he remains hopeful that today's high prices will lead to greater-than-expected EOR. He says he has been told by geologists that there is a lot more oil down there than conventional wisdom would have us believe.

Tom Petrie summarized the situation this way: "The economic characteristics of future oil production are changing profoundly, both in terms of longevity of production and the cost structure. It's not that the world is running out of oil. It's that we're running out of cheap oil and our ability to increase production."

And so, with EOR an important but limited approach to producing more oil, companies now are betting big on deepwater drilling, even though they realize that while there are significant reserves buried under the ocean floor, there likely is only enough for the world to tread water.

■ ■ ■

Think of it as deepwater's "Golden Triangle."

This is the phrase oil types use to describe the world's three primary deepwater drilling areas: the Gulf of Mexico, Africa, and Brazil.

It has been forecast that deepwater drilling expenditures will grow at a compounded annual growth rate of more than 7 percent and will total more than $20 billion a year by 2010, 85 percent of that spent in the Golden Triangle.

Basically, a deepwater well is one that is drilled in more than 1,000 feet of water. As more and more explorers go down farther and farther in search of oil (the technical limit in the Gulf of Mexico is said to be around 12,000 feet), the cost of deepwater drilling keeps getting more expensive. In a press release announcing its second quarter 2006 earnings results, Noble Corporation noted that "the average dayrate on the Company's deepwater units in the U.S. Gulf of Mexico capable of drilling in water depths 6,000 feet or greater increased 118 percent to $273,779 in the second quarter of 2006 compared to $125,886 in the second quarter of 2005." The company added, not that it really had to: "The deepwater market in the U.S. Gulf and Brazil remains strong."[5]

Needless to say, these deep-sea explorers are eventually going to want and need to recoup their superhigh costs. In this way the world's increasing reliance on deepwater oil will combine with its increasing reliance on oil from tar sands and other unconventional fossil-fuel sources to put steady upward price pressure on gasoline—pressure that likely will continue to be reflected in pump prices long after efficiency and biofuel start to relieve the strain on demand.

(Note: Deepwater drilling doesn't just mean oil; it also means natural gas. Greater deepwater reliance also is going to put long term upward price pressure on natural gas.)

To be sure, deep water is not the only frontier that is going to be explored to a much greater degree in the new oil industry. Another is areas north of the Arctic Circle which, in a cruel twist of fate, are becoming more accessible as global warming shrinks the polar ice cap. Indeed, as the ice continues to melt, it is getting easier to get at what, by some estimates, could be as much as 25 percent of the world's remaining oil and natural gas reserves. Needless to say, environmentalists are livid that the destruction they say is being caused by fossil fuel is fueling a search for more fossil fuel. How much of that oil and natural gas actually will get extracted remains to be seen. Who owns what is one question, with always-opportunistic Russia, plus Canada, Norway, the United States, and others all trying to stake their claims. Another important question is whether environmentalists will mount the mother of all environmental battles, one that makes the battle over where to drill for oil in environmentally sensitive Alaska child's play by comparison. (My bet is that they will.)

It is the prospect of greater reliance on deepwater oil and gas that causes Weeden & Co., Maxwell's firm, to highlight a number of oil field service companies that it thinks are companies to watch. During our discussions Maxwell named his top five: Todco, ENSCO International, Global Santa Fe, Transocean, and Diamond Offshore Drilling. He said the latter two make his list based on oil, while the first three make it primarily on the basis of natural gas drilling.

Transocean's comments in its August 2006 press release announcing its second quarter financial results typify the sort of robust business conditions all of these companies have been experiencing. Transocean said, "With strong demand for our fleet mobile offshore drilling rigs in both the domestic and international market sectors, the company's contract backlog has grown to approximately $19.4 billion at July 31, 2006, up from approximately $10.9 billion at Dec. 31, 2005."[6]

To be sure, on Wall Street in 2006 there were some who apparently did not think that deepwater service companies necessarily have a bright future in the new oil industry. The theory seemed to be that the ability of these companies to provide drilling equipment was going to catch up with the pace of deepwater exploration within a year or two, causing the prices for their services to fall. Based on this general theory, as well as on what some believed were the deepwater Gulf's disappointing results (this was before a major discovery by a consortium that included Chevron), share prices for deepwater drillers took a hit.

But this theory runs contrary to what experts say is actually happening, namely, regional supply deficits are increasing demand for this sort of offshore drilling equipment in other parts of the world such as West Africa, Southeast Asia, and the Middle East, resulting in an exodus of offshore drilling out of the Gulf. Reports of an exodus support the notion that "Every last drop of oil we can get is important," a notion that rings especially true when one talks with Marshall Adkins, the Houston-based director of energy research at Raymond James.

Adkins emphasized to me that, "For the first time in our lives, we have no oil bubble to fall back on." In other words, for the first time ever, the world has no cushion, no ready-to-produce supply of oil that can be quickly tapped to satisfy people's demand (which is why oil companies have set up camp in Canada's tar sands region).

Adkins made two points I had heard many times before. First, there is a groundswell of demand in China and India. Second, the mature oil fields in places like the United States and the North Sea are starting to run out. Then he mentioned something that, while I had heard it before, I suddenly realized I had paid way too little attention. "Here's what we do know," he began.

What Adkins "knows" can be summarized as follows: Contrary to statements by OPEC that it has more than enough oil to meet demand today, tomorrow, and for many years to come, OPEC oil production actually fell by about 1 million barrels a day through the first several months of 2006. "I find that bizarre," he said, noting that the drop-off occurred during a period when supplies were being stretched mighty thin.

When I asked him whether Saudi Arabia in particular might have just reached the point where it had decided to deliberately hold back on production in order to save something for future generations, Adkins, who has been a petroleum engineer for nearly a quarter century, replied, "Could be." But his tone clearly indicated that he did not think so.

Adkins said the only people who know for sure what's really going on are the people at the national oil companies, and they're not talking. Then again, if the reason for OPEC's "bizarre" behavior was a quarter century of inattentiveness to the care and maintenance of its oil fields, what could those people say? What would they be allowed to say by the politicians in charge?

Imagine that by 2015 or so, non-OPEC crude production had peaked and that, starting around 2010, it fell on OPEC to increase capacity in order to satisfy the world's growing appetite for oil. This is basically what ExxonMobil's chief executive has said must happen. In December 2004 at an oil industry meeting, Rex Tillerson, then the company's president, reportedly also said, "The resources available to OPEC are adequate to accommodate this increase and we are assuming that OPEC countries will make investments in a timely manner to meet rising demand."[7]

Look closely at the last part of that quote. The world's biggest oil company is "assuming" that somebody else will at least partially take care of the world's energy future. Not just anybody, mind you, but OPEC, the group that closed the spigot in the 1970s and that is now at ground zero of the terrorists and nationalists who are vexing the world. But wait. It gets worse.

Does OPEC really have "adequate" resources? In his book *Twilight in the Desert: The Coming Saudi Oil Shock and the World Economy* (New York: Wiley & Sons, 2005),[8] energy investment banker Matt Simmons argues that Saudi oil production basically is about to fall off a cliff and take the global economy with it. He maintains that Saudi fields are maturing and that maintenance problems are wreaking havoc. Many in the oil industry believe that Simmons is wrong, and thank God they do, because if it were the consensus that Simmons's fear is justified, there is no telling how high the price of oil might jump, and how much less we might all be worth on paper when we wake up tomorrow.

But I have to consider the fact that, as 50-year oil vet Maxwell has explained, a subtle but decisive change in who controls the purse strings in OPEC could have, by now, produced more than two decades of insufficient oil field investment. I must consider Adkins's point about OPEC's "bizarre" behavior, as well as the possibility that oil field depletion rates generally are being underestimated. I must further consider how little direct control Western oil companies have over the world's known remaining crude reserves.

Then, too, there is this: After doubling the number of rigs drilling "development" wells in 2006 versus 2005, in 2007 the Saudis are expected to further increase the number of rigs drilling development wells by 50 percent. Even with all of this additional drilling, however, "little change in production" is expected because "the additional wells simply are making up for the production declines in existing wells."[9]

Could it be that it isn't just Western governments but also Middle Eastern governments that are stuck in that *Twilight Zone* episode where the woman is riding as fast as she can in a futile attempt to correct her past mistakes? Could it be that 1 million barrels a day *less* production is as about as much as OPEC can now deliver to an increasingly hungry world?

If so, then the previously discussed prediction of CIBC chief economist Jeff Rubin that by 2010—likely too soon for substitutes and efficiency to have made much of an impact—the global demand for oil will exceed available supply by nearly 10 percent looks "rationally fearful."

Again, as Adkins noted, the only people who really know what is going on aren't talking. But if and when they do talk, there is no guarantee that what they say will accurately reflect the situation, given that OPEC members could always use the excuse—until the situation becomes unmistakable—of holding back on production for the sake of future generations to camouflage their quarter century of inattentiveness.

What can no longer be camouflaged is the steep falloff in production from Mexico's principal oil field. Mexico is an extremely important source of U.S. oil imports—number two behind Canada—which makes what the *Los Angeles Times* reported in July 2006 all the more distressing: "Output at Mexico's most important oil field has fallen steeply this year, raising fears that wells there that generate 60 percent of the country's petroleum are in the throes of a major decline."[10]

The field in question, Cantarell, is the world's second largest oil complex. Because it is mature, Cantarell's decline isn't unexpected. But the rapid rate at which it is now forecast to decline appears to be due largely to the shortcomings of Mexico's state-owned oil monopoly, commonly known as Pemex. As the *Times* article noted, "Critics have long lambasted state-owned Pemex as a hotbed of inefficiency and corruption that officials have treated more like an ATM than Latin America's largest company. . . . Federal officials last year siphoned $54 billion from Pemex to fund government spending that included a baseball stadium in Chihuahua and a gigantic flagpole in Neuvo Leon."

One can only hope that OPEC countries haven't been as reckless.

Despite the trouble Mexico's oil industry is in, "Pemex was not an overriding theme of the recent (Mexican) presidential election," the

Times article noted, inferring that the oil industry is such a source of pride to Mexicans that they may be in denial about its future.

Frankly, Washington also doesn't seem to completely understand the impact a steep decline in production from Cantarell could have on Americans, and not just at the pump. Think illegal immigration is bad now? Cantarell reportedly is responsible for more than half of Mexico's oil production. Mexico's oil industry reportedly is the source of roughly 40 percent of government revenue. Imagine how illegal immigration might surge if Cantarell "rolled over," to use an industry phrase. According to Pemex's own internal estimates, Cantarell production could drop as much as 71 percent in less than three years, the *Times* reported.

In the fall of 2006, energy analysts at one leading Wall Street investment firm were sitting around scratching their heads about why Cantarell's problems weren't being publicly discussed more. That's a very good question.

What is eerily similar about Mexico and OPEC is that officials of both have long downplayed any suggestion that meeting production targets is getting a lot harder. Mexico no longer can. OPEC still does. CIBC's Jeff Rubin has written that the "rising water rates [that] are plaguing Cantarell's production" also are affecting Saudi Arabia's giant Ghawar field and Kuwait's Burgan field. For sure that can't be good. In a March 2006 report,[11] Rubin also mentioned that Mexico's 6 percent annual growth rate in domestic gasoline consumption should exacerbate U.S. problems in terms of relying on Mexico for oil imports. Look at Chart 7 in that report, titled "US Oil Imports by Exporting Country" as of December 2005, and tell me if you aren't worried by the fact that of the top five (Canada, Mexico, Venezuela, Saudi Arabia, and Nigeria), only Canada isn't a potential problem for the United States. "Of all the present major suppliers to the US, only Canada is [in] a position to significantly increase oil exports to the US marketplace," Rubin wrote, although only through tar sands production, which, as previously discussed, I believe is a potential financial and environmental nightmare all its own. All of this further highlights the need for the United States to make China its energy partner before Beijing succeeds in rounding up the remaining available sources of crude, especially in Africa.

Even with a national or global Manhattan Project–style program aimed at energy independence, a radically restructured oil industry will not be able to shield us from Cantarell, Ghawar, and so on should they suddenly roll over for another five plus years. Whatever the future brings, the uncertainty surrounding the future ability of Mexico and OPEC to produce would seem to be more than sufficient grounds for dismissing the idea that deepwater oil service companies' business is going to peak within a couple of years.

Then too there is the general notion of *rig intensity*, which is especially important in a world dependent on mature oil fields. As the astute energy journalist Christopher Edmonds noted in an article on the business news web site TheStreet.com, "Rig intensity—the number of rigs needed to produce an additional increment of crude oil or natural gas—continues to increase as the decline rate in current wells accelerates."[12]

To be sure, some deepwater drilling business continues to be off-limits because it is in the Pemex-controlled region of the Gulf. As promising as that region is, don't expect it to be drilled anytime soon, certainly not before Cantarell's distress worsens. One of the global oil industry's greater ironies is that Pemex, which had record sales of more than $86 billion in 2005, "lacks sufficient funds for maintenance of equipment," as the *Times* article put it. As for bringing in foreigners to drill, the article makes clear that national pride stands in the way.

Even with Mexican waters excluded, however, as Adkins emphasized, "There's still a lot of unexplored (deepwater) territory." Petrie said that the oil discovery made in 2006 in the U.S. area of the Gulf of Mexico by the group that included Chevron only adds to the potential of the entire region.

It is thus that Maxwell's top five companies (Todco, ENSCO, Global Santa Fe, Transocean, and Diamond Shore Drilling) make the list of companies to watch, as does another previously mentioned outfit, Noble Corporation. Also well worth including, according to Petrie, are the well-known oil field services firms Halliburton (mentioned previously in the discussion of infrastructure providers), BJ Services, and Schlumberger. Still another that deserves watching, according to Wattley, is Weatherford International.

In 2006 Halliburton said it expects its net income and earnings per share to double over the next three to five years. "Those increases will be the result of the strongest demand for oil field services in years as well as acquisitions," Reuters reported.[13] BJ Services said, "We expect activity to remain strong into the foreseeable future."[14]

Schlumberger pointed to an increase in demand for its seismic technology as evidence that "our customers' concerns are as much a longer-term preoccupation with the renewal of reserves through defining new reservoirs, as they are concerns with short-term production volumes."[15] Weatherford reported strong earnings and entered into an agreement with Statoil of Norway to develop new fiber-optic–based sensing and communications systems to extend the life of oil and natural gas fields.

For all of these mentioned reasons, all of the aforementioned oilfield service providers—Schlumberger, BJ Services, Noble, Todco, ENSCO, Global Santa Fe, Transocean, Diamond Offshore Drilling, and Weatherford—make the watch list in the category of "Infrastructure Providers."

■ ■ ■

If these are the companies that will be doing the deepwater drilling, for which oil companies will they be working? Who are the deepwater explorers?

Deepwater exploration "is a phenomenon of the majors," said Adkins, explaining that major oil companies like ExxonMobil, BP, and Shell act like a consortium, pooling their technological talents and money in the hugely expensive search for deepwater oil and gas reserves.

Under the theory that, for the next 10 years (the transitional decade), every last drop of oil is going to be important to have, Adkins believes that major oil companies are a "great" buy now and should remain so for years to come. However, he too can see a future where oil is not the only transportation fuel, where substitute liquid fuels and efficiency are integral parts of a restructured oil industry. And he ponders the question: Which group of oil companies should do better in the new oil industry? Will it be the major oil companies or their smaller cousins, the independent oil companies?

Into the former category Adkins puts guys like ExxonMobil, British Petroleum, and Shell. Into the latter he puts folks like Apache Corporation, Anadarko Petroleum, Chesapeake Energy, and EOG Resources.

Regarding the latter group, Apache is an oil and gas producer with operations in the United States, Canada, and the United Kingdom North Sea, among other places. In 2006 Anadarko Petroleum acquired Kerr-McGee, one of the pioneers of deepwater drilling and a company exploring and developing offshore prospects in West Africa and Brazil, among other places. Chesapeake Energy is the self-described third largest independent producer of natural gas in the United States, with numerous land-based operations. EOG's oil and gas reserves are in the United States, Canada, offshore Trinidad, and the UK North Sea.

Adkins said that over the last 25 years, everyone at the majors who has wanted to take risks "has had their heads chopped off." Consequently, the "risk takers," as he described them, have gravitated to the independents.

Having a risk-taking mentality is going to be very important in the new oil industry. First and foremost, it could be the key to finding whatever crude oil remains to be found. In addition, it could be the key to whether an oil company picks up on the potential of biobutanol or an even better biofuel that may come out of some biotech laboratory. It could also be the key to whether an oil company recognizes the value of forming strategic alliances with the forest, agricultural, waste disposal, maybe even the candy industry, to insure a steady flow of cellulosic feedstock. It could lead to heretofore unimaginable alliances with car manufacturers and electric utilities. Overall, it could be the key to recognizing when an oil company should begin transitioning to a future that lies about 10 to 15 years out, not all that long a period of time in the oil industry.

Thus I have put these independent oil outfits—Apache, Anadarko, Chesapeake, and EOG—but not any of the majors on the watch list in a category titled "Oil Producers." The category has been ranked 11th out of 15. This may seem too low to some people, but in terms of shaping the future direction of the energy industry, oil producers, even with their advanced drilling techniques, will still likely be the old guard, not the young turks.

Of all the majors, probably BP acts most like an independent. Its marketing slogan, "Beyond Petroleum," sounds like a catch phrase for the new oil industry. BP's partnership with DuPont in biobutanol would seem to be evidence that the company intends to take risks as it branches out. But while BP may in fact be ahead of the pack, Adkins isn't convinced. "I think it is public relations," he said of BP's marketing phrase.

Do any of the majors understand the need to take risks?

"I don't think anybody has figured it out," Adkins said.

If Maxwell's calculations are correct, then oil companies that don't take risks could eventually find themselves simply liquidating assets. Indeed, Maxwell has estimated that no matter when crude oil production peaks globally, production by a number of major oil companies will peak within a few years. Specifically, he has estimated that RoyalDutch/Shell's production will peak in 2009 and ExxonMobil's in 2011. He foresees Chevron and BP reaching peak production in 2012. Occidental and Total, meanwhile, will peak in 2013. ConocoPhillips won't peak until 2016; however, this assumes the company is allowed by Venezuela to continue heavy oil production from the Orinoco Belt.[16]

Still, don't weep for Big Oil. (Not that anyone would who has had to fill up a car or truck in recent years.) Yes, major oil companies may lose even more direct control over the industry they built, but not before they have produced a heck of a lot more oil over the next several years. Moreover, depending on how they choose to invest their billions, major oil companies could wind up as the kingmakers—and the kings—of the new oil industry in their new role as energy investment bankers.

■ ■ ■

As Petrie mentioned, companies are now drilling many more wells per 40 acres of land. Combine that with all of the offshore activity and you get a lot of business coming the way of many companies involved with oil exploration and production whose names have yet to be mentioned.

The *upstream* oil and gas business—meaning that part of the oil industry involved in exploration and production—is really many interconnected businesses. What are some of these interconnected businesses?

- Drill bits. The drill bit is the gizmo that crushes or scrapes the rock as a hole is drilled down to where the oil or gas (hopefully) is located.
- Drillpipe. This is the tubular steel that connects the drilling rig or platform on the surface with the bit and other drilling apparatus at the bottom.
- Drilling mud. This is a phrase commonly used to describe liquids and gaseous fluids used in drilling.
- Blowout preventer. One can't have fluids without also having a blowout preventer, which basically is a large valve that acts to control the fluids.
- Decommissioning services. Given that many wells are now also starting to reach the end of their economic lives, well decommissioning services are increasingly important.

With a bow to Jim Cramer, who discussed specific companies involved in oil field services on a *Mad Money* program that aired on CNBC in May 2006,[17] I've added the following firms to the watch list in the category of "Infrastructure Providers": Smith International (for bits); Grant Prideco (pipe); Hydril (blowout preventer); AMCOL International (mud); and Tetra Technologies (well decommissioning). While these are by no means the only companies involved in this work, they are among the recognized leaders.

Some other companies that have yet to be mentioned are oil companies whose frontier (deepwater and so on) oil and natural gas potential should become increasingly important in the world over the next few years. One is Petrobras, the Brazilian oil company. In addition to having its own little piece of the ocean in which to drill, Petrobras also is big into sugarcane-derived ethanol. Another is Lukoil, the big Russian oil company, which has roughly 20 billion barrels of reserves, reportedly second in the world only to ExxonMobil. A third company, Imperial Oil of Canada, is kind of a frontier unto itself. Maxwell calls Imperial "a complete energy company," by which he means that Imperial has large tar sands, coal, and uranium reserves (uranium equates to nuclear energy.) One more, Talisman Energy, according to Maxwell, has recently found a lot of conventional oil. In 2006 the company also bet on natural gas in Canada, acquiring over 260,000 acres of land. Talisman called it an exciting development and part of the company's drive to find new sources of relatively low-cost conventional natural gas.

Each of these outfits—Talisman, Imperial, Lukoil, and Petrobras—makes the list of companies to watch in the category of "Oil Providers."

CHAPTER 7

The New Oil Economy?

How many news stories have you seen about angry Americans filling up the tanks of their cars and trucks? But while millions of drivers are fed up with high gasoline prices, everyone keeps filling up as if they don't have a choice.

That's because they don't. Not really. The only choice most people have today is to drive less, but many people can't drive a lot less because of their jobs and where they live. Others who could absolutely don't want to. Many Americans consider freedom of mobility their democratic right. The same sentiment is increasingly to be found in China, India, and so on.

The global economy is going to need a lot more energy, especially for the hundreds of millions of additional vehicles expected on global highways. But when it comes to oil, the world already is "drawing from the past," to use Charley Maxwell's words. What's more, non-OPEC crude production is expected to peak long before 2030. So without the structural changes inherent in the new oil industry, most of the additional oil the world is going to need will have to come from OPEC.

Lacking direct control over its own future, Big Oil is left to assume that OPEC will make the investments necessary to increase production in a timely fashion. But can it? Has OPEC been shortchanging oil field maintenance? What condition are OPEC's oil fields really in?

Even if OPEC is not another Mexico, how can the world possibly afford to increase its dependency on energy located in the most unstable region on earth? (A lot of the LNG the world will also be counting on will likewise come from the Middle East.) Does this not virtually guarantee that the war on terror will continue to cost American lives and money for decades to come and that America will never be able to end its addiction to imported oil?

There is no way to put a price tag on a soldier's life. But there is a price tag that can be put on the never-ending battle to make sure America's imported oil arrives safely. As painful as pump prices have gotten in recent years, they reflect less than half of the true cost of each gallon of gasoline Americans pump into their cars.

As defense analyst and economist Milton Copulos has pointed out, America pays a huge hidden cost for its imported oil. Copulos has estimated that when one factors in oil-related defense spending, as well as the cost of high oil prices in terms of jobs lost and other economic dampeners, the true cost of gasoline in the United States in the summer of 2006 was probably in excess of $11 a gallon.

Don't think we aren't all paying the entire $11, no matter how much less we might have forked out at the corner service station. As Pulitzer Prize–winning reporter Paul Salopek of the *Chicago Tribune* wrote in a series about oil that is worthy of a second Pulitzer, "Consumers don't dodge the bill for these masked expenditures. Instead, they pay for them indirectly, through higher taxes, or by saddling their children and grandchildren with a ballooning national debt—one that's increasingly financed by foreigners."[1]

Think about this: If the true cost of gasoline in the summer of 2006 was $11 or so a gallon, how much could it be in the summer of 2030 if OPEC's oil is even more important than it is today? How does $25 a gallon sound? Crazy? No more so than $3 gasoline would have sounded in the 1960s, prior to the first great global oil price shock. As energy investment banker Matt Simmons said, there is "no ceiling" to oil prices—not in the present-day oil industry.

All this is why proponents of the different sectors of the new oil industry (biofuel, efficiency, synthetic oil) should enjoy a warm welcome in Washington and other world capitals for years to come. They bring with them choices, alternatives, ways for people to keep driving and economies to keep growing in a politically safer, environmentally more sustainable fashion.

When it comes to energy, every winning investment idea is first a winning political idea. But as H. Ross Perot, one-time independent candidate for president of the United States, was fond of saying, the devil's in the details.

■ ■ ■

Simply put, America has two energy futures from which to choose—one a future of limitations, the other a future of possibilities.

As much as the present-day oil industry is a drain on the overall economy, the new oil industry could be a stimulant. Eliminate some of that $8 or more per gallon hidden cost of gasoline and this would free up hundreds of billions of dollars a year that the government could spend on job creation, deficit reduction, shoring up retirement and medical care programs, and so on.

Moreover, if people were willing to accept a new layer of government bureaucracy in their lives, the new oil industry just might be able to reduce energy consumption across the board—natural gas and electricity as well as oil; in the home as well as on the road—and do so while putting money in people's pockets. While such thinking may sound kind of crazy, as economist Jeffrey Sachs noted in his 2005 speech, "We have a billion people living in a degree of affluence that was unimaginable even a quarter-century ago."[2]

My translation: The global economic system is capable of creating wealth in ways that can be difficult to imagine.

It is important to note that, at present, the new oil industry is not an actual industry. It is more like a cluster of groups occupying the same general space, each one pushing what it sees as the answer to high oil prices, dependency on imported oil, and/or the worsening natural environment. As this book has tried to indicate, each group appears to have a piece of the road map showing the way out of the fix we're in. Without effective government policy, however, this road map likely will never get taped together. While things will still improve, our kids and grandkids may have to face the same fundamental problems we're facing. The consequence for investors would be that they would have to settle for fewer investment ideas turning out to be winners.

The best scenario for investors and the nation as a whole would be if the new oil industry were allowed to fire on all four cylinders—biofuel, efficiency, synthetic oil, and traditional oil.

Should tar sands and/or coal grab the inside track, environmentalists will move even more to block their development because of the green community's traditional concerns about pollution and reliance on fossil fuel. If biofuel grabs the inside track, especially before there are technological breakthroughs in cellulosic ethanol, a chorus of critics will charge that the nation can't afford biofuel because it pushes up the price of food, thereby fueling inflation, and risks making the nation dependent on imported food. If efficiency gets too far out in front, some will charge that the nation is simply exchanging dependence on foreign oil producers for dependence on foreign auto manufacturers. Others will charge that electric utilities are only interested in the extra revenue that may come their way thanks to kilowatt gasoline. Meanwhile, too much reliance on oil from the hurricane-exposed Gulf of Mexico would be criticized as being almost as dangerous as reliance on the politically turbulent Middle East.

For the new oil industry to pay off over the next 10 to 20 years to the fullest extent possible for nations and investors alike, the public needs to feel that it is in the driver's seat. People must be able to take something to the bank—literally.

■ ■ ■

Martin Feldstein, the George F. Baker Professor of Economics at Harvard University and the president and CEO of the National Bureau of Economic Research, has an idea, a really good idea. Feldstein, who was chairman of the U.S. Council of Economic Advisors under Ronald Reagan, has suggested creating a system he calls *tradable gasoline rights* (TGRs).

As outlined in an opinion piece in the *Wall Street Journal*—for which Feldstein serves as a member of the board of contributors—every adult would get a TGR debit card. Each time a person bought gasoline, they would pay with their TGR card as well as with money. Businesses that used trucks also would get allotments. A gallon of gasoline would cost one TGR. The government would determine the total number of gallons consumed by the nation per year and would give out that total number of TGRs. "In 2006, Americans will buy about 110 billion gallons of gasoline. To keep that total unchanged in 2007, the government would distribute 110 billion TGRs. To reduce consumption by 5 percent, it would cut the number of TGRs to 104.5 billion."[3]

Feldstein further explained:

> A key feature of these gasoline rights is that they are tradable. Individuals with more TGRs than they need could sell the excess, while those who want to use more gallons than their allocation would have to buy extra TGRs. The gasoline companies could act as clearing houses for these trades, using their gasoline pumps to sell TGRs in the same way that they sell gasoline or to buy TGRs in exchange for the cash needed to purchase gasoline. Other institutions like banks could also trade TGRs for cash. And individuals could of course buy and sell TGRs among themselves by letting others use their card.

Feldstein envisioned a system where, as he wrote, "The market price of a TGR would depend on the number of TGRs that the government distributed relative to the number of gallons that households would buy if there were no TGR system. The smaller the number of TGRs, the greater would be the price per TGR."

How would someone avoid using up his TGRs? According to Feldstein, "By driving less, driving at speeds that use less gas, or driving a more fuel-efficient car."

And why, exactly, should people go along with this further complication in their already complicated lives? In Feldstein's words, TGRs "could be distributed in a way that actually raises the income of a majority of households while giving everyone an incentive to reduce gasoline consumption."

Basically, TGRs sound like a way to put a monetary value on gasoline *not* used—on negaoil.

While Professor Feldstein has envisioned TGRs as part of the present-day oil industry, imagine if they were applied to the new oil industry. People could still stretch their TGRs by driving less, driving at speeds that used less gasoline, and driving more fuel-efficient cars. But the system could be configured so that people also could avoid using their TGRs by filling up with liquid fuel that contained a high percentage of biofuel. When plug-in hybrid vehicles become available, people could save TGRs by keeping their plug-in cars and trucks running on kilowatt gasoline.

Including these two additional options under a TGR system would motivate people who cannot drive less to find other ways to reduce their consumption of gasoline. People who do not want to drive less would be similarly motivated. The system would work to reduce gasoline consumption, and also the pollution this generates, in ways that are compatible with people's daily lives and with cultural norms. (Never forget: She'll have fun, fun, fun until her daddy takes the T-bird away.)

As previously discussed, plug-in hybrid vehicles will be a direct link between energy use in the home and on the road. Implicit in this is the notion that TGRs might be applicable for home energy consumption. But why wait for plug-in hybrid vehicles to become available? Why not incorporate home energy usage into a TGR system right off the bat?

Keep in mind that 25 years from now the world is expected to need not just a lot more oil but also a lot more electricity than it did in 2006 because the global population will have grown, emerging economies will have continued to develop, the United States itself will have continued to grow, and more people everywhere will have achieved or be striving for middle-class citizenship. How efficiently the world uses all forms of energy, as well as how diversified the world's energy base becomes, is going to make all the difference economically, environmentally, and in terms of nations' security.

TGRs would seem to be a good way to motivate people to save energy in their homes, a way to put a monetary value on one's negawatt as well as negaoil consumption.

One thing that can put people off from saving energy around the house is that they must be proactive on many different fronts. Whereas a car is a single-source use of energy, a home is a multiple-source use. Indeed, a modern home uses electricity to run:

- Air conditioning systems.
- Kitchen appliances such as refrigerators, ovens (both microwave and regular), and dishwashers.
- Clothes washers and dryers (plus that extra freezer down in the basement).
- Home entertainment systems (TVs, stereos, and so on).
- Home office systems (computers, printers, and so on).
- Indoor and outdoor lighting.
- Swimming pool heating systems (and, for some, a Jacuzzi).
- Clock radios, garage door openers, cell phone chargers, and a host of other miscellaneous uses.

In and of themselves, none of these home energy uses draws people's attention. Paying the monthly electric bill is something we do without thinking.

TGRs have the potential to change that. They have the potential to change people's behavior right down to the simple but, as it turns out, incredibly important act of changing a light bulb. A compact fluorescent light bulb (CFL) uses about two-thirds less energy than a standard incandescent bulb. This and the fact that a CFL lasts a lot longer than an incandescent can save a homeowner up to $100 in energy costs over the life of the bulb.

By focusing attention on the financial advantages of changing people's energy behavior around the house in dozens of small ways, TGRs have the potential to supercharge the energy technology revolution by creating a huge consumer demand for more energy-efficient houses, cooling systems, appliances, electronic gear, and so on. This would be in addition to a TGR-inspired increase in demand for more fuel-efficient cars and trucks. Another likely benefit would be that green power usage would surge as people installed solar and wind power systems as a way of not using their TGRs. Instead of being a bill nobody reads before paying it, the monthly electric bill could become a bill everybody reads very closely.

(If home as well as road energy use is to be a part of the system, the name probably would have to be changed from TGRs to TERs, the latter standing for tradable energy rights. For now, though, I'm sticking with TGRs out of respect to Professor Feldstein.)

Given the global nature of energy, there is every reason to believe that TGRs could become a global phenomenon. In Great Britain, ideas are already being discussed for what some have described as a "carbon credit card" system under which the government would give everyone a carbon allotment. People whose carbon footprint exceeded their allotment (thanks to driving a gas-guzzling vehicle and so on) would have to buy points from people who kept their footprint to a minimum by, for example, relying on public transportation. Whereas the British approach sees cutting energy use as a way to cut pollution, the TGR approach is directly intended to cut energy consumption, which in turn cuts pollution.

Energy consultant Glenn Wattley made an important point when he told me, "In Europe companies already trade carbon dioxide credits as a way to reduce greenhouse gas emissions. Trading TGRs would not be a complicating factor to consumers in the European Union. Furthermore, once such systems as trading CO_2 credits and TGRs are instituted, the public debate is minimized as people focus on making sure they benefit from such systems."

Another reason why TGR systems might prove popular in countries around the world is the emphasis so many countries are putting on new energy technology. In some instances, energy technology development seems farther along outside the United States—a good reason to consider a unified global TGR system, although the logistics of this admittedly would be complicated. For example, residential fuel cell development appears to be farther along in Japan, while rooftop wind power turbines appear farther along in Europe. (London has a fire station with a rooftop wind turbine intended to supply 8 percent of the electricity the station uses.)[4]

Japan especially might latch onto TGRs. The government there wants to cut its dependence on oil for transportation from 100 percent currently to around 80 percent by 2030, and to do so in part with a new kind of battery-powered ultra-small car that would be able to get 50 miles between recharges. A TGR system that combined home and road energy efficiency might serve Japan well as it tried to shift 20 percent of the nation's transportation fuel dependency from oil to electricity.

■ ■ ■

How might a TGR system actually work, and which companies might benefit and thus belong on the list of companies to watch?

As previously indicated, this whole thing is a nonstarter if people are not willing to accept a new layer of government bureaucracy in return for a chance to make money. If they are not, the new oil industry will still thrive (especially if there is skillful political leadership that balances the competing sectors), but its potential impact on other areas of the economy such as home remodeling, communications, and financial services won't be nearly as great.

If polls and other measures showed that a majority of people were willing, then the first step would be for government to decide how many TGRs should be issued and on what basis. This is a step that seems well worth taking if for no other reason than that it would allow politicians to approach the idea of a national energy policy from a fresh perspective. Everyone agrees that the United States does not presently have a national energy strategy. Everyone further agrees that one is urgently needed. It is those devilish details that keep getting in the way. Until now, the debate seems to have been all about which special interest can gain the inside track. To name but a few of the seemingly never-ending controversies: whether to drill for oil in environmentally sensitive areas; whether to mandate stronger fuel-efficiency standards; whether to force coal-fired power plants to run cleaner.

The political discussion about how to set up a TGR allotment system should begin with the understanding that the public interest comes first, not any special interest.

Let's get the discussion going. (Don't forget that participating in these sorts of discussions is the best way for investors to figure out which investment options have the best chance of paying off.)

From a technological perspective, it would seem clear that a nation's TGR system should be oriented toward promoting hybrid vehicles, both plug-ins and non-plug-ins. Hybrid technology goes with everything. Whether the accompanying technology is today's gasoline and diesel engines or tomorrow's fuel cell engine, "Hybrid is the enabling technology that makes all of those more efficient," according to a Toyota executive quoted in an article that ran on BusinessWeek.com.[5]

Engineers like Timothy Maxwell, professor of mechanical engineering at Texas Tech and expert on engines that use alternative fuels, emphasize that hybrids are, to use Maxwell's phrase, "the single most optimistic thing" for relieving the world's transportation fuel crisis over the next 15 to 20 years. Hybrids have just one downside, Maxwell told me: "They cost more."

Enter TGRs, which would help hybrid buyers offset that higher price over the lifetime of the vehicle, as well as help lower the sticker price by making hybrids more popular. As hybrids become more popular, more will be built, thereby generating economies of scale and increased competition among car manufacturers to be the recognized hybrid leader. Importantly from a car manufacturer's perspective, because hybrid technology goes with everything, every vehicle could be made a hybrid without undercutting research on other advanced engine technologies.

Even with the impetus of TGRs, however, it would take a number of years for there to be enough hybrids on the road to significantly reduce gasoline consumption. During this time a nation's ability to reduce its gasoline consumption would be heavily dependent on its use of biofuel.

While TGRs would be a good way to popularize flex-fuel vehicles, put-ting a lot of flex-fuel vehicles on the road would also be a multiyear process. (This optimistically assumes flex-fuel vehicles would not en-counter so much opposition from the oil industry that they would never get on the road.) By making it financially advantageous for people to fill up with biofuel, a nation would likely see an immediate significant reduc-tion in gasoline consumption. Moreover, there would be a new and very strong financial incentive for private industry to develop cellulosic ethanol, biobutanol, and whatever other biofuel might make scientific, economic, and political sense.

Just as TGRs should be able to motivate people to reduce their gaso-line consumption, they should likewise be able to motivate people to re-duce their electricity consumption, which would lessen the need to burn fossils fuels. (When plug-ins became available, the electricity they con-sume could be exempted.)

Anyone can quickly and inexpensively save energy around the house by doing simple things like caulking windows and doors and installing an inexpensive programmable thermostat. Millions of people doing millions of simple things to cut home energy consumption would sig-nificantly reduce demand for coal, natural gas, and home heating oil, the latter being one of those important nontransportation oil uses. All that would be needed to make TGRs a reality in the home would be a certifiable way of determining every home's energy use baseline. After that, usage could be regularly tracked by people through their monthly utility bills.

The British government has been thinking about paying for every homeowner to have an annual "carbon audit." In the United States, how-ever, there is no reason to burden government with this expense. Utilities already perform home energy audits and it seems only fair that, in ex-change for the money they may make by selling kilowatt gasoline, utili-ties should agree to give all of their residential ratepayers a free in-home energy audit that would serve as a baseline. Natural gas usage could be audited at the same time by combination gas-electric utilities.

Frankly, utilities should jump at the chance. Otherwise, they could find themselves beaten to the punch by retailers like Home Depot and Lowe's. For years now these guys have been keen on making home re-modeling easier by supplying all the materials and even lining up the necessary contractors. To provide free home energy audits might well be seen by them as a cost-effective way to increase business by spurring more homeowners to remodel.

It isn't hard to imagine Home Depot and Lowe's selling more of almost everything in their stores, from solar panels to insulation to energy-efficient appliances. In turn, this would put pressure on manufacturers of a whole host of energy-consuming products to make their offerings more and more energy-efficient. Given that the United States imports so much of this kind of stuff, the pressure would be global in nature, especially so if there were a U.S.–China partnership in place.

Since Home Depot and Lowe's both could be winners under a TGR system that rewarded home energy conservation and green power usage, both make the list of companies to watch in a category titled "Consumer Information Providers." This category ranks 13th on the list.

As much as Home Deport and Lowe's might benefit, any number of other well-known companies might, too, such as appliance and lighting manufacturer General Electric, which is already on the watch list in the category of "Infrastructure Providers." Homebuilders, a number of which already promote energy-efficient and environmentally friendly construction, could also benefit, as could home mortgage companies, some of which already offer energy-efficient home mortgages that generally allow people to borrow more on the theory that the less money they must spend on utilities, the more they should have available to pay the mortgage each month.

However, it is a company many may not have heard of that makes the list alongside Home Depot and Lowe's. The company is called The Alternative Energy Store. It is a place—in cyberspace as well as in Massachusetts—for people who are unfamiliar with and, hence, probably a little intimidated by how to go about making their home more energy-efficient and/or a mini green-power plant.

This description probably fits most of us, which is why, just as there is now YouTube, the broadcast-it-yourself video web site, as well as the social networking sites MySpace and Facebook, there would seem to be a coming need for a web site that serves as a community for ordinary people to learn the basics about energy efficiency and home-based green energy so they can take advantage of TGRs.

To be sure, the Alternative Energy Store isn't an unknown. It made the 2006 Inc.com 500, a list of the fastest-growing privately held companies, coming in at number 440. But whether it's the Alternative Energy

Store or some other outfit that hits the big time, this is a web model that looks promising. One day in August 2006, one of the site's "Featured Products" was a meter advertised as a way to "Measure for yourself how efficient your appliances really are." The "Featured Article" was about wind turbine systems for the home. The "Latest Post" concerned "What would be the cost of a PV system for the 'average' income household?"

As promising as this web model is, however, it still covers only half—the home half—of the TGR universe.

Consider the following: Of over 100 tire retailers on Long Island, New York, only 12 percent of them were carrying high-efficiency tires in August 2006, according to a press release issued that month by New York Senator Charles Schumer. "If most Long Islanders knew they could invest an extra $12 in a set of tires and then save up to $150 at the gas pump, they'd jump at the opportunity," the senator, who wants the federal government to require that replacement tires are as efficient as the originals, was quoted as saying.[6]

There is another web site that offers very good consumer information in the automotive area. While CalCars.org, which was discussed in regard to plug-in hybrid vehicles, currently targets people interested in plug-ins, it is easy to see how its mission could be expanded to include other useful information regarding automotive efficiency. While many web sites already offer general information, CalCars.org's advantage might be that it seems able to explain rather technical subjects in language anyone can understand. Thus does CalCars.org also make the watch list in the category of "Consumer Information Providers."

■   ■   ■

In putting together a TGR system, careful thought would have to be given to the relative value assigned to biofuel versus synthetic gasoline.

No doubt a case would be made by synthetic oil's supporters that gasoline made from tar sands, coal, natural gas, and oil shale should qualify as "not gasoline," the same as biofuel, even though synthetic gasoline *is* gasoline, just not refined from crude oil. Environmentalists would complain that synthetic oil is too environmentally destructive to warrant inclusion, while oil and coal companies and national security advocates would emphasize the diversity and political security of gasoline made from synthetic oil.

All are important points, but the overriding point is that Big Oil controls the distribution of transportation fuel. Just as TGRs won't work if the public doesn't accept a new layer of bureaucracy, this system is going nowhere unless Big Oil is on board. With most of the world's proven crude reserves beyond its direct control, and with new crude getting harder and more expensive to find, tar sands and natural gas are Big Oil's babies, its hope for the future. Probably the only way to get Big Oil on board with TGRs would be to recognize that there is value in buying gasoline that contains a percentage refined from unconventional fossil fuel sources. (One day, probably everyone will "fill up" from home. But I would not be surprised if, when that day comes, Big Oil, in its role as energy investment bankers, has already bought control of significant portions of the electrical grid and of leading green power manufacturers.)

It should be noted that, while making allowances for gasoline from unconventional fossil fuels would stick in the throat of environmentalists, it would be good news for synthetic oil investors, who basically would win whether a TGR system took root or not. The situation also is a reminder of why biobutanol's success is so important in the scheme of things. It is hard to imagine Big Oil ever embracing a biofuel that cannot be incorporated into its own gasoline distribution system. Hopefully, however, whatever value is placed on synthetic gasoline, it will be less than that given to biofuel, though here again we've got ourselves a devilish detail.

Currently, ethanol made primarily from corn constitutes about 10 percent of a significant percentage of gasoline sold in the United States. As such, gasoline containing corn-derived ethanol should be recognized as a way for people to save their TGRs. Still, the value of this first-generation ethanol must be sufficiently low to encourage the rapid development of both cellulosic ethanol and biobutanol, plus any other biofuels some latter-day Ben Franklin may have up his sleeve. Needless to say, corn ethanol's proponents may not see things the same way.

Yet another devilish detail will pop up the minute biofuel's development crosses into the area of genetically modified organisms (GMOs), which it probably already has. Some think that energy crops whose genetic makeup has been altered could turn out to be the closest thing to a silver bullet for preventing any more oil crises while simultaneously protecting the environment and nations' security, all without precipitating a food crisis. But using cellulosic ethanol will require GMOs to break down the woody, fibrous plant material.

GMOs generally make many environmentalists uneasy. Genetically modified energy crops could make some apoplectic.

The key to preventing the GMO issue from becoming a devilish detail may be to remind the environmental community that the more the world relies on genetically modified energy crops, the less chance there is that global environmental destruction will quicken in a search for naturally-growing cellulosic feedstock.

■ ■ ■

This brings us to the all-important question of how TGRs would get "spent."

Obviously, people who used more than their allotted TGRs—and there no doubt would be many, human nature being what it is—would have to buy additional TGRs. As previously noted, Professor Feldstein has suggested that gasoline companies could serve as clearinghouses for these trades.

Another approach that might work, especially if TGRs were a feature of home as well as road energy use, would be to give the job of clearing-house to the communications industry. People's cell phones are changing faster than the speed of light, new features being added all the time. It should not be hard to equip the now-ubiquitous cell phone such that it could be plugged into a gasoline pump that would electronically record how many TGRs the person was spending. Blackberries and laptop computers could be similarly equipped.

Interestingly, the wireless industry is at a stage in its development where new strategies are needed if its rapid pace of growth is to be maintained. (Currently 7 of every 10 Americans already receive wireless service.) As they look around for new services to offer, mobile carriers reportedly are hoping that their next big thing will be mobile data transmission. Carriers currently generate only about $7 or $8 a month from wireless data services. They are spending billions on expanding their networks so that they can provide high-speed wireless Internet. "Data is the great question. Everyone is building a network as if (data customers) are going to come," the CEO of one carrier has been quoted as saying.[7]

Well, if you build it they might come in droves if there were a TGR system that enabled people to track how many TGRs they had left, the same way they now track how many minutes they have left. Wireless companies could provide a seamless Internet-based data network that connected gasoline refiners, electric utilities, and others. One of the advantages of such an approach is that people are already familiar with how going over their allotted cell phone minutes costs them money. Anyone who exceeded their energy usage allotment could acquire additional TGRs simply by paying an extra fee on their monthly cell phone bill. In effect, wireless providers would function as a TGR bank, the place people go to buy extra TGRs.

It is way too soon to pick any particular companies in the wireless industry that might prosper from this, but because of the potential of TGRs to become the next big thing in wireless, wireless providers as a whole make the list of companies to watch in the category of "Consumer Information Providers," the same category where providers of "how-to" information such as Home Depot and Lowe's are to be found.

One other company needs to be added to this category: Google. In November 2006, Google's CEO told a reporter that he envisions a future where everyone gets a free cell phone in exchange for agreeing to accept targeted advertising. Google is so big and rich that it's conceivable that the company might be able to partner with oil companies and electric utilities on a TGR system that might, I suspect, become a magnet for advertisers.[8]

■ ■ ■

How would the wireless providers buy the TGRs that they would sell to the public? They might buy them from the government or, if you really wanted to make things interesting, from a financial services firm that *bundled*, to use a Wall Street term, TGRs and sold them by the thousand, the million, and so on.

Here is where another of Professor Feldstein's points needs to be emphasized, namely: "Other institutions like banks could also trade TGRs for cash." What's that line Yogi Berra says in the commercial for the insurance company Aflac? "They give you cash, which is just as good as money." Well, if TGRs were tradeable for money, they would be just as good as money.

I'm starting to really appreciate Professor Feldstein's insight, as expressed in the first paragraph of his *Wall Street Journal* opinion piece, that TGRs could be distributed "in a way that actually raises the income of a majority of households."[9]

Society being what it is, lower-income households might well use their cashed-in TGRs to buy food. But for the majority of people who don't have to worry about putting food on the table, cashed-in TGRs would represent a new source of investible cash.

Indeed, TGRs could prove to be a financial windfall for the financial services sector. They could prove to be a great marketing tool for selling all of the sundry financial products Wall Street wants wealthy and merely affluent people to purchase, starting with retirement accounts, college savings accounts, mutual funds, stocks and bonds, money market funds, and insurance. Basically, TGRs could be marketed to people as a way to take a bigger bite out of the apple of success. (Sorry, I'm no Madison Avenue copywriter.)

Of course, Wall Street might get a run for its money from every conceivable retailer, all of whom would want people to spend this newfound cash in their stores or on their web sites. Can't you just see annual TGR sales events at places like Macy's and Lord & Taylor? But it strikes me that the idea of wealth creation through smart energy management would be very potent in a country where so many people are rushing headlong toward retirement without enough money set aside to avoid having to work until they are 90 years old.

Indeed, wealth creation through energy efficiency (and "green" gasoline and electricity) could be a potent idea worldwide. Who wouldn't want the chance to be worth more, to have a more secure future, by installing CFLs, buying more fuel-efficient tires, driving a hybrid vehicle, and so on and so forth? While the wealth effect from smart energy management could taper off after a few years as all of the low-hanging fruit was picked, by then a lot of people might have prospered. One thing is certain: For countries such as the United States that are struggling to figure out how they are going to meet all of their future financial obligations, TGRs would seem to be well worth exploring.

A number of Wall Street leaders might be willing to accept the chairmanship of a blue-ribbon government commission that studied (but not to death) the feasibility of a national or international TGR system. One that comes to mind is the author of an important book whose title says it all: *Running on Empty*. The book's subtitle is *How the Republican and Democratic Parties Are Bankrupting Our Future and What Americans Can Do About It*.[10] As co-founder and chairman of the Blackstone Group, the chair of the Council on Foreign Relations, the former chairman of the New York Reserve Bank, and former President Nixon's international economic adviser, Pete Peterson would seem to be uniquely qualified to take Professor Feldstein's idea out for a spin in the new oil industry.

■ ■ ■

While TGRs would be designed for individuals, as Professor Feldstein has indicated, they could also be applied to commercial enterprises. Indeed, given that commercial and industrial customers consume roughly two-thirds of America's electricity, and that trucking and related enterprises consume a significant percentage of the diesel and gasoline burned in America, one would want to include them in a TGR system.

Incorporating commercial trucking into the system would serve to expand the use of both high- and low-tech ways for any commercial outfit to save on fuel the way UPS, the package delivery company, already does. High-tech, UPS uses computerized technology to minimize miles traveled. Low-tech, it tries to give drivers routes that require them to make right turns to the greatest extent possible. Why only right turns? Because in most places a vehicle can make a right turn before the traffic light has turned green if it has first stopped and its driver has checked to see if the coast is clear. Less time waiting for the light to change means less wasted fuel.

While the National Association of Manufacturers (NAM) and other groups have long been keen on reducing their members' power costs through such things as fluorescent lighting and variable speed drive motors, having written a pamphlet on the subject for NAM, I know from experience that small business owners are hesitant to spend on anything that doesn't have an immediate return. TGRs could help make such expenditures pay off more quickly.

To be sure, one probably would not want to treat a company the same as an individual under a TGR allotment system. Whereas a person could make money, it would seem to be better for a company to earn a tax credit.

■ ■ ■

In the planning for a TGR allotment system, special attention should be paid to the advantages Wall Street could offer. Indeed, Wall Street has the wherewithal to create a global system under which the new oil industry could become the new oil economy.

While every firm on Wall Street might in some way benefit from all this, there are some whose size, skill, and experience makes them natural choices to be put on the list of companies to watch. Goldman Sachs is one. Morgan Stanley is another. Merrill Lynch and Lehman are two more. Each already is a financial market leader in energy.

These are the final companies to make the watch list, a list that has ended up with 100 companies plus a couple of industries (wireless and defense) on it. Appropriately enough, they make it in the category of "Investment Bankers," alongside the energy industry's new investment bankers, ExxonMobil, Shell, and the like.

We have now come full circle. As usual, the more things change, the more they stay the same. The guys who have been in charge of the oil industry for more than 100 years—the big oil companies and the big investment banking firms on Wall Street—likely will still be in charge, although in the new oil industry they will be joined by other, equally heavy hitters from the biotech, automotive, and other industries.

Major oil companies may not want to change. But change, in the form of new technology, has started to be thrust upon them. So it has been at other times in the history of energy, times when demand began to exceed available supply and new thinking and new players were required to come up with new sources and new ways of consuming energy.

To be sure, conventional oil production—crude oil—will continue to be a vital part of the world's energy mix for years to come. But in the new oil industry that has started to take shape it will be one of a number of sectors that will need to both compete with and complement one another. It will be the job of government to come up with a strategy that does that, a strategy that hits the trifecta of energy security and environmental friendliness at a reasonable price. It will be investors' task to follow the new oil industry where technology and politics take it.

CHAPTER 8

The Complete List of 100 Companies to Watch

Why the Chevrolet Corvette Should Be the Symbol of the New Oil Industry

There are 100 companies, plus two overall businesses, on this list. They have been grouped in 15 categories that have been ranked in order of their potential significance in determining the future direction of the global oil industry. Where there is more than one company in a category, companies have been listed alphabetically.

CATEGORY 1: BIOBUTANOL TECHNOLOGY

DuPont (www.dupont.com)

Biobutanol has the potential to be one of the two most important game-changing new technologies. (The other is battery technology.) If this turns out to be the case, DuPont could ultimately become the company that makes one of the most important contributions to solving the world's oil problems.

Biobutanol is the biofuel even an oil company can love. For oil companies that embrace this biofuel, biobutanol could turn out to be the mother of all oil fields, one which, as long as there is garbage, will never run out and can never be nationalized by some pugnacious petro-ruler.

Biobutanol could be the perfect marriage of energy and agriculture—at least until an even better one may come along—with biotech serving as minister. But before DuPont can reap any glory, it must demonstrate that biobutanol can be produced cost-effectively. Even if biobutanol is shown to be cost-effective with first-generation biofuels such as sugar and corn, the extent of its long-term success will still depend on research in cellulosic ethanol (see the following section).

Like all other potential beneficiaries of the new oil industry, biobutanol and DuPont will have to successfully navigate the corridors of political power. Besides oil companies, opposition could come from proponents of plug-in hybrid vehicles who think the emphasis should not be on liquid fuel substitution but, rather, on liquid fuel elimination.

CATEGORY 2: ETHANOL AND BIODIESEL TECHNOLOGY

Ceres (www.ceres-inc.com)

Dyadic International (www.dyadic-group.com)

Genencor International (www.genencor.com)

Imperium Renewables (www.imperiumrenewables.com)

Iogen (www.iogen.ca)

Neste Oil (www.neste.com)

Novozymes (www.novozymes.com)

SunOpta (www.sunopta.com)

The real value of using biomass as transportation fuel lies in making use of feedstocks that currently go to waste, such as forest and agricultural residues and even household garbage.

Until waste products (and wild grasses) can be widely used, a country's dependency on using a food source to make ethanol will pose a potential threat to the supply and price of its food. Further, America's dependence on corn ethanol makes for a system that requires so much energy that the net energy benefit of the biofuel is small.

While corn ethanol is America's first-generation biofuel, so-called cellulosic ethanol will be its second. But first biotech companies must, among other things, develop better technology for breaking down the cellulose. Once this is accomplished, given that a biorefinery should be able to make biobutanol the same as cellulosic ethanol, the full value of biofuel should be achievable.

As with biotech generally, great biotech breakthroughs related to energy could come from any number of countries, companies, universities, and/or individuals. Two centuries ago Benjamin Franklin used then-modern technology to invent a stove that ended the energy crisis of the day—a firewood shortage. Who will be ethanol's corporate Ben Franklin? It could be one of the companies in this category; however, investors should remember that, in their new role as energy investment bankers, major oil companies, in partnership with universities and so on, could play a key role in the development of cellulosic ethanol—indeed, of all new energy technology.

CATEGORY 3: BATTERY TECHNOLOGY

A123 Systems (www.a123systems.com)

Altair Nanotechnologies (www.altairnano.com)

EEStor

Johnson Controls (www.johnsoncontrols.com)

Valence Technology (www.valence.com)

Other than biobutanol, no technological advancement may be more important to enabling the United States to hit the trifecta of reasonable energy prices, national security, and environmental friendliness than the development of batteries and battery-like devices for hybrid and all-electric (or nearly all-electric) vehicles.

Giving cars and trucks plug-in capability would significantly reduce the need for imported oil by shifting the system from a single source (oil) to multiple sources that include all of the fuel sources that make electricity.

It would enable cars and trucks to run cleaner while at the same time promoting the use of home-installed green power systems such as solar and wind. It should help eliminate that well-known medical condition known as "pain at the pump" by making transportation a more reasonably priced part of a person's monthly electric bill.

Plug-in vehicles will probably not only be more expensive, they also may not perform as hoped for due to their Achilles heel—the behavior of the people who drive them. But the fundamentals of plug-in hybrids with their lithium-ion batteries should propel them to market, though investors should never forget that when it comes to new technology, there's often something else waiting in the wings.

Indeed, what already may be waiting in the wings could be EEStor's ultracapacitors, battery-like devices that store huge amounts of electricity, enabling a car to perhaps travel some 300 miles on a single electric charging. In the long term, such a vehicle could profoundly change everything about energy.

CATEGORY 4: AUTOMOTIVE EFFICIENCY

Toyota (www.toyota.com)

Honda (www.honda.com)

Volkswagen (www.vw.com)

These three likely will be the "drivers" of a more efficiency-attuned global auto industry. The first two already have a reputation for efficiency that has served them well as gasoline prices have rocketed upward. Volkswagen could be on the cusp of a major revival as people rediscover VW's diesel and hybrid technology.

All three appear to have figured out what Detroit has yet to, namely, that everything goes with hybrid technology. Still, none are likely to be a Johnny-one-note, as illustrated by Honda's HCCI engine technology.

Ironically, as time goes on, automobile manufacturers could find themselves under attack by elements of the new oil industry's two other sectors—oil and oil substitutes—for making vehicles that use too *little* liquid fuel.

Might an auto company one day merge with an electric utility, biofuel company, or even an oil company? Only time will tell.

CATEGORY 5: INVESTMENT BANKERS

New

British Petroleum (www.bp.com)

Chevron (www.chevron.com)

ExxonMobil (www.exxonmobil.com)

Shell (www.shell.com)

Old

Goldman Sachs (www.gs.com)

Lehman (www.lehman.com)

JP Morgan (www.jpmorgan.com)

Merrill Lynch (www.ml.com)

Life ain't fair, the wise man said, and there may be no better example of this than the powerful positions the world's major oil companies likely will occupy in the new oil industry. Even as the world succeeds in reducing its dependency on oil through biofuels and greater efficiency, it likely will stay beholden to major oil companies.

Face it, thanks to all that money we've been giving them for years now, oil companies are swimming in cash. They've got enough money to pick and choose investments in whatever new area of energy looks good to them. To cite just one example: Chevron, through its technology ventures subsidiary, plans to collaborate with the University of California at Davis on technology for converting cellulosic biomass into transportation fuel.[1]

As Chevron and the others begin their transition to the far less oil-dependent world that could emerge within 5 to 10 years, they will continue to make a pretty penny by extracting every last drop of oil they can. Money begets money. Money reserves oil companies a seat at the table of policymakers who hopefully will guide the new oil industry so that it fires on all four cylinders.

As for the "old" energy investment bankers, Goldman, Lehman, Merrill, and Morgan have all demonstrated that they are adept at both financing and trading in energy. Whether or not they become the coordinators of a lucrative new financial market built on the principle of paying people to save energy (TGRs), the old investment bankers should continue to thrive in the new oil industry.

CATEGORY 6: COAL TECHNOLOGY

GreatPoint Energy (www.greatpointenergy.com)

Rentech (www.rentechinc.com)

Sasol (www.sasol.com)

Syntroleum (www.syntroleum.com)

So great is the U.S. military's concern about energy security that the Air Force hopes that in the future its jets will burn a different fuel, half of which is made from coal that has been turned into a liquid and refined into synthetic jet fuel.

So great is the Chinese government's concern about its energy security that it plans to build a number of big CTL (coal-to-liquid) facilities.

Thus is a new industry—liquid fuel from coal—born at the intersection of politics and science.

Sasol, Rentech, and Syntroleum could emerge as winners in a world where coal becomes a kind of everyman's fuel capable of compensating for future shortages of oil and natural gas. Sasol especially has bright global prospects with its related GTL (natural gas-to-liquids) technology.

Though a much smaller company, GreatPoint could have a bright future. Its technology could be key to using additional amounts of coal in ways that are more cost effective and less harmful to the environment. GreatPoint's "chemical cracking" approach requires less process steam/energy, a key cost factor.

CATEGORY 7: SYNTHETIC OIL AND LNG PROVIDERS

Arch (www.archcoal.com)

Canadian Natural Resources (www.cnrl.com)

CONSOL (www.consolenergy.com)

EnCana (www.encana.com)

Peabody (www.peabodyenergy.com)

Suncor (www.suncor.com)

Woodside Petroleum (www.woodside.com.au)

Some of them are coal companies. Others are tar sands companies. One is in LNG (liquefied natural gas). What they have in common is that they can provide a fuel source other than crude oil in a world where crude is getting harder and more expensive to find.

The coal guys (Arch, CONSOL, and Peabody) and the tar sands guys (Canadian Natural Resources, EnCana, and Suncor) should benefit from being politically secure energy sources. Among their respective individual attributes, EnCana is a leading promoter of carbon dioxide enhanced oil recovery (EOR), with a pipeline from North Dakota to fields in western Canada. As for Woodside, it should benefit from the world's growing need to utilize "stranded" natural gas reservoirs by liquefying the gas and then hauling it around the world by tanker ship.

Investors should remember that both coal and tars sands face stiff environmental opposition, though at this point it doesn't appear likely to get in the way, given the national security benefits of these unconventional fossil fuels. It boils down to: What price national security?

CATEGORY 8: BIOFUEL PRODUCTION

Aventine Renewable Energy (www.aventinerei.com)

Abengoa (www.abengoa.com)

Archer Daniels Midland (www.admworld.com)

Dynamotive Energy Systems (www.dynamotive.com)

Pacific Ethanol (www.pacificethanol.net)

VeraSun Energy (www.verasun.com)

The handwriting is already on the wall: ethanol made from corn is one day going to be supplanted by ethanol made from cellulosic sources such as wild grasses and waste products. But until that day comes, corn ethanol producers would appear to be in position to do well. All or some may continue to do well when cellulose arrives at center stage.

As the big boys on the block, ADM and Abengoa may do the best; however, only time will tell how well any of them do. Investors need to remember that in 2006 there basically were too many ethanol producers for the initial public offering (IPO) market to handle.

Still, estimates are that in 2012 corn ethanol may have grown into as much as a $45 to $60 billion a year market. That's not chicken feed. (No, wait—is corn used to feed chickens?)

Only time will tell whether Dynamotive has a bright future. It makes the list as a company working with biofuel for industrial boiler fuel and home heating oil, two other very important economic uses of oil. Adding it to the list serves to emphasize that curing a country's oil addiction means weaning a country off *all* of its oil uses.

CATEGORY 9: INFRASTRUCTURE PROVIDERS

ABB (www.abb.com)

AMCOL International (www.amcol.com)

Cheniere (www.cheniere.com)

Chicago Bridge & Iron (www.cbi.com)

Daewoo Shipbuilding (www.daewooshipbuilding.com)

Diamond Offshore Drilling (www.diamondoffshore.com)

ENSCO (www.enscous.com)

Fluor (www.fluor.com)

Foster Wheeler (www.fwc.com)

General Electric (www.ge.com)

GlobalSantaFe (www.globalsantafe.com)

Grant Prideco (www.grantprideco.com)

Halliburton (www.halliburton.com)

Hydril (www.hydril.com)

Hyundai Heavy Industries (www.english.hhi.co.kr)

Jacobs Engineering (www.jacobs.com)

McDermott (www.mcdermott.com)

Samsung Heavy Industries (www.shi.samsung.co.kr/)

Schlumberger (www.slb.com)

Shaw Group (www.shawgrp.com)

Smith International (www.smith.com)

Tetra Technologies (www.tatratec.com)

Todco (www.theoffshoredrillingcompany.com)

Transocean (www.deepwater.com)

Weatherford International (www.weatherford.com)

Infrastructure providers will be hard-pressed to keep up with demand for their services. They are going to be building the infrastructure for the new segments of the oil industry, such as biorefineries and LNG facilities, while at the same time tackling a task the possible enormity of which is only starting to be suspected, namely, the replacement of old energy infrastructure, some of it badly corroded.

Without infrastructure providers, every last drop of conventional energy, not just crude oil but also natural gas, will stay in the ground. None of the power plants that are going to be needed to satisfy an excruciatingly high rise in global electrical demand will get built. Neither will lots of other related infrastructure that's also critically needed, such as water treatment facilities.

Whenever a major hurricane impacts the Gulf of Mexico—which is where America's critical energy infrastructure increasingly will be found—infrastructure providers will have to make like a MASH unit in wartime. In the near term, unless the United States can quickly recover from whatever Mother Nature throws at it, the risk of war over energy will increase as anti-American petro-powers make like Dr. No with that aquarium of his that made little fish look like big ones. (Rent the movie.)

CATEGORY 10: TRANSPORTATION PROVIDERS

Burlington Northern (www.bnsf.com)

Canadian National (www.cn.ca)

Canadian Pacific (www.cpr.ca)

CSX (www.csx.com)

Frontline (www.frontline.bm)

Norfolk Southern (www.nscorp.com)

OMI Corporation (www.omicorp.com)

Overseas Shipholding (www.osg.com)

Teekay (www.teekay.com)

Union Pacific (www.up.com)

Somebody's got to move all that energy around. Whether it is oil, natural gas, or coal, in the coming days more of it will have to be transported over often longer distances in order to keep the global economy's wheels from coming off. Storage can only go so far, so the transportation providers' job will become increasingly critical.

Frontline, OMI, Overseas, and Teekay are tanker operators. Burlington Northern, Canadian National, Canadian Pacific, CSX, Norfolk Southern, and Union Pacific are railroads. Tanker operators especially would seem likely to have a thriving business in coming years. There's going to be all that liquefied natural gas to move around in addition to all that oil.

CATEGORY 11: OIL PRODUCERS

Apache (www.apachecorp.com)

Anadarko Petroleum (www.anadarko.com)

EOG Resources (www.eogresources.com)

Imperial Oil (www.imperialoil.ca)

Lukoil (www.lukoil.com)

Petrobras (www.petrobras.com)

Talisman Energy (www.talisman-energy.com)

As the saying goes, nothing lasts forever. These are some of the companies experts say have reserves which, because of their location, should have a reasonably long life at a time when the world is becoming increasingly dependent on its mature oil fields. (While the industry likes to call them *mature*, let's just call them what they really are—old.)

Some of these outfits are among the risk-taking independent oil and gas firms operating to a great extent in the potentially energy-rich Gulf of Mexico. Petrobras has its own offshore operations. Lukoil is in Russia, which is up there with Saudi Arabia in terms of being a global oil exporter. Lukoil's reserves rival those of ExxonMobil. Talisman and Imperial are two well-endowed Canadian energy firms. The latter is kind of a complete energy company with a wide range of energy reserves—not a bad position to be in, in a world where countries are constantly raising the value of fuel diversity.

One company that probably would make the list if it wasn't busy shooting itself in the foot is Mexico's Pemex. Actually, as a state-owned enterprise, Pemex isn't eligible. Still, it's worth mentioning Pemex as a cautionary tale of how the oil world could go downhill fast if, as some suspect, the major Middle Eastern oilfields have not been properly maintained over the last quarter century. While its biggest oil field is in an unnatural state of decline, Mexico still has good prospects in its area of the Gulf of Mexico, which bodes well for prospects in the U.S. area of the Gulf.

CATEGORY 12: ALTERNATIVE TRANSPORTATION PROVIDERS

Flexcar (www.flexcar.com)
Tesla Motors (www.teslamotors.com)
Zipcar (www.zipcar.com)
ZAP (www.zapworld.com)

Car-sharing companies like Flexcar and Zipcar represent an important element of what transportation may be tomorrow. The electrically powered vehicles from Tesla and ZAP also provide a forward look.

With car-sharing, it becomes easier *not* to own a car. Urban mobility is maintained by walking, public transportation, and, only when absolutely necessary, the automobile. Car-sharing further has the potential to popularize both hybrid and ultra-small vehicles. Indeed, it could become an important way to change people's thinking about what a car should offer in terms of fuel options and efficiency.

Tesla and ZAP are another way in which people's thinking may move beyond the notion that automotive efficiency is based on miles per gallon of gasoline. Thanks to plug-ins, electricity is going to become an important alternative transportation fuel. Tesla especially is a company to watch because, like a doctor is supposed to do no harm to his patient, a lot of motorists believe they should do no harm to the environment. A Tesla electric sports car helps accomplish that without—and this is crucial—sacrificing the performance the driver of a sports car naturally wants.

CATEGORY 13: CONSUMER INFORMATION PROVIDERS

Alternative Energy Store (www.home.altenergystore.com)

CalCars.org (www.calcars.org)

Google (www.google.com)

Home Depot (www.homedepot.com)

Lowe's (www.lowes.com)

Wireless Providers

In the future that could exist, people might get paid to save energy, not just on the road but in the home as well. Energy efficiency could become not only a way to eliminate much of the world's coming need for vast amounts of additional energy, but also a way to create wealth.

But whether the world ever utilizes a system such as tradeable gasoline rights (TGRs), the need to educate people about how they can reduce their personal energy consumption is likely to grow in coming years.

While many companies and web sites do this today, there is a need for bigger, more effective campaigns. The Alternative Energy Store represents a web model for showing people who might shy away from saving energy because it seems too complicated how easy it can be. Just as there are online communities for social interaction on a variety of subjects, this web site should be looked upon as an indication of how an online community might be constructed around the idea of saving energy. Were TGRs to become a reality, such a site could also serve as a quasi-financial site, offering rates of exchange for converting TGRs into money the way financial web sites offer rates of exchange on international currencies. Where should I take my leftover TGRs? Which bank, retailer, home mortgage lender, and so on is offering the best deal?

Meanwhile, by their sheer size, Home Depot and Lowe's could greatly expand people's understanding of home energy efficiency and the power of renewable energy sources such as the sun and the wind. They could provide this education in ways that enhance their core businesses. To be sure, both outfits already do a lot in this area, but especially if there was a TGR system in place, they might be able to create a tidal wave of home energy remodeling projects.

CalCars.org is in a position to be both a web site like the Alternative Energy Store and a hands-on company like Home Depot and Lowe's. Its mission is to make plug-in hybrid vehicles a reality as quickly as possible by educating the public on their importance and by demonstrating how today's non-plug-ins can be converted. In a world that should increasingly be all about hybrid technology, first non-plug-in and then plug-in, CalCars.org could see its mission grow and expand.

As for wireless providers, they might become the electronic backbone of a TGR system, enabling people to record how many TGRs they use when they fill up at a gas station and keeping track of the total number of TGRs a person has used and how many he or she has left in a given month. TGRs could become the way wireless providers sign up everyone who doesn't yet have a cell phone, while offering an additional revenue-generating service to existing customers—a win-win.

Wireless providers could get a run for their money from Google, the world's most dominant information provider. With its vast network, the company might on its own be able to create the infrastructure for a national or even global TGR system, in partnership perhaps with one or more of Wall Street's big boys.

CATEGORY 14: NONLIQUID FUEL PROVIDERS

Constellation Energy (www.constellation.com)

Exelon (www.exeloncorp.com)

Nanosolar (www.nanosolar.com)

NRG (www.nrgenergy.com)

PSEG (www.pseg.com)

Sharp (www.sharp.co.jp)

Suntech Power Holdings (www.suntech-power.com)

When plug-in hybrid vehicles sit in many people's driveways, at least some electric utilities and green power manufacturers could benefit from the nightly ritual of plugging in.

Obviously, if this happens, it won't be for at least a few more years. Still, it's worth noting that some utilities could be in position to benefit because they would get more productivity out of their coal and nuclear power plants, which generally must be kept running in the middle of the night when demand for power is quite low.

Solar power manufacturers generally are already faring well thanks to that other revolution, the one in stationary energy production and consumption. Any incremental increase they might see as a result of more people adding solar panels or roofing shingles to their homes is difficult to gauge. Still, the overall point here is that the more people merge in their minds their two energy universes—the one they occupy when they are moving and the one they occupy when they are standing still—the more likely they may want to make their own electricity and to do so in ways that don't pollute the environment. Solar power is the easiest such way. One's sun-supplied electricity could go directly into a plug-in vehicle or get sold back to one's local electric utility. Solar panels might even be fashioned into car roofs.

CATEGORY 15: DEFENSE COMPANIES

In a world that's addicted to foreign oil, where the United States spends roughly $2.70 per gallon to insure that its imported oil safely reaches America, Washington really has little choice but to almost literally throw money at defense companies.

One day, maybe 10 years from now, the new oil industry hopefully will have gone a long way toward curing the world's oil addiction. By then, hopefully, the world at least will be a recovering addict—and the category of "Defense Companies" will no longer be on this list.

Until then, however, defense companies should benefit from the need to prevent a disruption in the global flow of oil and, should one occur, from the need to reopen shipping lanes or do whatever else must be done to get the global economy back on its feet as quickly as possible.

Experts say no defense company stands out above the rest, which is why this category has no individual companies listed.

■ ■ ■

THE CHEVROLET CORVETTE—SYMBOL OF THE NEW OIL INDUSTRY

It is only fitting that on the last pages of this book, there should be a re-minder that, as much as the oil industry needs to change, the people charged to effect this change need to be ever mindful of Americans' time-tested love affair with their cars and trucks. Cars, mobility, the call of the open road—it is all part of who and what we are, of our psyche, our culture, our very understanding of what democracy means.

The Corvette does well enough in terms of miles per gallon of gas not to be considered a gas-guzzler. But you know what? With all of the effi-ciency technologies starting to be developed, even vehicles that have a reputation as gas-guzzlers may one day be gas-sippers.

Maybe the first step in licking America's addiction to imported oil should be to make it possible for people to keep driving their sports cars and SUVs without destroying the environment or taking out a bank loan. This should be possible through hybrids, HCCI, biofuel, and so on. Well-intended but misguided people should stop trying to get Americans to drive less and start enabling them to drive as much as they want or need to drive in a way that still meets the three goals of reasonable price, environmental friendliness, and energy security.

Raising gasoline taxes might have worked in the immediate aftermath of 9/11 but, generally speaking, too many Americans are under too much financial pressure in their everyday lives for any policy maker to think that raising the tax on one of life's simplest and (even with all those damn traf-fic jams) most rewarding pleasures will do anything but tick people off.

From a policy perspective, there's a case to be made that with all of the trouble the United States is having trying to export democracy, exporting America's cherished belief in the automobile is something that should be encouraged. It's the automobile as the ultimate *freedom* machine—an idea that ought to find fertile ground in China, India, and other still-developing countries where people are only just beginning to think of driving as their right.

To be sure, as part of this deal, America also should push harder for people to drive ultra-small cars in all the population-packed cities of the world. It should encourage people who don't really need to own a car to think in terms of car-sharing.

But by focusing on hybrid and other gas-saving technologies, as well as all the substitute motor fuels that burn cleaner and can come from domestic sources, it might one day be possible for even an SUV to be a recovering oil addict.

Nor should it stop there. People *want* to have as many creature comforts as they can in their homes. Most of these use electricity, which is why per-home power consumption has been steadily rising. Efficiency and green power must become things people do unthinkingly. There is no better way to motivate people to save energy and to switch to renewable energy sources than by making it pay—literally.

As unimaginable as TGRs may sound, the idea seems worth closer inspection by government and private industry. For a nation worried about how it is going to pay for its people's future health care, retirement benefits, and so on, TGRs conceivably might become a new way for its people to make and save money.

The future awaits.

2012 U.S. Biofuel Market Forecast

Biofuel	2012	2006
Corn Ethanol	$45–$60 billion	$6 billion
Cellulosic Ethanol	$1 billion	—
Biodiesel	$3–$4 billion	$200 million
Biobutanol	$1–$10 billion	—

Source: Michael Millikin, Green Car Congress

Summary: Biofuel production in the United States could experience up to a tenfold increase between 2007 and 2012. Much of this increase will result from government mandates; however, the market for the only established biofuel as of 2006, corn ethanol, could experience additional growth due to overall market conditions. While cellulosic ethanol (considered by many experts to be the next generation of ethanol production) and biodiesel will experience significant gains in production, the real wild card will be biobutanol, which could come out of nowhere starting around 2009 or 2010, and ultimately dethrone corn ethanol as the principal liquid substitute for gasoline that is made from biomass, sometime after 2015 or so—or sooner, depending on policy decisions in Washington. Biodiesel, it should be noted, will have a far bigger market outside the United States, especially in Europe.

Primer on Why Gasoline's True Cost in 2006 Was More than $11 a Gallon

While Americans have been paying upwards of $3 a gallon and more at the pump, pump prices represent only a fraction of gasoline's true cost. There are many hidden costs, beginning with the roughly $2.70 per gallon in defense expenditures that Americans indirectly pay through taxes and so on to insure that the oil the United States imports safely reaches its shores.

Defense expenditures are but one of gasoline's hidden costs. In 2006 a number of interconnected economic dampeners such as lost jobs and lower payroll taxes that were the result of America's imported oil addiction wound up making the true cost of gasoline (pump price plus defense expenditures plus economic dampeners) more than $11 a gallon, according to the man who is pioneering this sort of economic assessment.

Milton Copulos's work is very likely to hit the big media's radar screens before long. When it does, the economic case for the new oil industry will be in plain view. Investments in substitute fuels and efficiency that may have seemed too expensive will be viewed as financial bargains.

This document represents a valuable primer in the hows and whys of the true cost of America's oil addiction.

Testimony of Milton R. Copulos
President, National Defense Council Foundation
before the Senate Foreign Relations Committee
March 30, 2006

My name is Milton R. Copulos, and I am president of the National Defense Council Foundation.

I would like to thank Chairman Lugar for giving me the opportunity to speak with the Committee today and I would also like to commend him for his leadership addressing our nation's perilous energy dependence.

A Headlong Rush into Disaster

America is rushing headlong into disaster. What is worse, however, is that it is a disaster of our own design.

More than three decades have passed since the 1973 Arab Oil Embargo first alerted the nation to its growing oil import vulnerability. Yet, despite this warning, we are now importing more than twice as much oil in absolute terms than we did in 1973, and the proportion of our oil supplies accounted for by imports is nearly double what it was then. What makes this dependence even more dangerous than it was three decades ago is the fact that the global market has become a far more competitive place with the emerging economies of China, India and Eastern Europe creating burgeoning demand for increasingly scarce resources.

Indeed, over the past decade the Chinese economy has grown at a frenetic pace, officially estimated at 9.2 percent in 2005. India's growth rate for that year was 7.1 percent. In Eastern Europe, Belarus grew at 7.8 percent, the Czech Republic at 4.6 percent and the Ukraine at 4.4 percent. This compares with 3.5 percent for the United States, 2.1 percent for Japan and 1.7 percent for the European Union.

As a result of this explosive growth, oil consumption in the developing countries is expected to increase at a rate of 3 percent annually over the next two decades. But even this figure may severely understate the problem. Indeed, China alone has accounted for 40 percent of the total increase in world oil consumption over the past several years. Moreover China plans to add 120 million vehicles to its automobile fleet over the next decade, ultimately requiring 11.7 million barrels per day of new crude oil supplies. India, too, is expected to continue to require increasingly large amounts of oil with a projected increase of 28 percent over just the next five years.

Even conservative estimates suggest that nearly 30 million barrels per day of new oil supplies will be required by the year 2025 just to service the developing world's requirements. When Europe and the Americas are included the requirement is closer to 40 million barrels per day. It is doubtful that new supplies sufficient to meet this skyrocketing demand will be found from conventional sources.

Uncertain Suppliers

Nor is it just the potential physical shortfall of resources that is a source of concern. An even greater concern lies in the instability of U.S. sources of oil imports.

The top six sources of U.S. oil imports, Canada, Mexico, Saudi Arabia, Venezuela, Nigeria and Iraq, account for 65.1 percent of all foreign crude reaching our shores and 38.9 percent of total domestic consumption. Of these, four, Saudi Arabia, Venezuela, Nigeria, and Iraq, provide 38.2 percent of oil imports and 22.6 percent of total consumption. For a variety of reasons, none of the four I just mentioned can be considered a reliable source of supply.

Venezuela's President Hugo Chavez is a vocal opponent of the United States who has twice threatened to cut off oil shipments to the U.S.

Nigeria's production has been repeatedly disrupted by civil unrest, and some 135,000 barrels of oil per day are lost to theft.

Last month, a terrorist attack on the massive Saudi oil processing facility at Abqaiq was barely thwarted, but not before two of the terrorist's explosive-laden cars were detonated. Moreover, this was not the only instance of an attempt to disrupt the flow of Saudi oil. In the summer of 2002, Saudi Interior Ministry forces blocked an al-Qaeda plot to attack and cripple the loading dock at Ras Tanura which handles 10 percent of the world's oil supplies.

Attacks on oil facilities in Iraq are a frequent occurrence.

Nor are the attacks on U.S. oil supplies a coincidence. In December of 2004, al-Qaeda issued a fatwa that said in part:

> We call on the mujahideen in the Arabian Peninsula to unify their ranks and target the oil supplies that do not serve the Islamic nation but the enemies of this nation.

The fatwa went on to declare:

> Be active and prevent them from getting hold of our oil and concentrate on it particularly in Iraq and the Gulf.

Clearly, given the instability that characterizes four of our top six sources of oil, the question is not whether we will experience a supply disruption, but rather when. The disruption could occur as a consequence of a terrorist act, or could result from a politically motivated embargo. In the end, it doesn't really matter why a disruption occurs, because the consequences would be identical, and severe.

The Consequences of Disruption

The supply disruptions of the 1970s cost the U.S. economy between $2.3 trillion and $2.5 trillion. Today, such an event could carry a price tag as high as $8 trillion—a figure equal to 62.5 percent of our annual GDP or nearly $27,000 for every man, woman and child living in America.

But there is more cause for concern over such an event than just the economic toll. A supply disruption of significant magnitude, such as would occur should Saudi supplies be interdicted, would also dramatically undermine the nation's ability to defend itself.

Oil has long been a vital military commodity, but today has taken on even more critical importance. Several examples illustrate this point:

- A contemporary U.S. Army Heavy Division uses more than twice as much oil on a daily basis as an entire World War II field army.
- The roughly 582,000 troops dispatched to the Persian Gulf used more than twice as much oil on a daily basis as the entire 2-million-man Allied Expeditionary Force that liberated Europe in World War II.
- In Operation Iraqi Freedom, the oil requirement for our armed forces was 20 percent higher than in the first Gulf War, Operation

Desert Storm, and now amounts to one barrel of refined petroleum products per day for each deployed service member.

Moreover, the military's oil requirements will be even higher in the future.

Therefore, a shortage of global oil supplies not only holds the potential to devastate our economy, but could hamstring our armed forces as well.

The Hidden Cost of Imported Oil

While it is broadly acknowledged that our undue dependence on imported oil would pose a threat to the nation's economic and military security in the event of a supply disruption, less well understood is the enormous economic toll that dependence takes on a daily basis.

The principal reason why we are not fully aware of the true economic cost of our import dependence is that it largely takes the form of what economists call "externalities," that is, costs or benefits caused by production or consumption of a specific item, but not reflected in its pricing. It is important to understand that even though external costs or benefits may not be reflected in the price of an item, they nonetheless are real.

In October of 2003, my organization, The National Defense Council Foundation, issued "America's Achilles Heel: The Hidden Costs of Imported Oil," a comprehensive analysis of the external costs of imported oil. The study entailed the review of literally hundreds of thousands of pages of documents, including the entire order of battle of America's armed forces and more than a year of effort. Its conclusions divided the externalities into three basic categories: Direct and Indirect Economic Costs, Oil Supply Disruption Impacts and Military Expenditures.

Taken together, these costs totaled $304.9 billion annually, the equivalent of adding $3.68 to the price of a gallon of gasoline imported from the Persian Gulf.

As high as these costs were, however, they were based on a crude oil refiner acquisition cost of $26.92. Today, crude oil prices are hovering around $60 per barrel and could easily increase significantly. Indeed, whereas in 2003 we spent around $99 billion to purchase foreign crude oil and refined petroleum products, in 2005 we spent more than $251 billion, and this year we will spend at least $320 billion.

But skyrocketing crude oil prices were not the only factor affecting oil-related externalities. Defense expenditures also changed.

In 2003, our armed forces allocated $49.1 billion annually to maintaining the capability to assure the flow of oil from the Persian Gulf.

I should note that expenditures for this purpose are not new. Indeed, last year marked the 60th anniversary of the historic meeting between Saudi monarch King Abdul Aziz and U.S. President Franklin Roosevelt where he first committed our nation to assuring the flow of Persian Gulf oil—a promise that has been reaffirmed by every succeeding President, without regard to party.

In 1983 the implicit promise to protect Persian Gulf oil supplies became an explicit element of U.S. military doctrine with the creation of the United States Central Command, CENTCOM. CENTCOM's official history makes this clear stating in part:

> Today's command evolved as a practical solution to the problem of projecting U.S. military power to the Gulf region from halfway around the world.

I am stressing the long-standing nature of our commitment to the Gulf to underscore the fact that our estimates of military expenditures there are not intended as a criticism. Quite the opposite, in fact. Without oil our economy could not function, and therefore protecting our sources of oil is a legitimate defense mission, and the current military operation in Iraq is part of that mission.

To date, supplemental appropriations for the Iraq War come to more than $251 billion, or an average of $83.7 billion per year. As a result, when other costs are included, the total military expenditures related to oil now total $132.7 billion annually.

So, where does that leave us?

In 2003, as noted, we estimated that the "hidden cost" of imported oil totaled $304.9 billion. When we revisited the external costs, taking into account the higher prices for crude oil and increased defense expenditures we found that the "hidden cost" had skyrocketed to $779.5 billion in 2005. That would be equivalent to adding $4.10 to the price of a gallon of gasoline if amortized over the total volume of imports. For Persian Gulf imports, because of the enormous military costs associated with the region, the "hidden cost" was equal to adding $7.41 cents to the price of a gallon of gasoline. When the nominal cost is combined with this figure it yields a "true" cost of $9.53 per gallon, but that is just the start.

Because the price of crude oil is expected to remain in the $60 range this year, expenditures for imports are expected to be at least $320 billion this year. That amounts to an increase of $70 billion in spending for foreign oil in just one year. That increase would raise the total import premium or "hidden cost" to $825.1 billion, or almost twice the President's $419.3 billion defense budget request for fiscal year 2006. If all costs are amortized over the total volume of imports, that would be equivalent to adding $5.04 to the price of a gallon of gasoline. For Persian Gulf imports, the premium would be $8.35. This would bring the "real" price of a gallon of gasoline refined from Persian Gulf oil to $10.86. At these prices the "real" cost of filling up a family sedan is $217.20, and filling up a large SUV $325.80.

But, can anything be done about this enormous drain on our economy? The answer to that question is yes.

Solving The Problem

The simple truth is that we do not suffer from a lack of energy resources. Rather, what we suffer from is a lack of the political will and public consensus to use them.

As Pogo said, "We have met the enemy and they is us."

What then can we do?

The first step is to recognize that we face a twofold problem. The first part entails assuring adequate fuel supplies for the 220 million privately owned vehicles on the road today. These vehicles have an average lifespan of 16.8 years and the average age of our vehicle fleet is 8.5 years. Therefore we will require conventional fuels or their analogs for at least a decade, even if every new vehicle produced from this day forth runs on some alternative.

The second part of the problem is how to effect a transition to alternatives to conventional petroleum. This transition will take much longer than a decade—perhaps a generation or more—but the longer we delay beginning to make the change, the longer it will take to accomplish.

In the near term, say the next five to ten years, we essentially have two options. First, to make the greatest possible use of our readily accessible conventional domestic resources, particularly the oil and natural gas that lie off our shores. We should also consider using some of our

1,430 trillion cubic feet of domestic gas reserves as a feedstock for motor fuels produced through the Fischer-Tropsch process. Indeed, we currently have 104 trillion cubic feet of so-called "stranded" natural gas in Alaska and a pipeline with some 1.1 million barrels per day of excess capacity. Stranded gas could be converted into clean burning motor fuel and transported in the existing pipeline to the lower 48 states.

We can also expand our use of renewable fuels such as alcohol and biodiesel. A concerted program to make full use of them could significantly add to our motor fuel stocks within the stated time frame.

We should also encourage the acquisition of advanced vehicle technologies such as flex-fuel vehicles, hybrids and plug-in hybrids and vehicles that use propane or natural gas. At the same time, we should encourage the installation of biodiesel and E85 pumps in our nation's filling stations so that the infrastructure for alternative fuels can keep pace with the growth of the alternative fuel vehicle fleet.

Another point is to make sure that we do not forget to address non-transportation petroleum consumption. The fact that two-thirds of our petroleum is consumed in the transportation sector means that one-third is not. The opportunities to reduce oil consumption from non-transportation are greater than you might expect.

Take residential energy use for example. Roughly 12 percent of distillate use goes to home heating, most of it imported from the Middle East. Yet, there are alternatives readily available that could totally eliminate this use, and at the same time save consumers money. For instance, a developer in Moline, Illinois, is currently building homes that are between 85 percent and 90 percent energy efficient, and meet their heating and cooling requirements with geothermal energy. More important, these homes are being sold for 20 percent less than conventional housing sold in the same area. So consumers are not only saving energy, they are saving enormous amounts of money.

There is another commercial process that converts waste wood into a zero-sulfur industrial boiler fuel. Our Clean Forests program that removes deadwood and debris from national forests to prevent fires is generating an enormous amount of such waste wood, and that is just the tip of the iceberg. Oak Ridge National Laboratory estimates that a total of 1.366 billion tons of biomass is available for energy production each year. Utilizing this process, it could be turned into 5.6 million barrels of oil per day, or close to 27 percent of our total domestic requirements.

These, of course, are just two examples. Many more exist. The important consideration is that we have a wealth of options that could help in the near to intermediate term if we would only make use of them. To do this, however, we must have leadership.

In this regard, I should note that Chairman Lugar and his colleagues Senators Chaffee, Coleman, Nelson, and Obama deserve particular praise for their sponsorship of S.2025, the Vehicle and Fuel Choices for American Security Act, which is based on the Energy Security Blueprint of the Set America Free Coalition, of which I was a founding member. It is focused on reducing our dependence on foreign oil, not by compromising the American way of life, but by encouraging fuel choice, utilization of the vast array of America's domestic energy resources and accelerated deployment of advanced vehicle technologies. It is clear that this sort of bipartisan effort is exactly the kind of action that is required if we are to make any progress on this critical issue.

In the longer term, there are other domestic energy resources that can be brought into play. We have between 500 billion and 1.1 trillion barrels of oil contained in our huge oil shale resources. We have 496.1 billion tons of demonstrated coal reserves—27 percent of the world total. We also have 320,222 trillion cubic feet of natural gas in the form of methane hydrates. This is equivalent to 51.1 trillion barrels of oil. Indeed one onshore deposit in Alaska alone contains 519 trillion cubic feet of natural gas. That is equal to 82.9 billion barrels of oil.

We also have 4.85 billion pounds of uranium reserves. Harnessing this vital resource to provide electricity for our cities, towns and farms is only common sense. Moreover, it could serve to reduce the need to use natural gas for electricity generation, preserving it for higher uses.

There is one final point I want to make sure is not forgotten. Some portion of every dollar we spend on imported oil finds its way into the hands of individuals who wish to do us harm. The simple truth is that international terrorism stands on two financial pillars: oil and the drug trade. To the extent that we reduce the revenues generated by either of these activities, we hinder the ability of terrorists to operate.

To conclude, while our nation is in dire peril due to its excessive dependence on imported oil, the situation is far from hopeless. We have the resources necessary to provide our nation's energy needs if we can only find the political will to do so.

Valuable Energy News Web Sites

GREEN CAR CONGRESS

"Energy, Technologies, Issues and Policies for Sustainability," www.green congress.com

This is without a doubt the most thought-provoking Internet news web site, providing insights into a broad range of new energy technologies and the companies behind them. While its stories have first appeared elsewhere, Green Car Congress packages them in a way that captures the importance of the technological development at the heart of the matter. This web site has an amazingly informed group of individuals whose comments on each story often read like pages from an engineering text book. Another valuable feature is the site's search engine, which is far superior to many others in this area.

HYBRIDCARS.COM

www.hybridcars.com

As the name suggests, this site covers hybrid technology and the companies developing it. The site provides useful, actionable information for sophisticated and unsophisticated investors alike. The strength of this site lies in its backgrounders—articles that describe the ins and outs of hybrid technology and how it is being used in different ways by automotive manufacturers. There is a strong consumer component to the site for anyone thinking about buying a hybrid. What comes across is an attempt to be accurate and complete in information about hybrids.

ENERGY BULLETIN

www.energybulletin.net

It's easy to write this site off as so much ranting by deeply committed advocates of the "peak oil" theory. But while there is quite a bit of that in the stories referenced in the left-hand column, the right-hand column represents a valuable tool for investors to organize the most important energy news of the day in easy-to-understand categories. In every package of stories there are generally four or more just-published articles excerpted and with links to the original article. Among frequently appearing categories: Geopolitics, Climate, Food and Agriculture, Politics and Economics, Transport, Oil Industry, Renewables, Biofuels, Solar, and, of course Peak Oil. One quibble: The search engine could be better.

321ENERGY

www.321energy.com

This is a good web site for staying current with geopolitical developments around the world. The focus is heavily on fossil fuels. Headlines link back to the source, such as an Associated Press story about "Oil Firms Pressured by Russia," and a related story from Moscownews.com whose headline was "U.S. Tells Russia to Respect 'Rule of Law' in Oil Project Conflict." Admittedly, some stories are of limited value for an American investor, such as the one that was headlined "Can Nigerian Cars Survive on Ethanol?" Still, you get a clear sense that oil is indeed a global industry, and that the geopolitics of energy is all-important.

CLEAN EDGE—THE CLEAN-TECH MARKET AUTHORITY

"Helping Investors, Industry, and Society Understand and Profit from Clean Technology," www.cleanedge.com

As its boilerplate suggests, one of the selling points of this site is the economic research it presents. A lot of good financial information can be found at this address. What's also valuable about this site is one gets information about the revolution in stationary power sources—in particular, about solar and wind power. The dedicated energy investor will learn about upcoming conferences on topics like "Future Fuels" and "Investing in Clean Energy." A tip-off that this site is worth a regular look-see is its roster of sponsors, led by the energy venture capital firm I admire, Nth Power.

■ ■ ■

Of course there also are a number of energy blogs, although for my money, Green Car Congress's community of contributors probably offers the most interesting commentary on events. Others that investors may want to check out include The Energy Blog (http://thefraserdomain.typepad.com/), Cleantech blog (www.cleantechblog.com), Cleantech Investing (www.cleantechvc.blogspot.com), Biodiesel Blog (www.biodieselblog.com), and The Oil Drum (www.theoildrum.com).

Glossary

barrel of oil Although oil isn't transported in barrels, it is generally talked about in terms of barrels. It's worth remembering that a barrel contains 42 gallons of crude oil.

biobutanol A biofuel that one day may be made from almost anything that grows, including garbage, and mixed with gasoline to make a cleaner-burning fuel.

biodiesel A biofuel made for diesel-powered vehicles that also enables cleaner running; it is made from edible oils such as palm and soy.

Cantarell The big Mexican oil field that appears to be in a rapid state of decline and which may be a canary in the coal mine in terms of trouble for other mature oil fields.

carbon footprint The term given to the amount of carbon dioxide a person is responsible for generating through his or her everyday activities.

carbon sequestration The process by which carbon dioxide is buried underground to prevent it from building up in the atmosphere.

car-sharing An alternative to owning a car, best suited for urban living, where club members reserve a car to drive whenever they want.

cellulosic ethanol Ethanol made from the hard, woody parts of plant matter, a plentiful biomass resource.

charge depleting Refers to how the battery of a plug-in hybrid vehicle gets drained through use until the vehicle needs to be plugged in to be recharged.

charge sustaining   Refers to how a battery in a non-plug-in hybrid vehicle essentially recharges itself when the driver steps on the brakes.

Corvette   My personal choice for symbol of the new oil industry because of the image it conjures up of having fun behind the wheel—a cultural norm that mustn't be forgotten.

choke points   A reference to the two narrow shipping channels, susceptible to terrorists and unfriendly nationalists, through which much of the world's oil must travel.

commuter car   A term used to describe ultra-small cars that are extremely fuel-efficient that may become a common sight on city streets.

consumer information provider   Companies like Home Depot, and web sites like CalCars.org, which have the potential to popularize energy efficiency.

continuously variable transmission   An automotive engine technology that improves a vehicle's fuel efficiency.

conventional oil production   A term used to describe how crude oil is traditionally brought to the surface from wells under the ground. This book includes in this category wells drilled deep beneath the ocean floor.

crude oil   The liquid hydrocarbon source, as opposed to solid sources: coal, tar sands, and oil shale.

compact fluorescent lightbulb Super energy-efficient and long-lasting lighting source, it takes the place of a regular incandescent lightbulb.

CTL   Short for coal-to-liquids, a process by which coal, a solid fossil fuel, is turned into synthetic oil.

cylinder shutdown   An engine technology that improves fuel efficiency through sensing when a vehicle does not need all of its engine power.

deepwater drilling   A term that refers to oil exploration deep out in the ocean, such as in the Gulf of Mexico, where wells are drilled to depths of several thousand feet.

depletion rate   The calculated rate at which the oil or natural gas in a well is used up. These things are approximations; approximating correctly is critical to knowing how much oil remains.

drawing from the past A phrase oilmen use to describe how the current rate at which oil is being discovered is insufficient to replace what's being used at the current rate of consumption.

E85 The shorthand name for a liquid transportation fuel that is a blend of 85 percent ethanol to 15 percent gasoline.

Efficiency As used in this book, the term refers to the multitude of technologies, materials, and so on that enable a vehicle to improve its miles-per-gallon gasoline consumption; it refers generally to the more proficient consumption of energy.

EIA The U.S. Energy Information Administration, a key forecaster of future energy demand.

energy security Closely linked to national security, this term refers to need of a country for domestic or otherwise politically safe energy sources.

enhanced oil recovery (EOR) Refers to methods of coaxing out of the ground, primarily through gas injection, oil that doesn't naturally come to the surface.

enzyme pretreatment Refers to an important step in the processing of cellulosic ethanol into biofuel.

ethanol Made from grains or cellulose, this biofuel is blended with gasoline to make a cleaner-burning motor fuel.

everyman's fuel Refers to how coal is becoming more and more the go-to hydrocarbon source because of energy security and strains on the supply of crude oil and natural gas.

extreme commuter Those workers who drive 90 minutes or more, each way, to get to and from work; in future, whether by choice or necessity, their number are likely to grow.

first-generation biofuel A loose technical term often used to describe corn ethanol, currently America's principal biofuel.

Fischer-Tropsch Name of the technology, invented decades ago, that converts coal and so on into liquid hydrocarbons.

food versus fuel A term used to describe the problem of trying to meet demand/quotas for ethanol by growing corn and other food crops; refers to fear of diversion of too much farmland away from growing food.

Franklin stove   In the eighteenth century energy crisis America faced—a firewood shortage—Benjamin Franklin used then-new technology to invent this efficient solution to the problem.

freedom machine   The term this book uses to emphasize the power of the automobile in people's lives; captures the notion that the car is seen culturally as a kind of democratic right.

flex-fuel vehicles   Cars and trucks that can run on E85, the blend of 85 percent ethanol to 15 percent gasoline.

fuel-cell vehicles   Electrically powered vehicles that, sometime in the future, are counted on by some to burn cleaner and eliminate the need for gasoline, thanks to the use of hydrogen fuel made by a fuel cell.

fuel diversity   A term that describes the strategy for enhancing national security by utilizing a wide variety of fuel sources rather than relying on a single source such as oil.

geothermal power   A renewable energy system that utilizes the constant temperature of the earth to cool or heat a building.

Ghawar   Saudi Arabia's main oil field, which some fear may not have as much oil as the Saudi government maintains.

GTL   Short for gas-to-liquids, a process for liquefying natural gas (see CTL).

Golden Triangle   As used in the context of energy, refers to areas of ocean off the coasts of United States, Brazil, and West Africa that contain ample amounts of oil and natural gas; often thought of as the new frontier of oil and gas exploration and production.

HCCI   An automobile engine efficiency technology.

hidden cost of oil   A term used to describe the unseen costs of gasoline due to America's addiction to imported oil; includes expense of militarily defending shipping lanes and Middle East oil fields.

horizontal drilling   A key technology for extracting more oil from a well than what can be pulled out just by drilling straight down (vertical drilling).

hybrids   A word used generally to describe vehicles that have hybrid engines that can run on either electricity or gasoline.

infrastructure provider Any of a wide variety of engineering and construction companies that will be pressed to build the foundations of the new energy industry, such as biorefineries, while fixing the world's aging existing energy infrastructure.

kilowatt gasoline A term coined by this writer to describe use of electricity as a nonliquid transportation fuel that gets pumped into a plug-in vehicle's electric tank.

IEA Short for International Energy Agency, the influential European-based forecaster of long-term energy trends; not to be confused with EIA, the U.S. government forecasting unit.

lithium-ion batteries A type of more powerful battery being developed for plug-in hybrid vehicles.

LNG Short for liquefied natural gas, this term is used to describe a coming global industry where gas is cooled (liquefied) in order to ship it via tanker the way oil is; a way for tapping natural gas that is "stranded" in that it is not near an existing pipeline.

mobile energy A term used to describe energy production and consumption dedicated to things that move such as cars, trucks, and airplanes.

negaoil Just as there is oil, there can be negaoil, which is oil not used thanks to efficiency improvements (see *negawatts*).

negawatts A term coined by a leading energy efficiency expert to describe the quantity of electricity saved (i.e., not used) as a result of efficiency and conservation.

net metering Refers to consumers' ability to sell back to their local utility the power they generate themselves on-site, often by installing solar panels or roofing shingles; also known as *reverse metering*, it usually results in consumers receiving a credit on their monthly utility bill.

new oil industry A term coined by this author to encompass how the oil industry is changing with the development of liquid fuels that can substitute for gasoline plus technologies that cut down on the amount of liquid fuel required (see *negaoil*).

NExBTL A word coined by the company (Neste Oil) working on this advanced biofuel for diesel-powered vehicles; short for "next biomass to liquids."

nonliquid substitute fuel   A term used to differentiate between fuels that can substitute for gasoline made from crude oil (see *kilowatt gasoline*).

oil shale   One of the solid fossil fuels, basically rock-containing hydrocarbons; has the political attraction of being an energy source "made in the USA."

oil shock   A term that describes the effects of a sudden cutoff of the global flow of oil, such effects including shortages and prices spikes.

oil traders   Those guys you see on TV in colorful jackets frantically gesturing in something that looks like a trading pit; they are on the front lines of the minute-by-minute calculation of the price of oil in the spot market.

Orinoco Belt   That area of Venezuela containing a vast quantity of oil in the form of tar sands; seen as an increasingly important source of global hydrocarbons.

oxygenate   A process by which, through the blending of a clean-burning fuel such as ethanol, gasoline produces less harmful emissions.

peak oil   A term referring to the time when oil production reaches its physical limit and starts to decline, maybe rapidly. Exactly when peak oil will occur is the source of continuous debate within the oil industry.

PHEV40   A term that describes a plug-in hybrid electric vehicle that can run 40 miles solely on electricity, a range presently considered a sort of holy grail.

plug-ins   A term commonly used to describe a plug-in hybrid electric vehicle, which is a vehicle that can run on electricity from a battery that gets charged (fueled) through the simple and economical step of plugging it into an ordinary wall outlet.

rational fear   A term used in this book to underscore how people's emotions factor into the price of oil and how price levels that might not seem justified based on market fundamentals nevertheless can be topped.

regenerative braking   Refers to how electricity gets generated through heat capture when the vehicle's brakes are applied; this electricity gets used as fuel in a hybrid vehicle.

reserve base   A term that expresses the best estimates of how much oil or other resources a company, country, or the world has.

rig intensity   Refers to the number of wells required to produce a certain amount of oil or natural gas; can be an indication of how much oil/natural gas may remain at a given location.

right to drive   Not all of Americans' rights are outlined in the Bill of Rights; another, unwritten right, is the right to drive.

rolling over   A term that describes when the output from a mature oil field suddenly and precipitously begins to decline.

Saudi Arabia of coal   An expression used to emphasize the fact that, just like Saudi Arabia has a great deal of oil, the United States has a great deal of coal.

second-generation biofuel   Refers to substitute liquid fuels made from biomass that are technologically more advanced than corn ethanol—in particular, cellulosic ethanol and biobutanol.

shock absorbers   A term used in this book to describe investments that should hold their own in the event of an oil price shock.

solar panels and roofing shingles   The two most common ways to tap the renewable power of the sun to make electricity. Panels have been around awhile but shingles are relatively new and provide a less obtrusive way for homeowners to install a solar-electric system on top of their house.

solid fossil fuel   Refers to the fossil fuel energy sources naturally in solid form: coal, tar sands, and oil shale.

sour oil   Oil that contains more sulfur than *sweet oil* and, hence, is less desirable for being refined into gasoline and other products.

spot prices   In energy, the market prices of oil and other energy sources as set by oil traders on a minute-by-minute basis.

stationary energy   Refers to energy used outside of transportation, such as at the office and around the house (see *mobile energy*).

stranded natural gas   Reservoirs of natural gas not easily brought to market because they aren't near pipelines, and so on; liquefying the gas makes it more marketable (see *LNG*)

storage   Important but, in this author's opinion, overemphasized measure of how much energy the world has available. Storage is strictly a short-term measurement that doesn't reflect the world's preparedness for multiyear trends that will strain available energy supplies.

suboptimal farmland   Less-than-desirable farmland on which wild grasses could be grown for ethanol, thereby limiting the potential for a food versus fuel situation.

substitute liquid fuel   Any of the many liquids that can be an alternative for gasoline made from crude oil. The term encompasses both fuels made from biomass and those made from hydrocarbon sources other than crude oil.

sustainability   In the eyes of Wall Street, an increasingly desirable characteristic for a corporation to have; refers to products and operating procedures designed not to cause environmental problems nor use up the world's limited supply of fossil fuel.

sweet oil   Opposite of *sour oil*; a reference to that oil's low sulfur content, which makes it desirable for refining, in part because it produces more gasoline per barrel.

switchgrass   A wild grass that would make a good source for cellulosic ethanol; it was mentioned by President Bush in his 2006 State of the Union address.

synthetic oil   A general term that describes oil made from hydrocarbon sources other than crude oil—coal, tar sands, oil shale, and natural gas.

tar sands   Thick, sticky, sandy ground found in abundance in Canada and Venezuela containing very heavy oil that can be extracted through heating; a new—and expensive—frontier of oil production (see also *Orinoco Belt*).

thermal runaway   A serious problem associated with lithium-ion batteries. Significant progress reportedly is being made on solving this problem, which will be a major milestone in advancing battery technology for plug-in hybrids.

TGRs   A shorthand way of describing a system of tradable gasoline rights, which this book argues might be a way of enhancing energy efficiency across the board, basically by paying people to not use energy.

"Thar she blows!"   A phrase that brings to mind how the oil industry first underwent a major transformation back in the nineteenth century when demand for whale oil led to a severe supply shortage that resulted in people employing new technology to come up with new sources of oil.

transportation provider   A term used in this book to describe generally the all-important moving infrastructure of the new oil industry—in particular, oil tankers and railroads.

two-way potential   A term used in this book to describe how some investments could be useful both as a defensive hedge against a global oil shock and as potential beneficiaries of the changes taking place in the oil industry.

ultracapacitors   Battery-like devices capable of storing large amounts of electricity; they may be an improvement on lithium-ion batteries.

ultra-small car   Also known as the commuter car, it may have bright prospects in and around major cities as a way to simultaneously reduce gasoline consumption and traffic congestion.

unconventional fossil fuel   A broadly used term, which the book uses interchangeably with the term *solid fossil fuel,* to describe sources of hydrocarbon other than crude oil.

Notes

CHAPTER 1 The New Oil Industry

1. Paul Adams, "Mixed Signals Give Economists Pause," *Baltimore Sun*, April 25, 2006, http://www.baltimoresun.com.
2. The statement reportedly was made by Andris Kenteris, described in a September 17, 2006, article by Peter Capella of Agence France-Presse as "one of the people responsible for drawing up the European Union's new energy strategy."
3. "Strong Growth in World Energy Demand is Projected Through 2030," Energy Information Administration press release, June 20, 2006, http://www/eia.doe.gov
4. The IEA statistics appear in a November 8, 2006, article, "International Energy Agency Calls for Urgent Action to Reduce Use of Power," by Saeed Shah, *The Independent*, http://news.independent .co.uk.
5. Robert L. Hirsch, Roger Bezdek, MISI, Robert Wendling, MISI, "Peaking of World Oil Production: Impacts, Mitigation, and Risk Management," *SAIC* magazine, February 2005, http://www.saic.com/.
6. Daniel Gross, "Why Prices at the Pump May Have Little Bite," *New York Times*, Business section, May 7, 2006, 3.
7. Chris Woodyard, "Ethanol Gets Pricier But Could Plummet Next Year," *USA Today*, posted online June 21, 2006, http://www.usatoday .com/.
8. Hartgen's opinion piece appeared in the September 4, 2006, *Atlanta Journal-Constitution* on page A17; the quote from the Reason Foundation study appears on page 37.

205

9. Mark Landler, "Abroad at the Pump, Circumspection by the Barrel," *New York Times Week in Review*, May 7, 2006, 4.
10. Cambridge Energy Research Associates press release, April 24, 2006. http://www.cera.com.
11. Ronald Bailey, "Presidential Energy," *Wall Street Journal Online*, February 2, 2006, http://www.wsj.com/.
12. Jeff Rubin and Peter Buchanan, "Crude Prices Will Almost Double over Next Five Years," from Occasional Report #53, CIBC World Markets, April 13, 2005, http://www.cibcwm.com/.
13. Ted Conover, "Capitalist Roaders," *New York Times Magazine*, July 2, 2006, 32–33.
14. A transcript of Sachs's March 30, 2005 speech can be found on the web site of the Carnegie Council for Ethics in International Affairs, http://www.ceia.org/.
15. Energy Information Administration online Energy Kid's Page, "How Oil Was Formed," http://www.eia.doe.gov/kids/energyfacts/sources/non-renewable/oil.html#Howformed.
16. Joseph B. White, "One Billion Cars," *Wall Street Journal Online*, April 17, 2006, http://www.wsj.com/.
17. Jeff Rubin and Peter Buchanan, "OPEC's Growing Call on Itself," CIBC World Markets "Monthly Indicators," June 7, 2006, 6.
18. http://www.GasBuddy.com/.
19. Janet McBride and Peg Mackey, "Oil Industry Plans for Price Correction Not Crash," Reuters, August 17, 2006, http://www.reuters.com/.
20. Peter Maas, "The Breaking Point—Saudi Arabia, Soaring Demand and the Theory of Peak Oil," *New York Times Magazine*, August 21, 2005.
21. Tom Bergin, "Total Sees 2020 Oil Output Peak, Urges Less Demand," Reuters, June 7, 2006, http://www.reuters.com/.
22. Jeff Rubin and Peter Buchanan, "Advancing the Timetable for $100/Barrel Oil," CIBC World Markets "Monthly Indicators," September 7, 2005, 5.
23. "Oil at $100? It's No Longer a Pipe Dream," *Platts Energy Economist*, May 19, 2006, http://www.businessweek.com.
24. Stanley Reed, "Would $100 Oil Slam the Global Economy?" *Business Week* online, July 27, 2006, http://www.businessweek.com/.
25. Michael Brush, "It's Time to Invest for $100 Oil," MSN, August 2, 2006, http://www.moneycentral.msn.com/.
26. Rubin and Buchanan, "Crude Prices Will Almost Double."

27. Marla Dickerson, "Will Mexico Soon Be Tapped Out?" *Los Angeles Times*, July 24, 2006.

28. Keith Naughton, "The Long and Grinding Road," *Newsweek*, May 1, 2006.

29. See note 8.

CHAPTER 2   Terrorists, Nationalists, and Shock Absorbers

1. Prepared statement by Hillard Huntington, executive director, Energy Modeling Forum, Stanford University, before the Senate Foreign Relations Committee, March 30, 2006.

2. Richard N. Haass, "Let's Not Play the Oil Game," *Newsweek International*, May 15, 2006.

3. "IEA Says Demand on OPEC Crude to Increase 'Substantially,'" *Platt's*, November 7, 2006, found online at http://www.platts.com.

4. Jeff Rubin and Peter Buchanan, "OPEC's Growing Call on Itself," CIBC World Markets "Monthly Indicators," June 7, 2006, 6.

5. "Halting Iran Nuclear Program Trumps Oil Price—Bodman," Reuters, August 8, 2006, http://www.reuters.com.

6. Henry Kissinger, *Washington Post*, Opinion section, September 13, 2006.

7. Text of President Bush's 9/11 address, provided by the White House to the Associated Press, September 11, 2006, found online at http://www.washingtonpost.com/.

8. "Saudi Arabia Confirms Threat to Oil Facilities," Reuters, October 27, 2006.

9. "Iran Military Hints at Strait of Hormuz Blockade," Iran Focus, April 5, 2006, http://www.iranfocus.com/.

10. Secretary of State Condoleeza Rice, "We Have to Do Something about the Energy Problem," April 5, 2006, before Senate Committee on Foreign Relations, found online at http://www.EnergyBulletin.net/.

11. Daniel Dombey, Neil Buckley, and Carola Hoyos, "NATO Fears Russian Plans for 'Gas OPEC,'" *Financial Times*, November 13, 2006, http://www.ft.com.

12. J. F. O. McAllister, "Russia's New World Order: Buoyed by Expensive Energy and a Booming Economy, the Kremlin Is Once Again

Flexing Its Muscles Abroad—But Very Carefully," *Time* Europe, July 10, 2006, http://www.time.com/time/Europe/.

13. Cao Desheng, "China, U.S. Vow Closer Energy Ties," *China Daily*, September 14, 2006, at http://www.chinadaily.com.cn.

14. Terry Macalister, "Tanker Owners Set to Benefit from Rising Freight Rates," *Guardian*, September 12, 2001.

15. "Oil at 100 Dollars a Barrel Would Threaten Airlines: IATA Economist," Agence France-Presse, June 6, 2006, found at http://www.breitbart.com/.

16. Polya Lesova, "$100 Oil Would Hit Airlines, Car Makers Hard, S&P Says," *MarketWatch*, July 27, 2006, http://www.marketwatch.com/.

17. "Ten U.S. Cities Best Prepared for an Oil Crisis," SustainLane, http://www.sustainlane.com.

18. Sara Kehaulani Goo, "Car-Sharing Merges into the Mainstream," *Washington Post*, September 5, 2006, D01.

19. James Thorner, "The Resurgence of Rail," *St. Petersburg Times Online*, July 1, 2006.

20. Peter Smith, "The Railroad Industry: What's Different This Time," Morningstar, June 26, 2006, http://www.morningstar.com/.

CHAPTER 3   Substitute Liquid Fuels, Part One: Biofuel

1. Joel Makower, Ron Pernick, and Clint Wilder, *Clean Energy Trends 2006*, March 2006, Clean Edge Inc., http://www.cleanedge.com/reports/trends2006. pdf.

2. Statement of Alexander Muller, assistant director-general for the Sustainable Development Department of FAO, FAO press release, April 25, 2006, http://www.fao.org/.

3. "Strong Growth in World Energy Demand Projected Through 2030," June 20, 2006 Energy Information Administration press release, found online at http://www.eia.doe.gov.

4. "Kew Boss: 'World Must Wake Up to the Dangers of Biofuels,'" *The Independent*, September 9, 2006, found online at http://www.ClimateArk.org.

5. Earth Policy Institute, book bytes: "The Ecology of Cities," September 12, 2006, http://www.earth-policy.org/Books/Seg/PB2ch11_ss2.htm.

6. "Eco-Economy Updates: Supermarkets and Service Stations Now Competing for Grain," Earth Policy Institute, July 13, 2006, http://www.earth-policy.org/.

7. Iogen Corporation press releases, May 1, 2006, and January 8, 2006, http://www.iogen.ca.

8. "President Bush Discusses Advanced Transportation Technology in California," official text of President's speech on April 22, 2006, http://www.whitehouse.gov/news/releases/2006/04/20060422-3.html.

9. "Biofuels Market 'Ripe for Innovation,'" *Platinum Today*, July 18, 2006, http://www.platinum.matthey.com/.

10. Jon Birger, "Wanna Make a Bet on Biofuels?" *Fortune*, January 31, 2006, at CNNMoney.com, http://money.cnn.com/.

11. Lisa Haarlander, "Ethanol Boom Prompts the Andersons to Raise Equity," Reuters, June 29, 2006, http://www.reuters.com/.

12. Alex Halperin, "Will Ethanol Prove to Be Profitable Investment?" *BusinessWeek*, Halperin, June 12, 2006.

13. Nelson D. Schwartz, "Massive Oil Profits May Not Last," *Fortune*, February 3, 2006, found online at CNNMoney.com, http://money.cnn.com/.

14. WestLB AG press release, March 7, 2006, found at http://biz.yahoo.com.

15. Christopher Edmonds, "Prudhoe's a Warning of the Need for Fixes," Real Money, TheStreet.com, August 7, 2006, http://www.thestreet.com/pf/.

16. Dynamotive press release, August 24, 2006, www.dynamotive.com.

17. "SunOpta Goes to China," *Red Herring*, June 22, 2006.

18. "SunOpta to Partner with Royal Nedalco on Cellulosic Ethanol in North America," Green Car Congress, July 6, 2006, http://www.greencarcongress.com/.

19. "Dyadic Making Progress with Enzyme Mixtures for Cellulosic Ethanol," Green Car Congress, July 13, 2006, http://www.greencarcongress.com/.

20. Dyadic International press release, September 8, 2006, http://www.dyadic-group.com/.

21. Novozymes press release, June 27, 2006, http://www.novozymes.com/.

22. Genencor press release, May 1, 2006, http://www.genencor.com/.

23. "Ceres Hits Milestone in Switchgrass Genomics Program; Focus on Cellulosic Ethanol," Green Car Congress, July 10, 2006, http://www.greencarcongress.com/.
24. "Honda Co-Develops Process to Make Biomass Ethanol," Reuters, September 14, 2006, http://www.reuters.com/.
25. Georgia Forestry Commission press release, found online at Southern Regional Extension Forestry web site, http://www.sref.info.
26. See "BP-DuPont Biofuels Fact Sheet" on http://www.bp.com/; Reuters: "DuPont, BP Link Up for Biofuels Production," June 20, 2006, http://www.reuters.com/; Kerry A. Dolan, "A Competitor for Ethanol?" June 20, 2006, http://www.forbes.com/; DuPont press release May 16, 2006, http://www.dupont.com/.
27. Glenn Hess, "BP and DuPont to Make 'Biobutanol,'" Chemical & Engineering News, June 21, 2006, found online at http://pubs.acs.org/.
28. DuPont press release, May 16, 2006, http://www.dupont.com/.
29. Hess, "BP and DuPont to Make 'Biobutanol.'"
30. JGI press release, July 24, 2006, found online at http://www.jgi.doe.gov/.
31. Neste Oil Corp. press release, March 27, 2006, http://www.nesteoil.com.
32. Abengoa web site, http://www.abengoa.com/.
33. "Imperium Renewables Announces 100 Million Gallon Biodiesel Refinery," Clean Edge Inc., May 30, 2006, http://www.cleanedge.com/story.php?nID=4127.

CHAPTER 4 Substitute Liquid Fuels, Part Two: Unconventional Fossil Fuels

1. U.S. State Department Fact Sheet on Country Reports on Terrorism 2005, April 28, 2006, http://www.state.gov.
2. "Pentagon Plans Major Alternative Fuel Buys," by Adam Sarvana, June 7, 2006, found online at http://www.Military.com/; first appeared on http://www.InsideGreenBusiness.com/.
3. Secretary of the Air Force, Office of Public Affairs, September 13, 2006, found online at www.blackanthem.com.
4. Syntroleum press release, January 31, 2006, http://www.syntroleum.com/.

5. See Rentech web site, http://www.rentechinc.com/.
6. Wu Qi, "China Reins In Fast Growth of Coal-to-Liquid Fuel Projects," *Xinhua*, July 29, 2006.
7. Sasol press release, June 22, 2006, http://www.sasol.com/.
8. "The Renaissance of Coal," May 17, 2005, found online at http://www.emagazine.credit-suisse.com/.
9. International Energy Agency press release, October 26, 2004, http://www.iea.org/.
10. Keith Bradsher and David Barboza, "Pollution from Chinese Coal Casts Shadow Around Globe," *New York Times*, June 11, 2006, found online at http://www.kenai-peninsula.org.
11. See also "Turning Dirty Coal into Clean Energy" by Elizabeth Shogren, on NPR's *Morning Edition*, April 25, 2006, found online at www.npr.org/.
12. Raymond James's "Energy Stat of the Week," July 31, 2006, 1, http://www.raymondjamescm.com/.
13. Ibid., 2.
14. Ronald Barone, UBS Securities, "Sharing Less of the Wealth," *Nat-Gas Insight: Hot Summer Finally Cooling Off*, September 1, 2006, http://www.ubs.com/.
15. Scott Haggett, "Canadian Oil Production Seen Doubling by 2020," May 18, 2006, citing Canadian Association of Petroleum Producers' annual production forecast, found online at www.planet.ark.com/.
16. Tom Kenworthy, "Oil Shale Enthusiasm Resurfaces in the West," *USA Today*, June 2, 2006, 4A.
17. Rand Corporation Research Brief, "Gauging the Prospects of a U.S. Oil Shale Industry," 2005, 1, http://www.rand.org.
18. Woodside's presentation to North American analysts was found on its web site, http://www.woodside.com.au/.

CHAPTER 5   The Power of Efficiency

1. "Plug-In Hybrids Get Big Push from Calif. Utility," Reuters, September 5, 2006, http://www.reuters.com/.
2. American Public Power Association, *Public Power Weekly* 4 (January 30, 2006).

3. "President Bush Discusses Advanced Transportation Technology in California," official text of President's speech on April 22, 2006, http://www.whitehouse.gov/news/releases/2006/04/20060422-3.html.

4. U.S. Climate Change Technology Program Strategic Plan, September 2006, http://www.climatetechnology.gov.

5. Bradley Berman, "Pursuing New Power for Hybrids," *BusinessWeek* online, January 5, 2006, http://www.businessweek.com/.

6. Altair Nanotechnologies press release, June 14, 2006, http://www.altairnano.com/news.html.

7. Johnson Controls press release, February 20, 2006, http://www.johnsoncontrols.com/.

8. Feel Good Cars Corporation press release, April 11, 2006, http://www.feelgoodcars.com/. Feel Good Cars provides progress report on its plans to produce and distribute electric low-speed vehicles (LSVs) in the North American market.

9. Dan Zehr, "Charging into the Future—Cedar Park Startup Bets It Can Produce a Mass-Market Power Storage Device for Electric Cars," *Austin American-Statesman*, November 5, 2006, http://www.statesman.com.

10. The insurance company is Travelers. See Marshall Loeb, "Saving Money by Going Green," *MarketWatch*, January 6, 2006, http://www.marketwatch.com/; and "Insurance Company Offers Hybrid Car Owners 10 Percent discount," Reuters, June 1, 2006, http://www.reuters.com/.

11. Mark Clayton, "Toyota Moves to Corner the 'Plug-In' Market," *Christian Science Monitor*, July 20, 2006.

12. "Honda to Build Parts Factory for Hybrid Cars—Nikkei," Reuters, July 24, 2006, http://www.reuters.com/.

13. Steven Ashley, "Firing on Half Cylinders," ScientificAmerican.com, December 13, 2004, http://www.sciam.com/.

14. Scott Memmer, "CVT Enters the Mainstream," http://www.Edmunds.com/.

15. Daniel Gross, "Why Prices at the Pump May Have Little Bite," *New York Times*, Business section, May 7, 2006, 3.

16. Dave Freeman and Jim Harding, "Solar Cells Change Electricity Distribution," *Seattle Post-Intelligencer*, August 10, 2006.

17. Georgina Prodhan, "Sharp Sees Solar Power Costs Halving by 2010," Reuters, August 31, 2006, http://www.reuters.com/.

18. "Survey: US Consumer Awareness of E85 Flex-Fuel Vehicles High, Buying Interest Split About 50:50," Green Car Congress, July 26, 2006, http://www.greencarcongress.com/.

19. "The Ethanol Myth," ConsumerReports.org, October 2006, http://www.consumerreports.org/.

20. "Toyota Looks at Ethanol Development," *Sydney Morning Herald* Australia, July 19, 2006, found online at http://www.smh.com.au/.

21. Mark Clayton, "Plug-In Hybrids: A Here-and-Now Alternative," *Christian Science Monitor*, September 22, 2005, http://www.cs monitor.com.

22. "Fuel-Cell Car Hopes Played Down," British Broadcasting Corporation, March 11, 2003, found online at http://bbc.co.uk/.

23. Scott Horsley, "Hydrogen on the Highway: Driving a Fuel-Cell Car," *Morning Edition*, National Public Radio, November 29, 2005, found online at http://www.npr.org/.

24. Amy Raskin and Saurin Shah, AllianceBernstein LP, "The Emergence of Hybrid Vehicles—Ending Oil's Stranglehold on Transportation and the Economy," June 2006, found online at http://www .calcars.org/.

25. Ronald R. Cooke, "Oil Shortages? It's Happened Before. And It Will Happen Again," *The Cultural Economist*, September 15, 2006, found online at http://www.321energy.com/.

CHAPTER 6   Every Drop of Oil We Can Get Is Important

1. Day is scheduled to retire at the end of April 2007.

2. Australian Broadcasting Corporation, program transcript of Jonathan Holmes' report, "Peak Oil?" broadcast July 10, 2006, on the program *Four Corners*, found online at http://www.abc.net.au/.

3. Tom Cahill, "Age and Neglect Meet in Global Oil Pipelines," *Bloomberg News*, August 22, 2006.

4. Timothy Gardner, "US Says CO_2 Injection Could Quadruple Oil Reserves," Reuters, June 3, 2006, http://www.reuters.com/.

5. Noble Corporation press release, July 20, 2006, http://www.noble corp.com/.

6. Transocean Inc. press release, August 3, 2006, http://www.deep water.com/.

7. Sam Fletcher, "Exxon President Predicts Non-OPEC Peak in 10 Years," *Oil and Gas Journal*, December 12, 2004, found online at http://www.EnergyBulletin.net.
8. Matt Simmons, *Twilight in the Desert: The Coming Saudi Oil Shock and the World Economy* (New York: John Wiley & Sons, 2005).
9. Christopher Edmonds, "Energy Prices Can Shoulder the Load," TheStreet.com, August 24, 2006, http://www.thestreet.com/.
10. Marla Dickerson, "Will Mexico Soon Be Tapped Out?" *Los Angeles Times*, July 24, 2006.
11. Jeff Rubin and Peter Buchanan, "Drilling in Troubled Waters," CIBC World Markets "Monthly Indicators," March 6, 2006, 8–9.
12. See Note 9.
13. "Halliburton Sees Earnings Doubling in Coming Years," Reuters, June 8, 2006, http://www.reuters.com/.
14. BJ Services Company press release, July 25, 2006, http://www.bj services.com/.
15. Schlumberger Ltd. press release, July 21, 2006, http://www.slb.com/.
16. Charles T. Maxwell, "Oil Investing: Strategic Assumptions," Weeden & Co., March 30, 2005, http://www.weedenco.com/.
17. CNBC, Mad Money, May 24, 2006, http://www.moneycentral.msn.com/.

CHAPTER 7 The New Oil Economy?

1. Paul Salopek, "A Tank of Gas, a World of Trouble," part of a special report, "Twilight of the Oil Age," *Chicago Tribune*, July 30, 2006, http://www.chicagotribune.com.
2. The transcript of Sachs's March 30, 2005, speech can be found on the web site of the Carnegie Council for Ethics in International Affairs, www.ceia.org/.
3. The complete text of Prof. Feldstein's June 5, 2006, *Wall Street Journal* piece, "Tradeable Gasoline Rights," can be found on the web site for the Belfer Center for Science and International Affairs, John F. Kennedy School of Government, Harvard University, on the Publications page, http://bcsia.ksg.harvard.edu/.
4. "Fire Station Turns to Wind Power," BBC News, July 26, 2006, http://www.news.bbc.co.uk/.

5. "Toyota's Jim Press Discusses the Future," *BusinessWeek* online, May 17, 2006, http://www.businessweek.com/.

6. Charles Schumer, "New Fuel Efficient Tires Could Save Long Islanders $150 and Reduce U.S. Oil Dependency by 275,000 Barrels a Day," press release from Sen. Schumer's office, found online at www.senate.gov/~schumer/.

7. Jeffry Bartash, "Wireless Carriers Plot New Strategies," *MarketWatch*, September 22, 2006, http://www.marketwatch.com/.

8. "Google CEO: Free Cellphones for All, If . . ." Reuters, November 13, 2006, at CNNMoney.com, http://www.money.cnn.com/.

9. See note 3.

10. Peter G. Peterson, *Running on Empty: How the Republican and Democratic Parties Are Bankrupting Our Future and What Americans Can Do About It* (New York: Farrar, Straus and Giroux, 2004).

CHAPTER 8   The Complete List of 100 Companies to Watch

1. "Chevron and UC Davis to Pursue Joint Research into Next Generation Cellulosic Biofuels," Green Car Congress, September 19, 2006, http://www.greencarcongress.com/.

Index

A123 Systems, 111, 112, 114, 165
ABB, 170
Abengoa, 77–78, 169, 170
Adkins, Marshall:
  on deepwater exploration, 140,
    141, 142
  on depletion rate, 22
  on OPEC, 136–137, 138
  on recession and price of oil,
    15
Airline industry, 48–49, 50, 85–87
Al-Husseini, Sadad, 22
Alliance-Bernstein L.P., 125
Altair Nanotechnologies,
  111–112, 114, 165
Alternative Energy Store,
  155–156, 174
Alternative Transportation
  Providers sector, 50–53,
  173–174
AMCOL International, 144,
  170
Anadarko Petroleum, 141–142,
  172
Apache Corporation, 141–142,
  172

Arch Coal, 89, 168–169
Archer Daniels Midland
  Company, 63–64, 169,
  170
Arctic Circle, drilling in, 135
Austin American-Statesman, 112,
  113
Automobiles, as "freedom
  machines," 8–10, 16–17, 28.
  See also Corvette
Automotive Efficiency sector, 10,
  114–118, 122–126, 166
Aventine Renewable Energy
  Holdings, 64, 169

Barone, Ronald, 94
Battery Technology sector, 102,
  107–108, 110–114, 165–166
Berman, Bradley, 110–111
Bin Laden, Osama, 36
Biobutanol Technology sector,
  58, 69, 72–76, 157,
  163–164
Biodiesel fuel. *See* Ethanol and
  Biodiesel Technology
  sector

Biofuel Production sector, 6, 55, 63–64, 67–68, 77–78, 90, 169–170. *See also* Ethanol and Biodiesel Technology sector

biobutanol, 58, 69, 72–76, 157, 163–164

cellulosic ethanol, 58, 62–63, 68–72, 165

grain/corn ethanol, 56–62, 64–65, 165

market forecast for, 179

TGRs and, 153–154, 156–158

usage forecasts for, 57–58

BJ Services, 140, 141

Bloomberg News, 132

BMW, 124

Bodman, Samuel, 35

Brazil, 56–57

British Petroleum:

Alaskan oil field shutdown of, 132

biobutanol and, 72–76, 142

clean power plants and, 91

deepwater drilling and, 141

investment banking and, 66, 167

peak production and, 143

Brown, Jeffrey, 23, 34

Brown, Lester, 61, 63

Burgan oil field, 139

Burlington Northern Santa Fe, 54, 171–172

Bush, George H. W., 14

Bush, George W., 14, 107–108, 112

BusinessWeek, 25, 65

CalCars.org, 101–103, 119, 156, 174, 175

Canada, 93–96

Canadian National, 54, 171–172

Canadian Natural Resources, 96, 168–169

Canadian Pacific, 54, 171–172

Cantarell oil field, 26, 138–140

Carbon audits, 151

Carbon sequestration, 91–92

Car-sharing, 51–53

Carter, Jimmy, 14

Case, Steve, 53

Cellulosic ethanol, 58, 62–63, 68–72, 165

Ceres, Inc., 71, 79, 164

Charge depleting/charge sustaining batteries, 102

Chavez, Hugo, 39

Chesapeake Energy, 141–142

Chemicals industry, 49–50

Cheniere Energy, 41–42, 170

Chevrolet Corvette, 124, 125–126, 177–178

Chevron, 66, 143, 167

Chicago Bridge & Iron, 41–42, 170

China, 16–17, 19, 37, 39, 110

biofuels and, 56, 57, 69, 70, 124

CTL projects in, 84, 87–88, 91

energy "cold war" and, 42–44

China Daily, 44

Choke point scenario, 37

Christian Science Monitor, 122

Clayton, Mark, 115

Clean Edge Inc., 58, 193
Clinton, Bill, 14
Clooney, George, 50–51
Co$_2$-EOR, 133
Coal Technology sector, 6, 12, 81, 168
  coal-to-liquid (CTL) projects, 84–93
Commuter (ultra-small) cars, 10, 116–118
Compact fluorescent light bulb (CFL), 151
ConocoPhillips, 143
CONSOL Energy, 89, 168–169
Constellation Energy Group, 119, 175
Consumer Information Providers sector, 154–156, 158–159, 174–175
Consumer Reports, 121
Continuously variable transmission (CVT), 116
Conventional fuels, 6–7. *See also* Deepwater drilling; Enhanced oil recovery; Oil Producers sector
Copulos, Milton:
  on automobiles and Americans, 8, 28
  on biofuels, 68
  on defense companies, 45, 47
  on demand for gasoline, 18
  on hidden costs of gasoline, 46, 146–147, 181–189
  on Saudi Arabia, 36
Corio, Marie R., 117–118, 119

Corn ethanol. *See* Grain/corn ethanol
Corvette, 124, 125–126, 177–178
Cramer, Jim, 144
Crane, Sir Peter, 59
Credit Suisse, 89
CSX, 171–172
Cylinder shutdown, 116

Daewoo Shipbuilding and Marine Engineering, 42, 170
DaimlerChrysler, 115
Danisco (parent of Genencor), 70
Day, James, 128
Deepwater drilling, 81, 134–144. *See also* Infrastructure Providers sector
Defense Companies sector, 45–47, 176
Depletion rate, 22
Diamond Offshore Drilling, 135, 140, 141, 170
Diesel technology. *See* Ethanol and Biodiesel Technology sector
Domenici, Pete, 97
"Drawing from the past," 127, 145
DuPont, 72–76, 142, 163–164
Dyadic International, 69–70, 79, 164
Dynamotive Energy Systems, 68, 169, 170

E85 fuel, 57, 59, 121–122. *See also* Flex-fuel vehicles
Edmonds, Christopher, 67, 140
EEStor, 112–113, 165, 166

Efficiency, 5–6. *See also*
    Automotive Efficiency sector;
    Battery Technology sector;
    Flex-fuel vehicles; Nonliquid
    Fuel Providers sector; Plug-in
    vehicles
Electricity, 6. *See also* Nonliquid
    Fuel Providers sector
    TGRs and, 150–152, 154
    U.S. industrial sector's use of,
    18
EnCana Corporation, 96, 168–169
Energy Bulletin web site, 192
Energy cold war, 42–44
Energy Information Administration
    (EIA), 2, 58–59
Energy Policy Act of 2005, 60
Energy security, 1, 83–86, 105,
    117
Enhanced oil recovery (EOR), 92,
    127–134
ENSCO International, 135, 140,
    141, 170
Environmental issues:
    anxiety about, 1
    Arctic drilling and, 135
    CTL and, 83, 91–92
    ethanol and biodiesel fuels and,
    59–60
    plug-in vehicles and, 106
    tar sands and, 94
Enzyme pretreatment. *See*
    Cellulosic ethanol
EOG Resources, 141–142, 172
Ethanol and Biodiesel Technology
    sector, 56–57, 62, 69–72,
    76–79, 157, 164–165. *See also*
    Biofuel Production sector

Ethanol Producer, 64
Exelon Corporation, 119, 175
Extreme commuters, 28
ExxonMobil, 66, 141, 143, 167

Feel Good Cars Corporation, 112
Feldstein, Martin, 147–148, 158,
    159–160. *See also* Tradable
    gasoline rights
Financial Times, 40
Fischer-Tropsch (FT) technology,
    85–88
Flexcar, 52–53, 173
Flex-fuel vehicles, 52–53, 57, 59,
    121–122, 154
Fluor, 170
Food versus fuel conundrum, 61,
    83
Foody, Brian, 62
Ford, Gerald, 14
Ford Motor Co., 117, 124
Fortune, 64, 65
Foss, Michelle, 28
Foster Wheeler, 170
Franklin stove, 130
Freedom machine, automobiles as,
    8–10, 16–17, 28. *See also*
    Corvette
Frontline, 47, 172
Fuel cell vehicles, 122–123

Gasoline. *See also* Oil Producers
    sector
    estimated usage by plug-in
    vehicles, 103
    hidden costs of, 46, 146–147,
    181–189
    TGRs and, 149, 158

Gas-to-liquids (GTL) technology, 12, 88
Genencor International, 70, 71, 79, 164
General Electric, 91–92, 155, 170
General Maritime, 47
General Motors, 115, 124
Genetically modified organisms (GMOs), 157–158
Geopolitical instability. *See* Oil price shock
Georgia Forestry Commission, 72
Ghawar oil field, 26, 139
GlobalSantaFe, 135, 140, 141, 170
Golden Triangle, 134. *See also* Deepwater drilling
Goldman Sachs, 62, 162, 167
Google, 159, 174–175
Government policies, 3, 7, 29, 109–110. *See also* Tradable gasoline rights
    attempts to wean U.S. from dependence on foreign oil, 13–14
    biobutanol and, 73–74
    biofuels and, 59–61
Grain/corn ethanol, 56–62, 64–65, 165
Grant Prideco, 144, 170
Great Britain, 151, 154
GreatPoint Energy, 92–93, 168
Green Car Congress, 58, 191
Guardian, 47
Gulf of Mexico, 40–41, 134

Halliburton, 140, 170
Hartgen, David T., 8–9, 28
Hatch, Orrin, 107

Haysbert, Dennis, 50–51
HCCI (homogeneous charge compression ignition) engine technology, 115–116
Hedge funds, oil prices and, 24
Hidden costs of gasoline, 46, 146–147, 181–189
Hirsch, Robert L., 5, 18
Home Depot, 120, 154–155, 174–175
Home energy consumption:
    evolution of home heating industry, 129–131
    TGRs and, 150–152, 154
Honda:
    cellulosic ethanol and, 71
    efficient vehicles and, 10, 115–116, 123, 125, 166
Horizontal drilling, 131, 132
Hormats, Robert, 4, 16, 34, 110
Huntington, Hillard, 31, 32
Hybridcars.com, 191–192
Hybrid vehicles. *See* Plug-in vehicles
Hydril, 144, 170
Hyundai, 122, 124
Hyundai Heavy Industries, 42, 170

Imperial Oil, 144, 172
Imperium Renewables, 78–79, 164
India, 19, 88
Information. *See* Consumer Information Providers sector
Infrastructure Providers sector, 41–42, 66–67, 91–92, 135, 140–144, 170–171

International Air Transport
   Association (IATA), 48–49
International Energy Agency
   (IEA), 2, 32, 90
Investment Banking sector, 65–66,
   74, 162, 167–168
Iogen Corporation, 62, 69, 79,
   164
Iran, 33–35, 37, 40
Iraq, 33–35

Jacobs Engineering, 170
Japan, 152
Jet fuel, synthetic, 85–87
Johnson Controls, 112, 114,
   165
Joint Genome Institute, 76
JP Morgan, 167

Karim, Naz, 60, 62, 64–65,
   71
Kilowatt gasoline. *See*
   Electricity
Kissinger, Henry, 35
Kramer, Felix, 101–103, 108

Lehman Brothers, 162, 167
Liquefied natural gas (LNG),
   40–41, 98–99. *See also*
   Natural gas; Synthetic
   Oil and LNG Providers
   sector
Lithium-ion batteries. *See* Battery
   Technology sector
Lockheed Martin, 45
Los Angeles Times, 26, 138–140
Lovins, Amory, 6

Lowe's, 120, 154–155, 174–175
Lukoil, 144, 172

Matthews, Vincent, 15, 97, 129,
   132
Maxwell, Charles T.:
   on depletion rate, 22
   on drawing from the past, 127,
      145
   on Imperial Oil, 144
   on Middle Eastern
      governments, 131–132
   on oil shortfalls, 127, 129, 131,
      132, 133, 142–143
   on recession, 14–15
   on state-owned oil companies, 20
   on technology breakthroughs, 4
Maxwell, Timothy, 122, 153
Mazda, 123
McDermott, 170
Mercedes, 116
Merrill Lynch, 162, 167
Mexico, 26, 138–140
Millikin, Michael:
   on battery companies, 111
   on biofuels, 58, 64, 69, 71, 72,
      77, 179
   on plug-in vehicles, 108, 115
Mobile energy, 4
Morgan Stanley, 162
Morningstar, 54

Nanosolar, 120–121, 175
National Association of
   Manufacturers, 161
National security. *See* Energy
   security

Natural gas, 6. *See also* Gas-to-liquids (GTL) technology; Synthetic Oil and LNG Providers sector
  deepwater drilling and, 134–135
  depletion rate and, 22
  new supplies of, 128
  price spikes and, 12
  tar sands and, 94–95
Negaoil, 6–7, 27, 116. *See also* Tradable gasoline rights
Neste Oil, 77, 79, 164
Net (reverse) metering, 106
New oil industry:
  competition and, 26–27
  factors driving growth of, 1–3
  probable evolution of, 113, 147–148
  sectors of, 5–7
  tasks facing, 28–29
  web sites about, 191–193
New York Times, 7–8, 91
New York Times Magazine, 16
NExBTL, 76–77
Nigeria, 37–38
Nissan, 115, 123
Nixon, Richard, 14
Noble Corporation, 128, 134, 140, 141
Nonliquid Fuel Providers sector, 119–121, 154, 175–176
Norfolk Southern, 172
Novozymes, 70, 71, 78, 79, 164
NRG Energy, 119, 175
Nth Power, 78–79

Oil, 2, 17, 25–27. *See also* Oil Producers sector
  demand and cost of, 12, 15–24, 28
  peak oil debate and, 22–23
  types of crude, 17–18, 23–24
Oil price shock, 11–12, 17, 31–33, 41–42, 44–54
  China and energy "cold war," 42–44
  geopolitical instability and, 33–40
  weather issues and, 40–41, 46–47
Oil Producers sector, 44–45, 73–74, 141–142, 144, 172–173
  investment banking and, 65–66, 167
  loss of control of spending, 131–132
  possible attack on U.S. facilities of, 38
  prices and, 10–11, 20
  usage versus replacement and, 127–131
Oil shale, 12, 81, 96–98
OMI Corporation, 47, 172
Organization of Petroleum Exporting Countries (OPEC), 1, 19–20, 136–139, 145–146
Orinoco Belt, 39
Overseas Shipholding Group, 47, 172

Pacific Ethanol, 64, 169
Peabody Energy, 87, 89, 169

Peak oil debate, 22–23
Pearce, Brian, 49
Pemex, 138–140, 173
Pernick, Ron, 61, 78
Petak, Kevin, 3, 4, 17, 41
  on natural gas, 12, 22, 95, 98,
    128
Peterson, Pete, 161
Petrie, Thomas A., 4, 24, 127, 129
  on enhanced oil recovery, 131,
    133–134, 140
  in LNG industry, 41–42
Petrobras, 144, 172
PHEV40, 108
Pirates, 37–38
Platts Energy Economist, 25
Plug-in vehicles, 101–110
Political issues. *See* Government
  policies
Public Service Enterprise Group
  (PSEG), 119, 175
Putin, Vladimir, 40

Qatar Petroleum, 88

Railroad industry. *See*
  Transportation Providers
  sector
Rational fear, 25–27
Raymond James & Associates,
  94
Raytheon, 45
Recession. *See* Oil price shock
Red Herring, 69
Reed, Philip, 8, 10, 116–118,
  123–124
Renault, 117
Rentech, 87, 89, 168

Research Institute of Innovative
  Technology for the Earth
  (RITE), 71
Reuters, 36–37, 64, 133, 140
Reverse (net) metering, 106
Rice, Condoleezza, 38–39
Rig intensity, 140
Royal Dutch/Shell Group, 62, 143
Rubin, Jeffrey:
  on global demand for oil, 15,
    19–20, 25, 26, 138
  on Iranian exports, 34
  on Mexican exports, 139
Running on Empty (Peterson), 161
Russia, 39–40, 88

Sachs, Jeffrey, 16, 147
Salopek, Paul, 146
Samsung Heavy Industries, 42, 170
Sasol Ltd., 87–89, 168
Saudi Arabia, 20, 23, 26, 36–37,
    136–138
Schlumberger, 140–141, 171
Schumer, Charles, 156
Shale. *See* Infrastructure Providers
  sector; Oil shale
Sharp Corporation, 121, 175
Shaw Group, 171
Shell Oil, 66, 97–98, 141, 167
Simmons, Matthew R., 26, 137, 146
Smith International, 144, 171
Solar power, 120–121, 175–176
Sour crude oil, 17, 23–24
St. Petersburg Times, 54
Stagflation, 50
Standard & Poor's, 49, 50
State-owned oil companies, 20
Stationary energy, 4–5

Statoil, 141
Strait of Hormuz, 37
Strait of Malaca, 37
Substitute liquid fuels (SLFs), 5–6.
    See also Biofuel Production
    sector; Unconventional fossil
    fuels
Suncor Energy, 96, 169
SunOpta, 69, 79, 164
Suntech Power Holdings, 120,
    175
Super spikes. See Oil price shock
Sustainability, 75
SustainLane study, 51–52, 54
Sweet crude oil, 17, 23–24
Switchgrass, 58, 71
Synthetic Oil and LNG Providers
    sector, 89–90, 96, 98,
    156–158, 168–169
Syntroleum, 86, 87, 89, 168

Talisman Energy, 144
Tanker operators. See
    Transportation Providers
    sector
Tar sands, 12, 39, 81–82, 90,
    93–96, 127, 130
Taxes, oil prices and, 9–10
Teekay Shipping, 47, 172
Tesla Motors, 50–51, 173–174
Tetra Technologies, 144, 171
Thermal heat, for EOR, 133
3D seismic, 132
321Energy web site, 192
Tillerson, Rex, 24, 137
Todco, 135, 140, 141, 171
Toyota, 10, 115–116, 122–123,
    125, 166

Tradable gasoline rights (TGRs),
    147–162, 174–175, 178
    allotment/spending/trading of,
    158–162
    biofuels and synthetic gas and,
    156–158
    gasoline consumption and,
    148–150, 154
    home energy consumption and,
    150–152
    workings of, 152–156
Transocean, 135, 140, 141, 171
Transportation Providers sector,
    47–54, 171–172
Twilight in the Desert (Simmons),
    137

Ultra-small (commuter) cars, 10,
    116–118
Unconventional fossil fuels, 6, 55,
    81–84, 98–99. See also Coal
    Technology sector; Natural
    gas; Oil shale; Tar sands
Union Pacific, 54, 172
United Nations Food and
    Agriculture Organization, 58
Unocal, 44
UPS, 161
USA Today, 96–97
Utility companies. See Nonliquid
    Fuel Providers sector

Valence Technology, 111, 112,
    114, 165
Venezuela, 39
Venture capital, 78–79
VeraSun Energy, 64, 169
Volkswagen, 124, 166

Wall Street Journal, 19, 148, 160
Washington Post, 52
Waste products. *See* Ethanol and
    Biodiesel Technology sector
Wattley, Glenn, 61, 133, 140
    on CTL industry, 86–89, 93
    on price of oil, 15, 26, 29
    on TGRs, 151–152
Weatherford International,
    140–141, 171

Weather issues, 46–47
Wireless providers, 158–159,
    174–175
Woodside Petroleum Ltd., 98, 169
Woolsey, James, 106

Yergin, Daniel, 11

ZAP, 50–51, 173
Zipcar, 51–53, 173